Authors & Artists for Young Adults

ISSN 1040-5682

Authors & Artists for Young Adults

VOLUME 30

Thomas McMahon
Editor

GALE GROUP

Detroit
San Francisco
London
Boston
Woodbridge, CT

Thomas McMahon, *Editor*

Joyce Nakamura, *Managing Editor*
Hal May, *Publisher*

Catherine Goldstein, Alan Hedblad, and Deborah Morad,
Contributing Editors

Victoria B. Cariappa, *Research Manager*
Cheryl L. Warnock, *Project Coordinator*
Andrew Guy Malonis, Gary J. Oudersluys, *Research Specialists*
Patricia Tsune Ballard, Tracie A. Richardson, Corrine A. Stocker, *Research Associates*
Phyllis J. Blackman, Tim Lehnerer, Patricia L. Love, *Research Assistants*

Susan M. Trosky, *Permissions Manager*
Maria L. Franklin, *Permissions Specialist*
Sarah Chesney, Edna Hedblad, Michele Lonoconus, *Permissions Associates*

Mary Beth Trimper, *Production Director*
Cindy Range, *Production Assistant*

Randy Bassett, *Image Database Supervisor*
Gary Leach, *Graphic Artist*
Robert Duncan, Michael Logusz, *Imaging Specialists*
Pamela A. Reed, *Imaging Coordinator*

While every effort has been made to ensure the reliability of the information presented in this publication, Gale Research Inc. does not guarantee the accuracy of the data contained herein. Gale accepts no payment for listing; and inclusion in the publication of any organization, agency, institution, publication, service, or individual does not imply endorsement of the editors or publisher. Errors brought to the attention of the publisher and verified to the satisfaction of the publisher will be corrected in future editions.

The paper used in this publication meets the minimum requirements of
American National Standard for Information Sciences—Permanence Paper
for Printed Library Materials, ANSI Z39.48-1984.

Library of Congress Catalog Card Number 89-641100
ISBN 0-7876-3230-9
ISSN 1040-5682

10 9 8 7 6 5 4 3 2 1

Printed in the United States of America

Authors and Artists for Young Adults

TEEN BOARD

The staff of *Authors and Artists for Young Adults* wishes to thank the following young adult readers for their teen board participation:

Contents

Introduction

Authors and Artists for Young Adults is a reference series designed to serve the needs of middle school, junior high, and high school students interested in creative artists. Originally inspired by the need to bridge the gap between Gale's *Something about the Author*, created for children, and *Contemporary Authors*, intended for older students and adults, *Authors and Artists for Young Adults* has been expanded to cover not only an international scope of authors, but also a wide variety of other artists.

Although the emphasis of the series remains on the writer for young adults, we recognize that these readers have diverse interests covering a wide range of reading levels. The series therefore contains not only those creative artists who are of high interest to young adults, including cartoonists, photographers, music composers, bestselling authors of adult novels, media directors, producers, and performers, but also literary and artistic figures studied in academic curricula, such as influential novelists, playwrights, poets, and painters. The goal of *Authors and Artists for Young Adults* is to present this great diversity of creative artists in a format that is entertaining, informative, and understandable to the young adult reader.

Entry Format

Each volume of *Authors and Artists for Young Adults* will furnish in-depth coverage of twenty to twenty-five authors and artists. The typical entry consists of:

—A detailed biographical section that includes date of birth, marriage, children, education, and addresses.

—A comprehensive bibliography or filmography including publishers, producers, and years.

—Adaptations into other media forms.

—Works in progress.

—A distinctive essay featuring comments on an artist's life, career, artistic intentions, world views, and controversies.

—References for further reading.

—Extensive illustrations, photographs, movie stills, cartoons, book covers, and other relevant visual material.

A cumulative index to featured authors and artists appears in each volume.

Compilation Methods

The editors of *Authors and Artists for Young Adults* make every effort to secure information directly from the authors and artists through personal correspondence and interviews. Sketches on living authors and artists are sent to the biographee for review prior to publication. Any sketches not personally reviewed by biographees or their representatives are marked with an asterisk (*).

Highlights of Forthcoming Volumes

Among the authors and artists planned for future volumes are:

Douglas Adams
Allen Appel
Robert Aspirin
Nevada Barr
Olive Ann Burns
Jane Campion
Grace Chetwin
Robin Cook
Terry Davis
Gabriel Garcia Marquez
Allen Ginsburg
S. E. Hinton

Edward Hopper
John Jakes
Francisco Jimenez
Franz Kafka
Trudy Krisher
Stanley Kubrick
Lois Lowry
George R. R. Martin
Anne McCaffrey
Robin McKinley
Nick Park
Jackson Pollack

Tom Robbins
William Shakespeare
Neil Simon
Isaac Bashevis Singer
Sheri S. Tepper
Studs Terkel
Jean Ure
Vivian Vande Velde
Joan D. Vinge
Oprah Winfrey
Tad Williams
Frank Lloyd Wright

Contact the Editor

We encourage our readers to examine the entire *AAYA* series. Please write and tell us if we can make AAYA even more helpful to you. Give your comments and suggestions to the editor:

BY MAIL: The Editor, *Authors and Artists for Young Adults*, 27500 Drake Rd., Farmington Hills, MI 48331-3535.

BY TELEPHONE: (800) 347-GALE

Authors
& Artists
for Young
Adults

Sherwood Anderson

■ Personal

Born September 13, 1876, in Camden, OH; died of peritonitis, March 8, 1941, in Colón, Panama Canal Zone; son of Irwin M. (a harnessmaker) and Emma (Smith) Anderson; married Cornelia Lane, 1904 (divorced, 1916); married Tennessee Mitchell, 1916 (divorced, 1924); married Elizabeth Prall, 1924 (divorced, 1932); married Eleanor Copenhaver, 1933; children: two sons, one daughter. *Education:* Attended Wittenberg Academy, 1899.

■ Career

Writer. Worked as copywriter for advertising firm in Chicago, 1900; president of United Factories Co., in Cleveland, OH, 1906, and of Anderson Manufacturing Co., in Elyria, OH, 1907-12; advertising copywriter in Chicago, 1913; editor of two newspapers in Marion, VA, 1927-29; lecturer. *Military service:* U.S. Army, 1899; served in Cuba.

■ Awards, Honors

Prize from *Dial*, 1921.

■ Writings

Windy McPherson's Son (novel), John Lane, 1916, revised edition, B. W. Huebsch, 1922, reprinted, University of Illinois Press, 1993.

Marching Men (novel), John Lane, 1917, reprinted as *Marching Men: A Critical Text*, edited by Ray Lewis White, Press of Case Western Reserve University, 1972.

Mid-American Chants (poems), John Lane, 1918, reprinted, Frontier Press, 1972.

Winesburg, Ohio: A Group of Tales of Ohio Small Town Life (also see below), B. W. Huebsch, 1919, New American Library, 1956, reprinted with introduction by Malcolm Cowley, Viking, 1960, reprinted as *Winesburg, Ohio: Text and Criticism*, edited by John G. Ferres, Viking, 1966, reprinted as *Winesburg, Ohio: Authoritative Text, Backgrounds and Contexts, Criticism*, edited by Charles E. Modlin and Ray Lewis White, Norton, 1996.

Poor White (novel), B. W. Huebsch, 1920, reprint, New Directions Publishing, 1993.

The Triumph of the Egg: A Book of Impressions From American Life in Tales and Poems, B. W. Huebsch, 1921, new edition with an introduction by Herbert Gold, Four Walls Eight Windows, 1988.

Many Marriages (novel), B. W. Huebsch, 1923, reprinted as *Many Marriages: A Critical Edition*, edited by Douglas G. Rogers, Scarecrow, 1978.

Horses and Men: Tales, Long and Short, B. W. Huebsch, 1923.

A Story-Teller's Story: The Tale of an American Writer's Journey through His Own Imaginative

World and through the World of Facts, with Many of His Experiences and Impressions among Other Writers—Told in Many Notes—in Four Books and an Epilogue, B. W. Huebsch, 1924, reprinted as *A Story Teller's Story: A Critical Text,* edited by White, Press of Case Western Reserve University, 1968, revised edition with preface by Rideout, Viking, 1969, recent edition published as *A Story-Teller's Story,* Penguin, 1989.

Dark Laughter (novel), Boni & Liveright, 1925, reprinted with introduction by Howard Mumford Jones, Liveright, 1925.

Hands and Other Stories (selections from *Winesburg, Ohio: A Group of Tales of Ohio Small Town Life*), Haldeman-Julius, 1925.

The Modern Writer (nonfiction), Lantern Press, 1925, reprinted, Folcroft, 1976.

Sherwood Anderson's Notebook: Containing Articles Written During the Author's Life as a Story Teller, and Notes of His Impressions from Life Scattered through the Book, Boni & Liveright, 1926, reprinted, P. P. Appel, 1970.

Tar: A Midwest Childhood (semi-autobiography), Boni & Liveright, 1926, reprinted as *Tar, A Midwest Childhood: A Critical Text,* edited by White, Press of Case Western Reserve University, 1969.

A New Testament (prose poems), Boni & Liveright, 1927.

Alice [and] *The Lost Novel,* E. Mathews & Marrot, 1929, reprinted, Folcroft, 1973.

Hello Towns! (collection of newspaper articles), Liveright, 1929, reprinted, Dynamic Learning, 1980.

Nearer the Grass Roots [and] *An Account of a Journey, Elizabethton* (essays), Westgate Press, 1929, reprinted, Folcroft, 1976.

Perhaps Women (essays), Liveright, 1931, reprinted, P. P. Appel, 1970.

Beyond Desire (novel), Liveright, 1932, reprinted with introduction by Rideout, Liveright, 1961.

Death in the Woods, and Other Stories, Liveright, 1933, recent edition, 1986.

No Swank (articles), Centaur Press, 1934, reprinted, Appel, 1970.

Puzzled America (articles), Scribner, 1935.

Kit Brandon (novel), Scribner, 1936.

Plays: Winesburg and Others (includes *Jaspar Deeter, a Dedication, Winesburg, The Triumph of the Egg, Mother,* and *They Married Later*), Scribner, 1937.

Home Town (nonfiction), Alliance Book Corp., 1940, reprinted, P. P. Appel, 1975.

Sherwood Anderson's Memoirs, Harcourt, 1942, reprinted as *Sherwood Anderson's Memoirs: A Criti-*

cal Edition, edited by White, University of North Carolina Press, 1969.

The Sherwood Anderson Reader, edited by Paul Rosenfeld, Houghton, 1947.

The Portable Sherwood Anderson, edited by Horace Gregory, Viking, 1949, Penguin, 1970.

Letters of Sherwood Anderson, edited by Rideout and Jones, Little, Brown, 1953.

The Short Stories of Sherwood Anderson, edited by Maxwell Geismar, Hill & Wang, 1962.

Return to Winesburg: Selections from Four Years of Writing for a Country Newspaper, edited by White, University of North Carolina Press, 1967.

Buck Fever Papers (articles), edited by Welford Dunaway Taylor, University Press of Virginia, 1971.

A Teller's Tales, selected and introduced by Frank Gado, Union College Press, 1983.

Sherwood Anderson: Selected Letters, edited by Charles E. Modlin, University of Tennessee Press, 1984.

Letters to Bab: Sherwood Anderson to Marietta D. Finely, 1916-1933, edited by William A. Sutton, University of Illinois Press, 1985.

The Sherwood Anderson Diaries, 1936-1941, edited by Hilbert H. Campbell, University of Georgia Press, 1987.

Sherwood Anderson: Early Writings, edited by Ray Lewis White, Kent State University Press, 1989.

Sherwood Anderson's Love Letters to Eleanor Copenhaver Anderson, edited by Charles E. Modlin, University of Georgia Press, 1989.

Sherwood Anderson's Secret Love Letters, edited by Ray Lewis White, Louisiana State University Press, 1991.

Certain Things Last: The Selected Stories of Sherwood Anderson, edited by Modlin, Four Walls Eight Windows, 1992.

Work represented in anthologies. Contributor to periodicals, including *Dial.*

■ Sidelights

On the last day of February, 1941, at age 64, Sherwood Anderson set off on a new adventure: he and his fourth wife, Eleanor Copenhaver, sailed on the *Santa Lucia* on a goodwill mission to South America. The titular spokesman for small-town America, once known around the world for his groundbreaking fictional techniques in *Winesburg, Ohio*—a man who influenced an entire generation of American writers—intended to get to know his neighbors to the south just as he had those denizens of Ohio about whom he had once so incisively written. He went looking for a Latin American Everyman; he found his own end.

Ben Hecht, an old friend from Anderson's Chicago days and a fellow writer, talked with him shortly before the sailing and published a piece on Anderson's strange mission. In the event, it would serve as both summation of a man's career and as eulogy. Hecht wrote: "Sherwood Anderson is off to find something that vanished out of the world he knew and wrote about. It

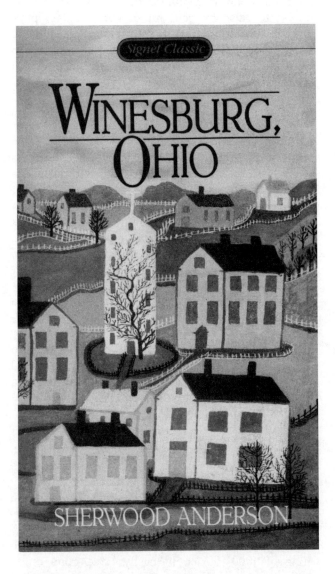

Considered Anderson's ground-breaking masterpiece, this work is a collection of related stories that explores the deep and intimate secrets in ordinary people's lives.

disappeared out of the land. It was the America he knew—that moody, whimsical, inarticulate hero of the pre-radio, pre-movie hinterlands. Something scotched him. And Sherwood, his great biographer, is off to strange lands, where he can forget his hero is dead."

If Anderson's last journey was a quixotic one, it was not out of the ordinary for him. His entire creative life had been one long process of seeking, of trying to go beyond the givens. But this final trip was doomed before it began: sometime in the last two days on land, at farewell parties given the Andersons, Sherwood swallowed a toothpick. By the third day of the sailing, the toothpick had penetrated his intestine and brought on peritonitis. By March 4, the illness had progressed so far that morphine would do nothing to block the pain. His wife had him brought ashore in the Canal Zone, and taken to the Gorges Hospital at Colón. He died there four days later.

By the time of his death, Anderson had already faded from the firmament of top-rank writers in America. Obituary writers were kinder than the critics. Publication of his *Memoirs* the year following his death occasioned a retrospective glance by the latter group at Anderson's achievements. Writing in the *Nation*, Margaret Marshall found his novels and essays to be "a study in non-discipline," while Lionel Trilling voiced the opinion of the avant garde in *Kenyon Review* that Anderson's later works "were all too clearly an attempt to catch up with the world, but the world had moved too fast." Most damning—and insightful—of all were Maxwell Geismar's comments in the *Yale Review:* "Sherwood Anderson had the ill luck, as was T. S. Eliot's, to become an ancestor before he had become mature."

Anderson himself was self-deprecating about his achievements. In his posthumously published *Memoirs* he wrote: "There has been something of struggle but little enough of the heroic in my life. For all my egotism I know I am but a minor figure." Yet this "minor figure" was a pioneer of the short story, influencing that form "more strongly that anyone except, possibly, Edgar Allan Poe," according to Ray Lewis White in *The Achievement of Sherwood Anderson*. In a handful of stories, such as "I Want to Know Why," "The Egg," "I'm a Fool," "The Man Who Became a Woman," "Death in the Woods," and "Brother Death," as well as in his book of interrelated tales, *Winesburg, Ohio,* Anderson rebelled against what he termed the "poison plot," and concentrated instead on character and mood. He plumbed the language of rural and middle America for a new and naturalistic language; he scavenged the recesses of the unconscious to bring these people to vivid life. Additionally, Anderson influenced a generation of writers from William Faulkner and Ernest Hemingway—whose first works he was instrumental in helping to have published—to Thomas Wolfe and James T. Farrell.

Slowly critical fashion concerning Anderson began to change, beginning in the 1960s and continuing until the present when his *Winesburg, Ohio* has become part of the canon, read in high school English classes. Anderson the writer has found his way into college syllabuses and onto the classics bookshelves. He has come a long way from humble beginnings in Clyde, Ohio; Anderson the man of letters is a character straight out of the pages of his own fiction.

They Called Him "Jobby"

Born on September 13, 1876, Anderson was a child of the nineteenth century. He grew up mainly in the town of Clyde, Ohio, which had a population of about 2,500 when the Andersons moved there in 1883. Though the railroad had passed through Clyde since the 1850s, the town had missed the boom of a Columbus or Toledo. It was prosperous, yet still "betrayed traces of the unsettled West," according to an Anderson biographer, Kim Townsend. Thus Anderson was the product of America's pre-industrial heartland, and this early influence never left the boy or man. He was full of not only the boosterism that characterized the period, but also the freethinking individualism that America promised yet so rarely delivered.

The third child in a family of five boys and one girl, Anderson early on earned the nickname in Clyde of "Jobby," for he was forever working at odd jobs to help the family out economically. His studies came in second to such labor, and he did not finish his high school degree until he had become a man in his own right and left his family behind. This was not a mere matter of truancy on Anderson's part, but an act of necessity, for the family's father, Irwin, was a harnessmaker

in a time when that trade was ending. The father's subsequent itinerant work as a house painter fared not much better, as he was fonder of playing his horn in the local band and regaling people with his Civil War stories than he was of working.

"Anderson's family was among the poorest" in Clyde, according to Townsend in his *Sherwood Anderson.* Yet they were far from the lowest on the social ladder, and young Sherwood grew up with the sons of the most powerful people in town. These humble beginnings, however, left a mark on Anderson the man. Once he left Clyde after his beloved mother's death, he was determined to raise himself out of such genteel poverty. As Townsend put it, "Anderson's rise in the world would be accomplished by his moving up from job to job, not up from one school grade to another."

In Search of the American Dream

Anderson's mother died in May of 1895 when he was 18. This effectively severed the author's ties with Clyde, and with his family. The following year he left for the bright lights of Chicago. Initially he stayed in a boarding house run by a former resident of Clyde, and ultimately found a job in a cold-storage plant hauling frozen meat, followed by another such job in a warmer warehouse. When his older sister and two of his brothers came to town, they shared two rooms in a tenement. With the outbreak of the Spanish-American War, Anderson was quick to join up, escaping a seamy reality for the adventure of war. In the event, he spent his time in the Ohio National Guard far from any action: his company did not embark for Cuba until four months after the armistice had been signed.

Back in the United States in 1899, Anderson settled for a time in Clyde, and then moved to Springfield to enroll in the Wittenberg Academy and finish his high school education. He had just turned twenty-three when he began what was his senior year of high school. Living at a local boardinghouse, he did well in school, graduating in June of 1900. He could easily have gone on to college, but Anderson was hungry for life. He took a job as an advertising solicitor for a publishing company and headed off again to Chicago to make his fortune.

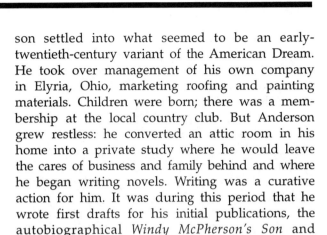

This novel concerns people's relationships with machines at the turn of the century through the eyes of inventor Hugh McVey. *Art (c) T. H. Benton and R. P. Benton Testamentary Trusts/Licensed by VAGA, New York, NY.*

Soon Anderson was writing advertising copy, changing agencies and employers as his skills increased. He began to prosper; Chicago began to take note of the young ambitious man from Clyde. He became something of a dandy, sporting spats and a dinner coat. Anderson would look back at this period as a training ground for the writer he became; the changing roles of advertising copy was his school of creative writing. Some of his early advertising pieces even showed the folksy approach that was later evident in his short stories.

In 1903 Anderson met Cornelia Platt, the well-educated daughter of a well-connected businessman; a year later they were married and Anderson settled into what seemed to be an early-twentieth-century variant of the American Dream. He took over management of his own company in Elyria, Ohio, marketing roofing and painting materials. Children were born; there was a membership at the local country club. But Anderson grew restless: he converted an attic room in his home into a private study where he would leave the cares of business and family behind and where he began writing novels. Writing was a curative action for him. It was during this period that he wrote first drafts for his initial publications, the autobiographical *Windy McPherson's Son* and *Marching Men*.

In 1912, virtually in the middle of dictating a letter, Anderson could no longer support the twin worlds he had created. He suffered a nervous breakdown and went missing for four days, turning up finally in a drugstore in Cleveland, still in his business suit but with mud up to his knees. After a spell in a hospital, Anderson returned to his family, but never came home again. He sold what was left of his business and returned to Chicago to take up advertising copywriting once again. He and Cornelia tried a form of reconciliation, spending several months with their children at a remote hunting lodge in Missouri's Ozark Mountains in 1913-14, but the break was too deep. Once back in Chicago, Anderson moved off on his own, preparing himself to be a writer.

Winesburg, Ohio

The Chicago that Anderson went back to was a city that provided a fine atmosphere for creative artists. During these years the Chicago Renaissance was in full swing, and Anderson, supporting himself by day with ad work, fell in with these men and women by night. In addition to such luminaries as Carl Sandburg and Theodore Dreiser, there were also artists such as Floyd Dell, Ben Hecht, Margery Currey, Margaret Anderson, Burton Rascoe and Ferdinand Schevill. Anderson was exposed to the new ideas of the new century: the psychoanalytic theories of Sigmund Freud and the writings of Gertrude Stein, D. H. Lawrence, and James Joyce. These were bohemian days for Anderson, who let his hair grow long and began sporting a beard, and when he formed a modern marriage with the artist and dancer Tennessee Mitchell, it was only part of the territory of such a life style.

But Anderson was no mere poseur: he worked on his fiction. By 1914 he published his first short story, "The Rabbit-Pen," in *Harper's*. It was an auspicious beginning for a fledgling writer, albeit at age thirty-eight. The two novels from his Elyria days were published in 1916 and 1917; though they received some attention in the press, there was little in them to prepare readers for the series of interrelated short stories he had been working on in 1915 and 1916 and published only in 1919.

A short story, "Sister," published in the *Little Review* in late 1915 was perhaps more telling of the writer's development, for in it Anderson begins

This collection of Anderson's best stories show why the author is regarded to be one of America's most influential twentieth-century writers. *Art (c) Estate of Grant Wood/Licensed by VAGA, New York, NY.*

SHERWOOD ANDERSON

The Egg and Other Stories

to use more straightforward language and to plumb the subject matter of small-town America that would become his signature. This story was also the first published representation of what Anderson would call the "grotesque": a human psychologically and perhaps also physically deformed by the lack of love and understanding. Several early pieces of what would later be gathered together for the book, *Winesburg, Ohio,* were published in *Masses* and *Little Review,* and in them Anderson can be seen groping his way toward a new way of storytelling about a new character in American literature. Anderson enlarged his lists of grotesques for these stories, and also began adapting his language to the rhythms of the American heartland, blending both of these elements with the ancient oral tradition.

In *Winesburg, Ohio,* Anderson tells the story of small-town America and of the lonely and frustrated people who inhabit that space. Though the book is regional in setting, the stories collected in it tell a much larger story. In simple, straightforward language, Anderson cuts through the gloss of character and reveals the true human underneath. What unity *Winesburg, Ohio* has is achieved by a common setting and tone, by the theme of the solitary life that runs throughout the stories, and by the progress of a sort of main character, George Willard, whose development is followed through several of the stories. Anderson's book of grotesques is, in fact, often seen through the eyes of young George Willard, reporter for the *Winesburg Eagle,* and it is through him that many of the secrets of the town are let out. First appearing in the story "Hands," he learns about women in "Nobody Knows" and "An Awakening." In the end, like Anderson in his real-life Clyde, George Willard leaves Winesburg after the death of his mother and the piercing experiences of "Sophistication."

The entire sequence, however, begins with "The Book of the Grotesque," in which an old writer explains his theory of how people become grotesques because, as Walter B. Rideout noted in *Dictionary of Literary Biography,* "they cling rigidly to single-minded perceptions of themselves and life." After this introduction there follows twenty-one tales about various inhabitants of Winesburg, Ohio, most of them frustrated somehow in their lives. They lead isolated lives and are examples of the grotesques that the old writer noted. Willard is one of the few of these inhabitants to gain any self-knowledge, to display any understanding of the human predicament or any growth.

George Willard, son of Tom and Elizabeth, wants desperately to become a writer, but is only covering surface reality as a reporter for the local newspaper. His father, a boorish man, runs the local hotel and his mother, frustrated in her marriage, takes her pleasure in her son and his goals, as well as in her conversations with the local GP, Dr. Reefy. George progresses from callow youth to compassionate man in the pages of this book that is not really a novel. He grows beyond exploitation of his fellow humans—treating both people and language more fairly by the time he determines to depart Winesburg. He embraces intimacy, both of a sexual and nonsexual type; his emotional closeness to his friend, Helen White, enables him to break through his own thin skin of needs in order to feel sympathy and more importantly, empathy for the other inhabitants of Winesburg. But even George Willard's development is dealt with indirectly; there is no sense of "novel" in these collected tales. "What is wanted is a new looseness; and in *Winesburg* I have made my own form," Anderson later wrote in his *Memoirs*. "There were individual tales but all about lives in some way connected. . . . Life is a loose flowing thing."

These stories, almost all of them written on the backs of pages of an earlier, unpublished novel, were from the start intended to hold together in this loose format. The continuing theme of loneliness and of lives frustrated in their sexuality or in dreams was as important in the loose unity as were the stories of George Willard. Some of the grotesques presented have a horrid quality to them, but on the whole, Anderson's portraits are full of compassion and simple lyricism about these lives of "quiet desperation," as they are typified in the book. There is Wing Biddlebaum from "Hands," a semi-recluse who often relies on young George to keep him company in the evening. In fact, many of the stories take place at dusk or in the evening, yet another unifying motif in the work. Wing's hands—expressive and emotive—got him into trouble when, as a young teacher at an all-male school, he was accused of touching his young pupils inappropriately. This misunderstanding has filled Wing's life with a sort of misery; his desire for human fulfillment has been thwarted because of the incident.

Winesburg is full of other such colorful grotesques, all presented in impressionistic flashes; chosen at moments of epiphany rather than spread out in plot-driven stories. There is Wash Williams who wants desperately to find love beyond the physical; Elmer Cowley who wants to belong; the Rev. Curtis Hartman who tries to square his religion with his erotic urges; and Dr. Reefy whose deepest thoughts are consigned to scraps of paper stuffed into his pockets and left to form illegible "paper pills" along with assorted pocket lint. These plotless stories, such as "Hands" and "Queer," examine lives led in isolation because of convention or personal weakness, or look at moments of self-awareness and spiritual epiphany as in "The Untold Lie" and "An Awakening."

The Critical Reception

Reviewers were quick to see the originality in Anderson's work, published in 1919 by the same firm, Huebsch, which had introduced Joyce and Lawrence to an American audience. Maxwell Anderson, a reviewer for *The New Republic*, pointed out Anderson's revised version of the short story as artistic form: "As a challenge to the snappy short story form, with its planned proportions of flippant philosophy, epigrammatic conversation, and sex danger, nothing better has come out of America than *Winesburg, Ohio*." Llewellyn Jones, writing in the *Chicago Evening Post*, called the book a "poem," noting that "most of the tales in this book have that strange air of seeming inconsequence that only life has, that conscious art strives so hard to avoid." The inevitable comparison to Edgar Lee Masters' *Spoon River Anthology* was also made. Master's verse work, published in 1915, was also an evocation of small-town life and it is interesting to note in this regard that Anderson's new wife, Tennessee Mitchell, was a one-time companion of Masters. The literary firebrand, H. L. Mencken, noted in *Smart Set* that in Anderson's tales "one gets all the joy that goes with the discovery of something quite new under the sun—a new order of short story, half tale and half psychological anatomizing, and vastly better than all that has gone before. Here is the goal that *The Spoon River Anthology* aimed at, and missed by half a mile." Mencken also commented that "Anderson is a man of whom a great deal will be heard hereafter." It was a prescient judgment. Anderson's old friend from Chicago days, Floyd Dell, now in New York, reviewed the book

If you enjoy the works of Sherwood Anderson, you may also want to check out the following books:

William Faulkner, *Go Down, Moses and Other Stories*, 1942.
Ernest Hemingway, *The Snows of Kilimanjaro and Other Stories*, 1961.
Thornton Wilder, *Our Town*, 1938.

for *The Liberator,* and called it a "magnificent collection of tales," concluding that Anderson "has broadened the realm of American fiction to include aspects of life of the first importance."

Later critics were equally positive about Anderson's groundbreaking work. Though the work lingered for two decades, Anderson's death in 1941 occasioned a retrospective look at the writer's achievements and initiated what later became a cottage industry in Anderson studies. The American novelist and critic Waldo Frank, writing in *Story,* was one of the first to reject Anderson's own cultivated image as an artistic primitive and to closely examine the aesthetic and technical elements of *Winesburg, Ohio.* Re-reading the book after many years, Frank noted that the "first impressive realization . . . is that *Winesburg* has form . . . the work is an integral creation." Frank went on to compare this "lyrical form" to that of Balzac, Chekhov, Maupassant, and other masters of the short story. "The positive substance of the book," Frank observed, "is the solitariness and struggle of the soul which has lost its ancestral props: the energy of the book is the release from these old forms into a subliminal search for new ones." Frank concluded that "Sherwood Anderson is a mature voice singing a culture at its close; singing it with the technical skill of literally, the *past master.*"

The respected critic and editor Irving Howe, in his *Sherwood Anderson,* examined Anderson's use of imagery and symbolism in *Winesburg,* noting that the book may be read "as a fable of American estrangement, its theme the loss of love. The book's major characters are alienated from the basic sources of emotional sustenance." Acknowledgments by both the writer William Faulkner and James T. Farrell of the debt they owed to the

older author spurred on the revitalization of Anderson studies. Faulkner, whose first novel *Soldier's Pay* was published due to Anderson's influence, wrote in the *Atlantic* in 1955 that upon first meeting Anderson, "I knew that I had seen, was looking at, a giant in an earth populated to a great—to great—extent by pigmies, even if he did make but the two or three gestures commensurate with gianthood." One of those gestures, by implication, was *Winesburg, Ohio.* Farrell, another protégé, wrote in *Perspective* that "Sherwood Anderson influenced me . . . perhaps more profoundly than any other American writer."

Later critics examined aspects of *Winesburg, Ohio* from its supposed rejection of small-town virtues to its use of narrative form. Malcolm Cowley, in an introduction to a 1960 edition of the book, noted that Anderson's work was "far from the pessimistic or destructive or morbidly sexual work it was once attacked for being. Instead it is a work of love, an attempt to break down the walls that divide one person from another, and also, in its own fashion, a celebration of small-town life in the lost days of good will and innocence." Rex Burbank, writing on the book in his critical analysis *Sherwood Anderson,* concluded that Anderson's work avoided the extremes of both revolt against provincialism as well as romanticized and sentimental depiction of an idyllic village life. Anderson's book "has outlasted both . . . precisely because it goes well beyond both of those oversimplified extremes to acknowledge both the worth and the tragic limitations of life in the small Midwestern towns and—by easy geographical extension—of all human life," Burbank noted.

The wealth of critical analyses of these simple tales has continued to grow over the years, with internal debates over the sort of reality presented in the book, of contrasting beliefs about the theme of isolation and of Anderson's theory of the grotesque. Yet most of these critics agree that *Winesburg* was not only Anderson's finest work, but also one that helped shaped American letters. Writing in *Dictionary of Literary Biography,* David D. Anderson noted that this book of stories "is the keystone of Anderson's literary reputation, and it is an impressive achievement." The same critic went on to point out that *Winesburg* "is a work in which Anderson not only defines the problem of human isolation but asserts that it can be overcome, if only in moments, if we learn to transcend the walls that society and biology have erected among us." This collection of tales has become a textbook of the short story form and individual stories from it have been widely anthologized for study. As Ellen Kimbel wrote in *The American Short Story: A Critical History, 1900-1945*, "in *Winesburg, Ohio*, the American short story was suddenly and resoundingly thrust into the twentieth century."

Life After *Winesburg*

Anderson's book of loosely united tales "brought its author more critical than financial success," observed Rideout in *Dictionary of Literary Biography*. After its publication he was still forced to write advertising copy to make ends meet. Though the book's fame spread around the world, heralding a literary revolution, its author continued to churn out glowing copy on cars and fashion. He next turned his creative talents to the novel, publishing what many consider to be one of his best efforts in that form, *Poor White*, in 1920. In this novel, Anderson takes the pre-industrial Midwestern town as seen in *Winesburg* into the twentieth century, using it as a symbol of the development of America as a whole. This time the town is Bidwell, transformed by the dreams of progress of two young men, Hugh McVey and Steve Hunter, who start a factory there employing the formerly agrarian local workers. Meanwhile, a second storyline involves Clara Butterworth who has just returned from college. The daughter of a primary investor in the new factory, Clara meets Hugh and they quickly fall in love and elope. Hugh, like Anderson himself as a younger man, has been growing dissatisfied with the business life he has created. Ultimately, he reaches out to a more poetic life, rejecting the world of commerce, and at the end he and Clara are also struggling to establish a new relationship with one another.

Another novel, *Dark Laughter*, is perhaps Anderson's most popular, and one heavily influenced by the writings of both James Joyce and D. H. Lawrence. Once again Anderson writes of individuals in revolt against the restrictions of modern life. In the book John Stockton has grown weary of his life as a journalist in Chicago, and one day simply leaves it all—including his wife—behind him for a life of adventure. He changes his name to Bruce Dudley and takes a job in a factory. There he meets Aline Grey, wife of the owner of the factory, and both are powerfully attracted to each other. Hired as a gardener to the Greys, Dudley and Aline finally commence an affair that leads to Aline's pregnancy. The two leave together in the end, Aline's husband abandoned and confused. Dark laughter of the house servants is heard, confirming Aline's affair.

But Anderson's lasting achievement during the 1920s were two short story collections, *The Triumph of the Egg* and *Horses and Men*, which contain some of his best stories apart from those in *Winesburg, Ohio*. The former collection contains two impressive tales: "I Want to Know Why," which starts off the collection, and "The Egg," both of which "are among Anderson's best," according to David D. Anderson in *Dictionary of Literary Biography*. The first story is set in the late-nineteenth century at a racetrack and concerns a young boy who loves horses and cannot understand why grown men substitute these with low things such as prostitutes. Throughout the story is the theme of the inability to understand contradiction not only in society but also in each human. "The Egg" again uses an adolescent narrator, the son of a restaurant owner who takes great pleasure in displaying a collection of deformed, preserved chickens to his customers. The collection is, Anderson noted in *Dictionary of Literary Biography*, "a significant achievement as a unified collection," but here the unifying element was theme rather than locale or character.

Horses and Men contain another pair of widely anthologized stories: "I'm a Fool" and "The Man Who Became a Woman." Again present in this unified collection is the theme of despair and frustration at the constrictions of modern life. The collection also again opens with a story set at a racetrack: "I'm a Fool" is the story of a youth who grows up following the Ohio racetrack circuit and who ultimately despairs at his own rough background. One of Anderson's best stories is "The Man Who Became a Woman," another tale of racetracks and of a youthful lover of horses. A further collection of stories published late in Anderson's life, *Death in the Woods*, rounds out his achievement in the form. Two stories of note appeared in that collection: "Death in the Woods" and "Brother Death." In the former, an old lady who takes care of family and animals freezes to death in the woods on her way back from the market. Her body is found several days later, unharmed but stripped bare by the very dogs that were accompanying her. The narrator tells of the effect of this sight when he came upon it as a youth, and of the residual effect it has had; the awesome beauty of the circular nature of the life and death of this woman. Appearance and reality, eternal dualities for Anderson, were examined in "Brother Death," in which a younger brother dies because of a heart condition while at the same time an older brother dies spiritually, browbeaten by his father.

A Faded Literary Icon

Sherwood Anderson's primary literary achievements came about during a ten-year-period of intense work. His best works were published between 1916 and 1926, including semi-autobiographical pieces such as *A Story-Teller's Story* and *Tar: A Midwest Childhood*. In the early 1920s he traveled to Europe, where he met Gertrude Stein and James Joyce, and also made the acquaintance of the young Ernest Hemingway. Anderson quickly became a grand old man of American letters; with only a decade of writing under his belt, he was yet a man in his fifties and had a demeanor to encourage such a role. As such, he fostered American letters, encouraging young writers such as Hemingway, Faulkner, Farrell, and Wolfe among others. As thanks, he won parodies and caricatures of himself from both Hemingway and Faulkner.

In 1923, Anderson divorced his second wife and settled in New York's Greenwich Village, where he met Elizabeth Prall, the manager of a bookstore, and the couple married in 1924. By 1925 he had an assured income of $100 per week from his new publisher Liveright for the delivery of one manuscript per year. Publication of *Dark Laughter* and its subsequent fine sales enabled Anderson to buy a home in Virginia on Ripshin Creek. Lecturing helped to fill out Anderson's income in these years, and he left advertising behind for good.

But all was not right in Anderson's Eden. He began to feel that he had written himself out. The checks from Liveright thus became a constant reminder of his own lack of creative vitality. Additionally, his relationship with Prall began to deteriorate: the couple would separate in 1929 and divorce three years later. To fill his creative void, Anderson bought two weekly newspapers in nearby Marion, Virginia, and edited them both

until 1929 when he handed them over to his son, Robert.

In the 1930s, Anderson was drawn briefly to communism and leftist causes and began to write social commentary, such as *Beyond Desire*. This final period of his life was marked by relative stability, brought on in part by his fourth marriage, to Eleanor Copenhaver, daughter of a Marion, Virginia superintendent of schools and a woman 20 years younger than Anderson. In 1933 he published his last collection of stories, *Death in the Woods*, and in 1935 he wrote his last novel, *Kit Brandon*.

Anderson's final years were marked by regular travels between New York in the winter and Virginia the rest of the year. Anderson put down roots again in Virginia and felt himself to be part of the community there and had seemingly reconciled himself to a secondary role in American letters. A younger generation of writers had come to the forefront, eclipsing him. When he died in the Panama Canal Zone in 1941, he was a largely forgotten man of letters, though his achievement lived on with other writers who had learned from him. Faulkner, one of those authors who benefited from the help of the older writer, summed up Anderson's status when he said, "He was the father of my generation of American writers and the tradition of American writing which our successors will carry on."

■ Works Cited

Anderson, David D., *Dictionary of Literary Biography*, Volume 86: *American Short-Story Writers, 1910-1945*, Gale, 1989, pp. 3-30.

Anderson, Maxwell, "A Country Town," *New Republic*, June 25, 1919, pp. 257-69.

Anderson, Sherwood, *Sherwood Anderson's Memoirs*, Harcourt, 1942, p. 3.

Burbank, Rex, *Sherwood Anderson*, Twayne, 1964.

Cowley, Malcolm, introduction to *Winesburg, Ohio*, new edition, Viking, 1960, pp. 1-15.

Dell, Floyd, review of *Winesburg, Ohio*, *The Liberator*, September, 1919, p. 47.

Farrell, James T., "A Note on Sherwood Anderson," *Perspective*, June, 1954, pp. 83, 87.

Faulkner, William, "Sherwood Anderson: An Appreciation," *Atlantic*, June, 1955, p. 29.

Frank, Waldo, "'Winesburg, Ohio': After Twenty Years," *Story*, September-October, 1941.

Geismar, Maxwell, "Babbit on Pegasus," *Yale Review*, autumn, 1942, p. 183.

Hecht, Ben, "Adios," *Letters from Bohemia*, Doubleday, 1964, pp. 98-99.

Howe, Irving, *Sherwood Anderson*, Morrow, 1951, p. 101.

Jones, Llewellyn, review of *Winesburg, Ohio*, *Chicago Evening Post*, June 20, 1919.

Kimbel, Ellen, "The American Short Story: 1900-1920," in *The American Short Story: A Cultural History, 1900-1945*, edited by Philip Stevick, Twayne, 1964, pp. 33-69.

Marshall, Margaret, "Notes by the Way," *Nation*, May 16, 1942, p. 574.

Mencken, H. L., review of *Winesburg, Ohio*, *Smart Set*, August, 1919.

Rideout, Walter B., "Sherwood Anderson," *Dictionary of Literary Biography*, Volume 9: *American Novelists, 1910-1945*, Gale, 1981, pp. 19-35.

Townsend, Kim, *Sherwood Anderson*, Houghton Mifflin, 1987, pp. 6, 7, 15.

Trilling, Lionel, "Sherwood Anderson," *Kenyon Review*, summer, 1941, p. 293.

White, Ray Lewis, "Introduction," *The Achievement of Sherwood Anderson*, University of North Carolina Press, 1966, p. 3.

■ For More Information See

BOOKS

Anderson, David D., *Sherwood Anderson: An Introduction and Interpretation*, Holt, 1967.

Anderson, David D., editor, *Sherwood Anderson: Dimensions of His Literary Art*, Michigan State University Press, 1976.

Anderson, David D., editor, *Critical Essays on Sherwood Anderson*, G. K. Hall, 1981.

Bridgman, Richard, *The Colloquial Style in America*, Oxford University Press, 1966.

Dictionary of Literary Biography, Volume 4: *American Writers in Paris, 1920-1939*, Gale, 1980.

Dictionary of Literary Biography Documentary Series, Volume 1, Gale, 1982.

Geismar, Maxwell David, *The Last of the Provincials: The American Novel, 1915-1925*, Houghton, 1947.

Kazin, Alfred, *On Native Grounds*, Reynal & Hitchcock, 1942.

Rideout, Walter B., editor, *Sherwood Anderson: A Collection of Critical Essays*, Prentice-Hall, 1974.

Rosenfeld, Paul, *Port of New York*, Harcourt, 1924.

Schevill, James, *Sherwood Anderson: His Life and Work*, University of Denver Press, 1951.

Small, Judy Jo, *A Reader's Guide to the Short Stories of Sherwood Anderson*, G. K. Hall, 1994.

Sutton, William A., *Exit to Elsinore*, Ball State University Press, 1967.

Sutton, William A., *The Road to Winesburg: A Mosaic of the Imaginative Life of Sherwood Anderson*, Scarecrow, 1972.

Taylor, Welford Dunaway, *Sherwood Anderson*, Ungar, 1977.

Trilling, Lionel, *The Liberal Imagination: Essays on Literature and Society*, Viking, 1950.

Twentieth-Century Literary Criticism, Gale, Volume 1, 1978, Volume 10, 1983.

Walcutt, Charles C., *American Literary Naturalism: A Divided Stream*, University of Minnesota Press, 1956.

Weber, Brom, *Sherwood Anderson*, University of Minnesota Press, 1964.

PERIODICALS

American Literature, December, 1989, p. 731; December, 1991, p. 781.

Antioch Review, spring, 1988, p. 278; fall, 1989, p. 505.

Choice, January, 1990, p. 794.

Esquire, September, 1992.

Georgia Review, spring, 1988, p. 208.

Los Angeles Times Book Review, May 26, 1991, p. 8.

Modern Fiction Studies, summer, 1986, p. 273; winter, 1990, p. 533, 557.

National Review, June 5, 1987, p. 44; May 31, 1985, p. 42.

New Statesman & Society, September 29, 1989.

New York Review of Books, January 30, 1986, p. 16.

New York Times Book Review, July 10, 1988; February 25, 1990, p. 25; December 20, 1992.

Studies in Short Fiction, fall, 1991, p. 572.

Tribune Books (Chicago), September 13, 1987, p. 10.

Wilson Library Bulletin, November, 1989, p. 110.

Winesburg Eagle, 1975—.

World Literature Today, spring, 1988, p. 286.*

—Sketch by J. Sydney Jones

T. A. Barron

■ Personal

Born March 26, 1952; married Currie Cabot; five children. *Education:* Princeton University, B.A., 1974; studied at Oxford University on a Rhodes scholarship.

■ Addresses

Home and Office—545 Pearl St., Boulder, CO 80302.

■ Career

Writer and venture capital entrepreneur.

■ Writings

Heartlight, Philomel, 1990.
The Ancient One, Philomel, 1992.
(With photographer John Fielder) *To Walk in Wilderness: A Rocky Mountain Journal*, Westcliffe Publishing, 1993.
The Merlin Effect, Philomel, 1994, Tor, 1996.

(With photographer John Fielding) *Rocky Mountain National Park: A One Hundred Year Perspective*, Westcliffe Publishing, 1995.
The Lost Years of Merlin, Putnam, 1996.
The Seven Songs of Merlin, Putnam, 1997.
The Fires of Merlin, Philomel Books, 1998.
Where Is Grandpa?, Putnam, 1999.
The Mirrors of Merlin, Philomel Books, in press.

■ Work in Progress

The Wings of Merlin, expected 2000.

■ Sidelights

Writer T. A. Barron, a self-described "wandering bard," has said in an on-line interview that is posted on the Amazon.com cyber bookstore home page, that his life has always been filled with words. The former Rhodes Scholar grew up on a Rocky Mountain ranch near Colorado Springs, Colorado, and his prose reflects a lifelong passion for nature and the great outdoors. "Wherever moss, trees, and streams are the first citizens— that's where I am from. Sense of place inspires and infuses everything I write," Barron told Amazon.com. "My very best ideas spring from life itself, especially the wonders of the natural world. If you open all your senses to their wildest, stretching your spiritual roots as deep as a great redwood, the universe beckons. Add a pinch of inspiration and anything is possible." What Barron has created with his inspirational recipe is an eclectic bibliography that includes a trilogy about a plucky teenage heroine named Kate Gordon, which melds science fiction, fantasy, and myth with environmental activism and good old-fashioned adventure; the first four novels in a projected five-part epic saga about the legendary magician Merlin; a Henry David Thoreau-inspired book about a hiking expedition the author undertook in the Colorado wilderness; a book about Rocky Mountain National Park; and a children's book about the death of Barron's own father. "I write books I would like to read," Barron said in a question-and-answer interview that he has posted on his own official Web site. "That means each story must have a character, a relationship, a place, a dilemma, and an idea that I care about."

A personal involvement with the themes that he deals with in his books has been a central element of Barron's writing. As a boy, he was an avid reader—everything from sports stories to biographies of Abraham Lincoln and Albert Einstein, to Greek and Norse myths. Barron also loved writing down his own thoughts and feelings; he was just five when he began producing a personal magazine for family and friends called "The Idiot's Odyssey." "I kept writing during my college years at Princeton, and during my time as a Rhodes Scholar at Oxford," Barron recalled in a message to readers that he posted on his own Web site. He told interviewer Claire Martin of the *Denver Post* that while he was a student at Princeton he had "tried hard not to major in anything, and came close to majoring in geology, history, religion, and other things." In the late 1970s, during his years at Oxford, Barron took a year off and used his earnings from summer jobs to travel widely throughout Europe and Asia. He also wrote his first novel during this period. However, when the book was rejected by more than forty publishers, Barron shelved his plans to become a writer. Instead, he returned to the United States and enrolled at Harvard law school with the idea of becoming an environmental lawyer. Eventually he changed his mind, and instead embarked upon a business career with a small New York-based venture capital firm.

All the while, Barron continued to secretly dream of one day becoming a writer. For a five-year period in the early 1980s he stopped trying to write fiction, but ideas for books still filled his head. "A novel is like a good stew," Barron told Gilbert M. Sprague of *Publishers Weekly* in a 1990 interview. "You have to let it simmer for a while to get a really tasty meal." Barron knew what he was talking about, for he had struggled for more than four years to finish his first novel. When finally he did so, it was as a result of a series of events in his life which caused everything to fall into place for him, when he began writing again in earnest. "In a one-year period of time, three things happened in rapid succession. A very good friend of mine died of cancer, I met and married my wife . . . and our first child was born." These concurrent circumstances "prompted me to write a story about birth, life and death," Barron told Sprague. Barron began writing during every spare moment he had: early mornings, in the evenings after work, in taxis, while traveling on business, even while he was in meetings. He was struggling to complete a science fantasy novel called *Heartlight*.

Meets with L'Engle

It was at this point in his life that good fortune—in the person of Newbery Award-winning author Madeleine L'Engle—smiled on Barron. By chance, he met L'Engle, and she asked to read what he was working on. "For a long time, I didn't give it to her, but finally gave in. Then, some wonderful things happened," Barron told *AAYA*. According to Claire Martin of the *Denver Post*, when L'Engle read *Heartlight*, "She saw strength and promise in the manuscript, which combined a quest, astronomy, butterfly lore, and the complex relationship between grandparent and grandchild." As a result, L'Engle passed Barron's novel on to her agent; this "jump-start[ed] Barron's career as a writer." The agent submitted *Heartlight* to Philomel, a children's book imprint of Putnam Publishing, and one of the editors there agreed the story had potential. So she met with Barron to talk about his manuscript, offering encouragement and suggestions. Then, without a contract or even a firm commitment that Philomel would publish anything that he wrote, Barron set about revising the novel. His efforts paid off when Philomel published *Heartlight* in the fall of 1990.

This development marked a watershed in Barron's life. He realized he now had a difficult decision to make: he could continue with his business career, or take a gamble by chasing his longtime dream of being a full-time writer. "Life is too short not to follow your passions," Barron told Amazon.com. "In 1990, I moved back to Colorado and started writing in the attic of my home, with the help of my wife and our five young children," Barron recalls in the message to his fans that he has posted on his official Web site. "So I still often get up before dawn to write—but now I can keep going after breakfast."

"I write books I would like to read. That means each story must have a character, a relationship, a place, a dilemma, and an idea that I care about."

—T. A Barron

Heartlight, Barron's first novel, introduced Kate Gordon, the teenage heroine who is also the central figure of two subsequent books. In this adventure, Kate and her grandfather, a famous astrophysicist, use a new invention he had created to travel to a distant galaxy to learn why the Earth's sun is losing its power. There they discover that the star Trethonial, which should already have burned out and become a black hole, instead is surviving by drawing energy from other suns in the universe. Kate's religious faith helps her save the Earth and its sun, as she convinces both Trethonial and her grandfather that death is both an important part of God's pattern and a central element of life's eternal cycle.

Barron faced a daunting challenge in his effort to create Kate as a believable flesh-and-blood character. He recalls, "To do it I had to find the voice of the young girl within myself—not easy for a man [then] in his late thirties. The reward, however, was equally enormous. . . . What ever made me do such a thing? The credit goes to our first child, a girl named Denali. When she was born, I was working hard on *Heartlight.* I didn't know whether the lead character would be a boy or a girl, but I did know that the book would be about the idea that every life matters somehow."

Reviewers were divided in their opinions of Barron's literary debut. *Voice of Youth Advocates* contributor Lucinda Snyder Whitehurst felt that *Heartlight* was "entertaining and intellectually stimulating." She went on to point out that substantial use of religious symbolism in the book does not "overwhelm the story," but rather "provides a framework for action and a promise that everything happens for a reason." Roger Sutton of the *Bulletin of the Center for Children's Books* was less impressed. "There is simply too much going on here, in a plot riddled with abrupt shifts and clichéd fantasy motifs," he concluded.

Continues Kate Gordon Stories

For his part, Barron was determined to forge ahead in his new career. He explained in his Amazon.com interview that by the time he had finished writing *Heartlight,* he felt that he "had come to know his [Kate Gordon character] so well and had grown so fond of her" that he "wanted to find out what happened to her next." As a result, Barron continued Kate Gordon's fantasy adventures in two subsequent tales: *The Ancient One* and *The Merlin Effect.* In the former, Kate and her great-aunt Melanie battle to save an Oregon old-growth redwood forest from unscrupulous loggers. The trees happen to be growing on Native American sacred grounds, and they have a spiritual value as well as an economic one. One day, while Kate is in the forest with her great-aunt's owl-handled walking stick, she is mysteriously transported back in time 500 years. There she becomes involved in an earlier struggle over the same land. Kate's actions in the past affect events in the present when she helps the forces of good triumph over some evil lizard people led by a creature named Gersha, who has the body of a human and the head of a Tyrannosaurs Rex.

As had been the case with *Heartlight,* critics were divided in their opinions of *The Ancient One.* Influenced by American Indian myths, and the works of C. S. Lewis, Madeleine L'Engle, and Edgar Rice Burroughs, "Barron has woven a boldly original novel that is as thought-provoking as it is fun to read," wrote *Publishers Weekly* reviewer Sybil Steinberg. Meanwhile, Sally Estes of *Booklist* chided Barron for writing a tale that she felt was "vastly overwritten, melodramatic, and so cliché- and adjective-ridden that the almost too strong environmental message is clearly lost." However, Estes did allow that "Despite the excesses, readers will be drawn in . . . and will want to know the outcome." Kathleen Leverich of the *New York Times Book Review* also had mixed praise for *The Ancient One.* "Fantasy mavens will find plenty here to enthrall them. And there's the rub," observed Leverich. "For colorful as this action-adventure is, it's an interruption of a book that's far more interesting and august. The fantasy paraphernalia is fine, but what is compelling is Mr. Barron's view of the natural world." Reviewer Carolyn Cushman of *Locus* disagreed entirely; she dismissed *The Ancient One* as the work of an author with a polemic "axe to grind"— namely the virtues of environmentalism and Native American rights. "When Barron forgets her [sic] message and just lets the magic happen the plot moves quickly, with some amusing bits of weirdness," Cushman wrote.

"A novel is like a good stew. You have to let it simmer for a while to get a really tasty meal."

—T. A. Barron

After publication of *The Ancient One,* Barron took a brief "time out" to collaborate with photographer John Fielder on *To Walk in Wilderness,* an account of a month-long hike Barron took in the Colorado wilderness. (The pair teamed up a second time in 1995 for a book about Rocky Mountain national park.) When Barron settled back in at his desk, he resumed work on the third book in the Kate Gordon series, which is called *The Merlin Effect.* This time out, Barron tells the story of Kate's adventures when she helps her father search for a sunken Spanish galleon in the waters off southern California's Baja Peninsula. The galleon is thought to hold the magical Horn of the wizard Merlin, which according to legend has the power to bestow immortality. While searching for this artifact, Kate rescues a whale that gets tangled in her father's underwater search equipment, and she gets sucked down into a giant whirlpool during a storm. There she battles Merlin's mortal enemy, recovers the long lost Horn, and returns it to its rightful place. Reviewer Linda Perkins of *Wilson Library Bulletin* praised *The Merlin Effect* as "convincing, compelling science fantasy." Suzanne Curley of the *Los Angeles Times*

Book Review wrote that it was a "wild and woolly" tale with "enough down-to-earth quality to appeal even to those who don't strictly consider themselves fantasy enthusiasts." Lisa Dennis of *School Library Journal* commented that while "Barron's writing style is neither as smooth nor" as "well developed" as some other authors who write for the same young adult audience, *The Merlin Effect* is an "intriguing mixture of contemporary life, historical detail, science, myth, and magic."

Aside from all of the favorable reviews that *The Merlin Effect* garnered, from its author's perspective, it proved to be the most important book in the Kate Gordon trilogy. While researching the book Barron immersed himself in the mythology of Merlin. In the process, he became fascinated with the timeless story of this legendary wizard. As a result, he plunged into work on an ambitious five-book series that focuses on Merlin's origins and his adventures prior to his arrival in King Arthur's court at Camelot. In *The Lost Years of Marlin,* the first book in the series, Barron "begins to unravel the mystery," as he explained in his Amazon.com interview. The story opens with an unknown boy washing up on the coast of Wales. "At that point," Barron notes, "he has no idea who he is, or what he may become—let alone that he will ultimately rise to universal wisdom. The epic reveals the great discoveries, challenges, gains, and losses that ultimately prepare him to be the wizard Merlin."

The Merlin legend has a timeless appeal, and *The Lost Years of Merlin* found favor with readers and critics. Reviewer Kathleen Marszycki of *Voice of Youth Advocates* commented that the first few chapters of Barron's new novel were "fairly slow going," but after that the pace picked up considerably. "This is a good bet for those who enjoy fantasy, mythical quests, and of course, Merlin, the greatest wizard of them all," Marszycki wrote. Mary Jo Drungil of *School Library Journal* praised Barron's depiction of the Merlin character as "excellent"; she concluded that it more than made up for the weak depiction of minor characters. This and the "fast-moving plot [are] sure to keep readers turning pages," she concluded.

Delves Further into Merlin Lore

In the second and third books in the series, *The Seven Songs of Merlin* and *The Fires of Merlin,*

If you enjoy the works of T. A. Barron, you may also want to check out the following books and films:

Welwyn Wilton Katz, *Whalesinger,* 1990.
Gregory Maguire, *I Feel Like the Morning Star,* 1989.
Mary Stewart's Merlin trilogy, including *The Crystal Cave,* 1970, *The Hollow Hills,* 1973, *and The Last Enchantment,* 1979.
Excalibur, a film directed by John Boorman, 1981.

Barron continues the story of the young wizard's spiritual awakening. In *The Seven Songs of Merlin,* he is reunited with his mother Elen, whom he has not seen for many years. However, when the two embrace, Elen is poisoned by a deathshadow that was meant for her son. In order to save her, Merlin must meet the challenge of mastering the seven wizard songs within one lunar month. "A few contrivances aside, the tale is spellbinding . . . and readers will relish . . . [both] the action and the well-crafted setting," wrote Sally Estes of *Booklist.* A reviewer for *Publishers Weekly* disagreed, terming the novel "a patchy tale" that "may not do enough to pique readers' interest, especially avid Arthurian legend fans."

Barron regards *The Fires of Merlin,* the third book in the five-part series, as pivotal since it deals with the main character's coming of age and passage into manhood. Even as he is suffering a crisis of faith in his own magical powers, the young wizard is thrown into a life-and-death struggle against an evil dragon called Valdearg and the powers of darkness, who are intent on draining all of the magic from the mythical kingdom of Fincayra. "One adventure leads to another without a clear sense of dramatic arc or resolution, but the action hardly pauses long enough for one to notice," wrote reviewer Kathleen Beck of the *Voice of Youth Advocates.* Sally Estes of *Booklist* predicted, "Fans will definitely be clamoring for more."

Barron has in the works the last two novels in the Merlin series. *The Mirrors of Merlin* will be published in the fall of 1999, while the final book (as yet untitled) is scheduled for 2000, just in time for the millennium. "Why am I spending almost a decade writing about Merlin?" Barron mused. "Because he is much, much more than a great wizard. His story is, in truth, a metaphor—for the idea that all of us, no matter how weak, or confused, have a magical person down inside, just waiting to be discovered."

■ Works Cited

"Amazon.com talks to Thomas A. (T. A.) Barron," http://www.amazon.com/exec/obidos (January 28, 1999).

Barron, T. A., "The World of T. A. Barron—The Official Web site," http://www.tabarron.com (January 28, 1999).

Beck, Kathleen, review of *The Fires of Merlin, Voice of Youth Advocates,* February, 1999, p. 44.

Curley, Suzanne, "A Centuries-Old Mystery," *Los Angeles Times Book Review,* January 22, 1995, p. 8.

Cushman, Carolyn, review of *The Ancient One, Locus,* July, 1992, p. 58.

Dennis, Lisa, review of *The Merlin Effect, School Library Journal,* November, 1994, p. 118.

Drungil, Mary Jo, review of *The Lost Years of Merlin, School Library Journal,* September, 1996, p. 201.

Estes, Sally, review of *The Ancient One, Booklist,* September 1, 1992, p. 46.

Estes, Sally, review of *The Seven Songs of Merlin, Booklist,* September 1, 1997, p. 105.

Estes, Sally, review of *The Fires of Merlin, Booklist,* September 1, 1998.

Leverich, Kathleen, review of the *Ancient One, New York Times Book Review,* February 14, 1993, p. 21.

Marszycki, Kathleen, review of *The Lost Years of Merlin, Voice of Youth Advocates,* October, 1996, p. 216.

Martin, Claire, "Colorado Author Is Living His Dream," *Denver Post,* October 28, 1998.

Perkins, Linda, "Caught Between," *Wilson Library Bulletin,* January, 1995, pp. 117-18, 127.

Sprague, Gilbert M., "T. A. Barron," *Publishers Weekly,* December 21, 1990, pp. 17-18.

Steinberg, Sybil, review of *The Ancient One, Publishers Weekly,* July 27, 1992, p. 63.

Sutton, Roger, review of *Heartlight, Bulletin of the Center for Children's Books,* December, 1990, p. 78.

Review of *The Seven Songs of Merlin, Publishers Weekly,* July 21, 1997, p. 202.

Whitehurst, Lucinda Snyder, review of *Heartlight, Voice of Youth Advocates,* April, 1991, p. 40.

■ **For More Information See**

PERIODICALS

Booklist, September 1, 1992, p. 46.
Bulletin of the Center for Children's Books, December, 1990, p. 78.
Journal of Youth Services in Libraries, winter, 1999, pp. 10-12.
Kirkus Reviews, July 15, 1992, p. 918; September 15, 1994, pp. 1264-65.
Locus, July, 1992, p. 58.
New York Times Book Review, June 2, 1991, p. 29, November 26, 1996, p. 20.
Publishers Weekly, July 27, 1992, p. 63; August 1, 1994, p. 80.
School Library Journal, January, 1991, p. 88.
Voice of Youth Advocates, April, 1991, p. 40; April, 1999.

—Sketch by Ken Cuthbertson

James Berry

Award honor book, 1988; Signal Poetry Award, Thimble Press, 1989, for *When I Dance: Poems;* Order of the British Empire, 1990; Chomondeley Award for Poetry, Society of Authors, 1991; Coretta Scott King Award honor book, and *Boston Globe-Horn Book* Award, both 1993, and both for *Ajeemah and His Son.*

■ Personal

Born in Jamaica; immigrated to England in 1948. *Hobbies and other interests:* Cricket and music, especially jazz, reggae, and classical.

■ Addresses

Home—London, England.

■ Career

Writer and editor. Educator and conductor of writing workshops for children, 1977.

■ Awards, Honors

C. Day Lewis Fellowship, 1977-78; National Poetry Competition Award, 1981, for "Fantasy of an African Boy"; Grand Prix Smarties Prize for Children's Books, Book Trust, 1987, for *A Thief in the Village and Other Stories; A Thief in the Village and Other Stories* was named a Coretta Scott King

■ Writings

(Editor and author of introduction) *Bluefoot Traveller: An Anthology of Westindian Poets in Britain,* Limestone Publications (London), 1976, revised edition published as *Bluefoot Traveller: Poetry by West Indians in Britain,* Harrap, 1981.
Fractured Circles (poetry), New Beacon Books, 1979.
Cut-Away Feelins; Loving; and, Lucy's Letters, Strange Lime Fruit Stone (Stafford, England), 1981.
Lucy's Letters and Loving, New Beacon Books, 1982.
(Editor) *Dance to a Different Drum: Brixton Festival Poetry 1983,* 1983 Brixton Festival (London), 1983.
(Editor) *News for Babylon: The Chatto Book of West Indian-British Poetry* (anthology), Chatto, 1984, Bloodaxe Books, 1998.
Chain of Days, Oxford University Press, 1985.
A Thief in the Village and Other Stories, Hamish Hamilton, 1987, Orchard Books, 1988.
The Girls and Yanga Marshall (short stories), Longman, 1987.
Anancy-Spiderman, illustrations by Joseph Olubo, Walker, 1988, published as *Spiderman-Anancy,* Holt, 1989.

When I Dance: Poems, Hamish Hamilton, 1988.

Ajeemah and His Son, HarperCollins (New York City), 1992.

The Future Telling Lady and Other Stories, HarperCollins, 1993.

Celebration Song: A Poem, illustrated by Louise Brierley, Simon and Schuster Books for Young Readers (New York City), 1994.

(Editor) *Classic Poems To Read Aloud,* illustrated by James Mayhew, Kingfisher (New York City), 1995.

Hot Earth, Cold Earth, Bloodaxe Books (Newcastle upon Tyne), 1995.

Rough Sketch Beginning, illustrated by Robert Florczack, Harcourt Brace (San Diego), 1996.

Don't Leave an Elephant To Go and Chase a Bird, illustrated by Ann Grifalconi, Simon and Schuster, 1996.

Everywhere Faces Everywhere, illustrated by Reynold Ruffins, Simon and Schuster, 1997.

First Palm Trees, illustrated by Greg Couch, Simon and Schuster, 1997.

Isn't My Name Magical?, illustrated by Shelly Hehenberger, Simon and Schuster, 1999.

Contributor of poetry to books, including *Black Poetry,* edited by Grace Nichols, Blackie, 1989.

■ Sidelights

James Berry "has acquired a considerable reputation for fusing two cultures into a sensitive understanding of both in prose and poetry," according to a *Junior Bookshelf* critic. The same reviewer went on to comment that Berry "draws upon his West Indian memories for subject matter and his wide acquaintance with the richness of English language as a means of expression." The recipient of numerous honors, Berry "is not just another fist-raising polemicist," according to *Booklist's* James Parisi. In his poems, as in his short stories and novel for young readers, Berry paints not only a self-portrait, but also a sketch of his people, the conflicts, "injustices, and coming to conscious identity of a colonized race," according to Parisi.

Berry himself noted in his acceptance speech for a 1993 *Boston Globe-Horn Book* award that as a child he only slowly understood the legacy of slavery and oppression that touches people of all races. "Denial and exclusion easily become part of a total dispossessing," Berry noted. "What is necessary is to move beyond the world of exclusion and of denial." Kwame S. N. Dawes, in *Writers of Multicultural Fiction for Young Adults,* observed that Berry's preoccupations with race and identity questions began as a teenager in his Jamaican village where the privileged position of the whites vis-à-vis the blacks was all too apparent. The slave history of the island deeply affected the future poet as well. "Alarmed by the implication of inferiority that such a background suggested, Berry has committed his work to trying to retrieve the humanity and dignity of blacks all over the world," Dawes wrote. Berry's mission is not one of vengeance according to Dawes. "Instead, he has sought in his work to create dialogue through a two-way process of culture sharing and respect." In story collections such as the prize-winning *A Thief in the Village and Other Stories, The Girls of Yanga Marshall,* and *The Future-Telling Lady and Other Stories,* Berry has celebrated the quotidian of growing up black in Jamaica, writing of aspirations, hopes, and dreams both fulfilled and unfulfilled. In his collections of trickster tales dealing with the spiderman named Anancy, Berry has brought oral tradition to life, calling up the West African past of the peoples of the Caribbean. In his poetry, such as *When I Dance,* he introduces readers not only to the experiences of a different time and world, but also to the musical possibilities of Creole language and English. His prize-winning novel, *Ajeemah and His Son,* has also moved readers on several continents and made real and deeply personal the horrifying experience of slavery. Yet through it all, Berry maintains the light touch; his is the voice of reconciliation rather than simply condemnation. His job as a writer, as he has often noted, is to build bridges between cultures and races, to tell the stories of those whom history often ignores.

The Jamaican-British Connection

Berry was born in rural Jamaica in 1924, one of six children. A close family, the children grew up by the sea, living a subsistence lifestyle on their own crops and animals. He enjoyed "a gregarious, outdoor, rural country life," as he noted in his *Horn Book* acceptance speech. Yet always there was a great yearning in the young Berry to learn what had gone on in the world before he was born. "When I was about ten years old, I began to be truly bewildered by my everyday Jamaican rural life," Berry wrote. "I felt something of an alien and an outsider and truly imprisoned." In part this was due to the "lacks" surrounding his life: lack of information, lack of reading matter, lack of a sense of being a worthwhile person simply because of his skin color. Reading and writing came easily for the young Berry; one school textbook was generally shared between all members of his family. "But I had an inner life that could not be shared," he noted in *Horn Book.* There were Bible stories and the Anancy traditional folktales about that spiderman trickster which helped to open his "inner seeing," but these also emphasized the lack of more formal written tales.

At age seventeen, Berry went to the United States as part of a labor scheme during the war years.

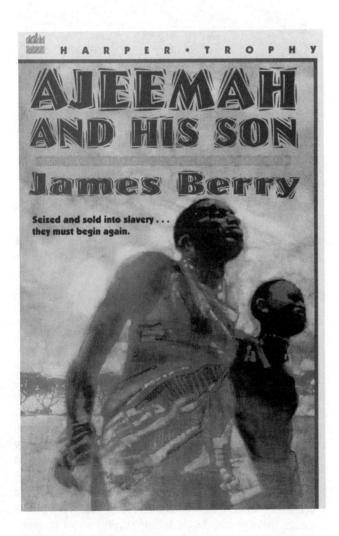

This award-winning novel chronicles the cruel life of a father and son as they are taken from their homeland to labor as slaves in Jamaica.

He stayed for four years, but went back to his coastal Jamaican village, disillusioned by the treatment of blacks in the United States. He stayed on in Jamaica until 1948, but finally the limited opportunities of island life sent him off to London, just as many others from the West Indies had done before him. In London Berry worked to put himself through night school in telegraphy, and stayed in that field for many years until he was ultimately made 'redundant,' losing his job to automation. Such career termination carried with it a state pension in Britain, and this redundancy came at a fortuitous moment for Berry, for he had begun to write by this time, publishing short stories and creating stage plays. Now, out of a job, he could devote himself full-time to his craft.

Early chap book publications, as well as his advocacy of black writing in Britain, led to his editing an anthology of West Indian, or Westindian, poets in Britain, *Bluefoot Traveller,* and to conducting writers' workshops in the schools. In 1977 he worked for a year as writer-in-residence in a comprehensive school in London, an experience that convinced Berry of the need for children's books about black life. However, another decade and several adult volumes of poetry and stories intervened before Berry set himself to right that situation.

Stories Out of Jamaica

Berry had been gone from his native Jamaica for almost four decades before publication of his first juvenile book, *A Thief in the Village and Other Stories,* yet frequent visits had kept him in touch with his roots, allowing him to celebrate the importance of simple things in this collection. Neil Bissoondath, writing in the *New York Times Book Review,* felt that Berry's collection of stories for teens "fills a gap that has existed for years in West Indian writing." Bissoondath went on to note that in his own household, where books were treasured, there had been no stories of people like himself; nothing about the children of the West Indies. "Our daily life, it seemed, was too pedestrian to provide drama between hard covers," Bissoondath wrote. "Now James Berry, in his sprightly and realistic tales of Jamaican life, proves this to be untrue."

A variety of boys and girls are presented in the nine short stories set mostly in a coastal town some eighty miles from Kingston. In one story, "Becky and the Wheels-and-Brakes-Boys," a girl gets a long-awaited bicycle. "I know total-total that if I had my own bike, the Wheels-and-Brake-Boys wouldn't treat me like that," Becky tells readers in this opening tale to the collection. In the title story, a Rastafarian man is wrongly accused of stealing, and the villagers allow their own prejudices to cover up the more respected member of the village who is actually guilty of the crime. There are tales of underdogs and children struggling for acceptance from their peers. The object of belonging, as Dawes pointed out, "is usually something physical," such as Becky's bike or a mouth organ in "The Mouth-Organ Boys," and even a mongoose, in "Elias and the Mongoose." A reviewer for *Publishers Weekly* noted that "Berry's prose is liquid and cool," that the stories "are musical in print, even before they are read aloud," and that Berry produced an "epiphanic" collection: the stories wrap themselves "around ordinary incidents and transforms them into lore."

Writing in *Bulletin of the Center for Children's Books*, Betsy Hearne concluded that the language was "rhythmic" and that the scenes in the stories "will take readers beyond suburban America to a subsistence society that is nonetheless complex in family relationships and community dynamics." A critic in *Junior Bookshelf* called Berry's initial juvenile effort a "lovely collection," noting that they "focus on family life, of poverty, of joy and sadness, and all have the atmosphere of Jamaican life, tightly bottled and ready to fizz out on opening." Bissoondath noted in the *New York Times Book Review* that these "are simple stories of restricted possibility, but Mr. Berry delves deep, revealing and examining the dreams of the children. . . ."

Berry told an interviewer for *Publishers Weekly* that the stories in the collection "were straight out of my own childhood and later observations." He went on to note that in "the Caribbean, we were the last outpost of the Empire. No one has reported our stories, or the way we saw things. It's the function of writers and poets to bring in the left-out side of the human family." Berry told his stories in the language of the people he was featuring, a rhythmic mixture of local dialect and more formal English. "It's so important to me to use authentic voices," Berry told *Publishers Weekly.* "Readers need to learn to appreciate black people's voices. Sounds are community. We may

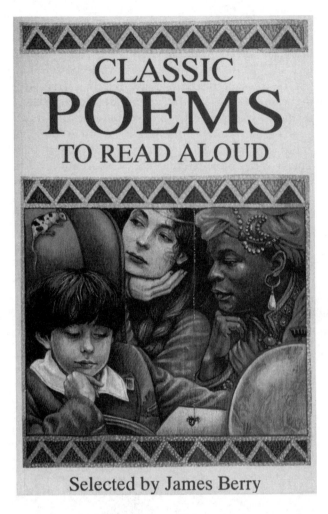

Berry has also edited poetry collections, including this one for children that gathers together verses past and present from around the world.

damage children by putting down something so closely knitted to their early years. Life has given us a rich variety of language. And if we celebrate one language over the many, we are deprived. When people share, they are joyful and enriched."

More such linguistic enrichment has come with Berry's other works for young readers, including *The Girls and Yanga Marshall,* a further collection of four tales from the Caribbean, built around the central theme of the desire to resolve conflicts, and with *The Future-Telling Lady and Other Stories.* The latter collection, geared toward middle-grade readers, combines five contemporary Caribbean tales with one African American folktale featuring "young people between the ages of 10 and 14 who, in the course of the story, learn something about themselves," according to Lyn Miller-Lachmann writing in *School Library Journal.* "Berry's poetic, often onomatopoeic, style captures the language and daily rhythms of rural and small-town Jamaica," noted Miller-Lachmann, and that his "sense of humor will attract readers." *Booklist*'s Hazel Rochman commented that "Berry tells his stories of contemporary Jamaica with a joyful exuberance, rooted in the oral tradition, that demands they be read aloud," while *Horn Book*'s Ellen Fader observed that the "strikingly original stories . . . show tremendous range in subject matter and mood" and that "Berry's language sings with grace, beauty, and respect."

With his 1988 *Anancy-Spiderman*, Berry introduced that West African trickster into the literature. This particular clever character is supposed to outwit his opponents and even whisper stories into children's ears at night, tales told in a mixture of Creole and English. Reviewing the American publication of the collection, a contributor in *Bulletin of the Center for Children's Books* concluded that there was "no question that this is a living tradition." Berry has written two further Anancy tales, *Don't Leave an Elephant to Go and Chase a Bird* and *First Palm Trees*. These picture books reveal different aspects of the trickster. In the former title, Anancy receives a corncob from Skygod. Giving this gift to a hungry woman, he receives a gourd in exchange. Anancy continues to trade up all day until greed leads to his undoing by a herd of elephants. In *First Palm Trees*, Anancy desperately wants to win the king's reward for creating the first palm trees in the world. When he tries to bribe the Spirits into making such a tree and then splitting the reward with him, Anancy learns a lesson of cooperation as each Spirit in turn rejects his offer in favor of working together. A *Kirkus Reviews* critic noted that "Berry uses a lovely West Indian lilt" in this "rollicking, original read-aloud."

Out of Slavery

While writing his second collection of short stories, Berry suddenly realized that there was a missing aspect to his tales. Only as an adult had he come to see the irony of how he and his siblings and friends would play on the ruins of an old slave plantation sugar mill in Jamaica. Growing up he heard bits and pieces of the slave his-

If you enjoy the works of James Berry, you may also want to check out the following books:

Mary E. Lyons, *Letters from a Slave Girl: The Story of Harriet Jacobs*, 1992.
Scott O'Dell, *My Name Is Not Angelica*, 1989.
Frances Temple, *A Taste of Salt*, 1992.

tory of his island; as an adult he brought himself to read of this ignoble past. The missing element from his story collection was the ingredient of slavery—connecting Jamaica with Africa and the slave trade. "Then the full idea struck me," Berry wrote in *Horn Book*. "I was excited. I'd come to know in my writing that whenever the spark of an idea so struck and heated me that sweat instantly poured down my armpits, I was really onto something."

What Berry was onto was the story of a father and his son kidnaped in the early nineteenth century from their African home and shipped into slavery. *Ajeemah and His Son* is a short but hard-hitting book. *Horn Book*'s Gail Pettiford Willett noted that in "eighty-three pages James Berry has given us a most powerful book that will leave the reader with many of the same intense feelings as its characters" Ajeemah and his son. Dawes commented that *Ajeemah and His Son* is Berry's "most ambitious children's book to date," and that it "is telling evidence that Berry is a writer of children's literature to be contended with."

Ajeemah and his son, Atu, are en route to present the bride price—two pieces of gold hidden in Ajeemah's sandals—for Atu's bride-to-be, Sisi. Suddenly set upon by slave traders, they are shipped like cattle to Jamaica. Berry captures the emotions that overcome Ajeemah and Atu as they are taken away, Willett wrote. Once in Jamaica, the father and son are separated, never to see one another again. Both work the Jamaican sugar plantations, but each has a different fate. The father learns to survive, leaving his African roots behind and marrying again, siring a daughter, and ultimately living to be a free man again once the West Indian slaves are freed. But Atu, turned bitter and brutal by the experience, ends his life in suicide.

Hearne, writing in *Bulletin of the Center for Children's Books,* called Berry's prose "hypnotic," noting that he "telescopes a story covering thirty-three years" into a mere eighty-three pages. "The pace achieves a kind of poetic momentum," observed Hearne. "Intense scenes and rhythmic dialogue punctuate the narrative and focus the characters as singular individuals pinioned by history." In a starred *Booklist* review, Rochman wrote that Berry is "a fine poet, and he tells his story with the rhythm, repetition, and lyricism of the oral tradition, tells his story as passionately as the personal account of capture, journey, sale, and toil." Award committees agreed with the critics on

Berry's 1997 poetry collection celebrates life in Jamaica with its musical blend of English and Creole.

this book, and Berry suddenly found himself a well known writer on this side of the Atlantic.

A Writer of Many Parts

Berry has also published several volumes of poetry for young readers and has edited others. His award-winning *When I Dance* was published in 1988 and deals with many of the same concerns as his short fiction. As John Mole noted in a *Times Educational Supplement* review, the poems in this collection are told in the rich-textured language of Berry's Caribbean dialect, "but they exclude no one." Deborah Fenn noted in the *Times Literary Supplement* that these "poems in Creole surprise, excite and engage by the unfamiliar appearance of words on the page, which, written more phonetically than standard English, create the immediacy of a particular voice." Fenn concluded that the poems, divided into eight sections, explore interests and preoccupations of young children as well as probe their private thoughts, and that Berry "brilliantly" achieves the adolescent perspective.

Berry has also written a lyrical poem of the birth of Jesus for the picture book *Celebration Song,* and three further collections: *Rough Sketch Beginning, Everywhere Faces Everywhere,* and *Isn't My Name Magical.* In *Rough Sketch Beginning,* Berry creates a poem about an artist sketching ideas for a landscape painting while the illustrator of the book mirrors that experience in the artwork. Michael Cart, writing in *Booklist,* called this book "beautifully written, lavishly designed, and ingeniously illustrated." A popular collection of forty-six poems, *Everywhere Faces Everywhere* is "lyrical, sometimes topical," according to Cart. "Berry speaks with wit and warmth in a variety of poetic voices, including narrative and dramatic. And as always, he demonstrates an extraordinary gift for richly imaginative simile and metaphor." A reviewer for *Voice of Youth Advocates* called this collection "delightful," and commented that it "will appeal to young adults who enjoy poetry." A critic in *Kirkus Reviews* called *Everywhere Faces Everywhere* "a mosaic-like collection," with poems in styles from haiku to ballad. There is rap, graffiti language and proverb here as well, all in Berry's unmistakable "lyrical" voice.

With his poetry, short stories, and one novel, Berry has filled in that "lack" he felt as a youngster growing up in Jamaica, creating a world of literature which celebrates the black Caribbean experience, both in language and culture. He has given voice to those previously left out of that world which exists between hard covers. Berry wrote in his acceptance speech in *Horn Book* that "To unify ourselves into one human family with an expanded and harmonious human spirit in any kind of abundant one-world is a millions-of-years job. I believe that the sharing of experience through stories is a great contribution towards that. Wanting to share an experience through a story is this wonderful saving grace that we possess."

■ Works Cited

Review of *A Thief in the Village, Junior Bookshelf,* October, 1987, p. 229.

Review of *A Thief in the Village, Publishers Weekly,* January 29, 1988, p. 429.

Berry, James, *A Thief in the Village and Other Stories,* Orchard, 1988.

Berry, James, "Ajeemah and His Son," *Horn Book,* January-February, 1994, pp. 50-52.

Bissoondath, Neil, "The Importance of Simple Things," *New York Times Book Review,* May 8, 1988, p. 30.

Cart, Michael, review of *Rough Sketch Beginning, Booklist,* May 1, 1996, p. 1500.

Cart, Michael, review of *Everywhere Faces Everywhere, Booklist,* May 1, 1997, p. 1496.

Dawes, Kwame S. N., "James Berry," *Writers of Multicultural Fiction for Young Adults,* edited by M. Daphne Kutzer, Greenwood Press, 1996, pp. 43-51.

Review of *Everywhere Faces Everywhere, Kirkus Reviews,* March 15, 1997, p. 458.

Review of *Everywhere Faces Everywhere, Voice of Youth Advocates,* October, 1997, p. 258.

Fader, Ellen, review of *The Future-Telling Lady and Other Stories, Horn Book,* March-April, 1993.

Fenn, Deborah, review of *When I Dance, Times Literary Supplement,* March 3, 1989, p. 232.

Review of *First Palm Trees, Kirkus Reviews,* November 15, 1997, p. 1704.

"Flying Starts: New Faces of 1988," *Publishers Weekly,* December 23, 1988, pp. 27-28.

Review of *The Future-Telling Lady and Other Stories, Junior Bookshelf,* April, 1992, pp. 68-69.

Hearne, Betsy, review of *A Thief in the Village and Other Stories, Bulletin of the Center for Children's Books,* July-August, 1988, p. 223.

Hearne, Betsy, review of *Ajeemah and His Son, Bulletin of the Center for Children's Books,* November, 1992, p. 65, 66.

Miller-Lachmann, Lyn, review of *The Future-Telling Lady and Other Stories, School Library Journal,* February, 1993, p. 92.

Mole, John, "Rap, Pap and Poetry," *Times Educational Supplement,* November 11, 1988, p. 51.

Parisi, James, review of *Chain of Days, Booklist,* December 1, 1985, pp. 524-25.

Rochman, Hazel, "To Be a Slave," *Booklist,* October 1, 1992, p. 315.

Rochman, Hazel, review of *The Future-Telling Lady and Other Stories, Booklist,* February 15, 1993, p. 1061.

Review of *Spiderman-Anancy, Bulletin of the Center for Children's Books,* December, 1989, p. 78.

Willett, Gail Pettiford, review of *Ajeemah and His Son, Horn Book,* March-April, 1993, p. 210.

■ For More Information See

BOOKS

Black Authors and Illustrators of Children's Books, second edition, Garland, 1992.

Children's Literature Review, Volume 22, Gale, 1989, pp. 7-11.

Seventh Book of Junior Authors and Illustrators, H. W. Wilson, 1996.

Twentieth-Century Children's Writers, 5th edition, St. James Press, 1999.

PERIODICALS

Bulletin of the Center for Children's Books, April, 1997, pp. 273-74.

New York Times Book Review, April 25, 1993, p. 24; December 3, 1995, p. 68; May 15, 1998, p. 23.

Publishers Weekly, January 18, 1993, p. 470; October 10, 1994, p. 69; December 11, 1995, p. 70; November 24, 1997, p. 73.

School Library Journal, June, 1988, p. 101; February, 1993, p. 92; May, 1995, p. 111; March, 1996, p. 185; June, 1997, p. 131; December, 1997, p. 105.

Times Educational Supplement, November 29, 1985, p. 24; November 20, 1987, p. 30; June 3, 1988, p. 48; December 6, 1991, p. 32; February 14, 1997, p. 7.*

—*Sketch by J. Sydney Jones*

Dee Brown

Military service: U.S. Army, 1942-45. *Member:* Authors Guild, Western Writers of America, Society of American Historians, Beta Phi Mu.

■ Personal

Born February 28, 1908, in Alberta, LA; son of Daniel Alexander and Lulu (Cranford) Brown; married Sara Baird Stroud, August 1, 1934; children: James Mitchell, Linda. *Education:* Attended Arkansas State Teachers College (now University of Central Arkansas); George Washington University, B.L.S., 1937; University of Illinois, M.L.S., 1952.

■ Addresses

Home—7 Overlook Dr., Little Rock, AR 72207-1619.

■ Career

U.S. Department of Agriculture, Washington, DC, library assistant, 1934-39; Beltsville Research Center, Beltsville, MD, librarian, 1940-42; U.S. War Department, Aberdeen Proving Ground, Aberdeen, MD, technical librarian, 1945-48; University of Illinois at Urbana-Champaign, librarian of agriculture, 1948-72, professor of library science, 1962-75.

■ Awards, Honors

Clarence Day Award from American Library Association, 1971, for *The Year of the Century: 1876;* Christopher Award, 1971; Buffalo Award from New York Westerners, 1971, for *Bury My Heart at Wounded Knee;* named Illinoisan of the Year by Illinois News Broadcasters Association, 1972; Best Western for young people award from Western Writers of America, 1981, for *Hear That Lonesome Whistle Blow: Railroads in the West;* Saddleman Award from Western Writers of America, 1984.

■ Writings

NOVELS

Wave High the Banner (based on life of Davy Crockett), Macrae Smith, 1942.
Yellowhorse, Houghton (Boston), 1956.
Cavalry Scout, Permabooks, 1958.
They Went Thataway (satire), Putnam (New York City), 1960, reprinted as *Pardon My Pandemonium,* August House (Little Rock, AR), 1984.
The Girl from Fort Wicked, Doubleday (New York City), 1964.
Creek Mary's Blood, Holt (New York City), 1980.
Killdeer Mountain, Holt, 1983.

Conspiracy of Knaves, Holt, 1986.
The Way to Bright Star, Forge, 1998.

NONFICTION

Grierson's Raid, University of Illinois Press (Champaign), 1954.
The Gentle Tamers: Women of the Old Wild West, Putnam, 1958.
The Bold Cavaliers: Morgan's Second Kentucky Cavalry Raiders, Lippincott (Philadelphia), 1959.
(Editor) George B. Grinnell, *Pawnee, Blackfoot, and Cheyenne*, Scribner (New York City), 1961.
Fort Phil Kearny: An American Saga, Putnam, 1962, published in England as *The Fetterman Massacre*, Bar-rie & Jenkins, 1972, reprinted as *The Fetterman Massacre*, University of Nebraska Press (Lincoln), 1984.
The Galvanized Yankees, University of Illinois Press, 1963.
The Year of the Century: 1876, Scribner, 1966.
Action at Beecher Island, Doubleday, 1967.
Bury My Heart at Wounded Knee: An Indian History of the American West, Holt, 1970, abridged edition for children by Amy Erlich published as *Wounded Knee: An Indian History of the American West*, Holt, 1974.
Andrew Jackson and the Battle of New Orleans, Putnam, 1972.
Tales of the Warrior Ants, Putnam, 1973.
The Westerners, Holt, 1974.
Hear That Lonesome Whistle Blow: Railroads in the West (also see below), Holt, 1977.
American Spa: Hot Springs, Arkansas, Rose Publishing (Little Rock, AR), 1982.
(Contributor) *Growing Up Western: Recollections*, Knopf (New York City), 1990.
Wondrous Times on the Frontier, August House, 1991.
When the Century Was Young: A Writer's Notebook (autobiographical) August House, 1993.
Images of the Old West, with paintings of Mort Kunstler, Park Lane Press (New York City), 1996.
(Editor) Stan Banash, *Best of Dee Brown's West: An Anthology*, Clear Light Publishers (Santa Fe, NM), 1997.

WITH MARTIN F. SCHMITT

Fighting Indians of the West (see also below), Scribner, 1948.
Trail Driving Days (see also below), Scribner, 1952.
The Settlers' West (see also below), Scribner, 1955.

The American West (contains *Fighting Indians of the West, Trail Driving Days*, and *The Settlers' West*), Scribner, 1994.

JUVENILE

Showdown at Little Big Horn, Putnam, 1964.
Teepee Tales of the American Indians, Holt, 1979, reprinted as *Dee Brown's Folktales of the Native American, Retold for Our Times*, illustrated by Louis Mofsie, Owl Books, 1993.
(With Linda Proctor) *Lonesome Whistle: The Story of the First Transcontinental Railroad*, (abridged edition of *Hear That Lonesome Whistle Blow: Railroads in the West*), Holt, 1980.

Editor of "Rural America" series, Scholarly Resources, 1973. Contributor of articles to periodicals, including *American History Illustrated, Civil War Times*, and *Southern Magazine*. Editor of *Agricultural History*, 1956-58.

Brown's books have been published in more than twenty languages, including Latvian, Russian, and Icelandic.

■ Sidelights

Dee Brown is the author of some thirty books of fiction and nonfiction, including the critically acclaimed and worldwide bestseller, *Bury My Heart at Wounded Knee*. Published in 1970, that history of the "winning" of the American West as told from the viewpoint of the Native Americans who were dispossessed in the process has sold over five million copies and has been translated into fifteen languages. *Bury My Heart at Wounded Knee* is also indicative of Brown's interests, techniques, and themes. Most of his works, both fiction and nonfiction, deal with Western history, are told in a strong narrative voice by focusing on individual lives emblematic of certain periods and concerns, and examine with a critical eye the side effects of the westward march of "progress."

Writing in *Dictionary of Literary Biography Yearbook: 1980*, Winifred Farrant Bevilacqua insightfully summed up Brown's literary achievement. "Viewing history as the interaction of many dynamic and prosaic factors," Bevilacqua wrote, "in fairly orthodox regional studies as well as in openly critical accounts, Dee Brown has, over the years, examined nearly every chapter in the saga of the westward movement. His best work, generally based on original documents, has portrayed the destruction of ancient Indian cultures and investigated other aspects of the toll exacted by the nation's westward expansion." Reviewing Brown's memoirs, *When the Century Was Young,* in the *Washington Post Book World,* John Espey noted that "Brown is a master of the plain style, modulating it skillfully to fit whatever engages his sense of wonder and discovery."

Brown began this "plain style" in 1942 with a fictional account of Davy Crockett, and has continued it throughout a career spanning nearly six decades. In 1998, at age ninety, he published yet another historical novel, *The Way to Bright Star,* chronicling the picaresque adventures of a fifteen-year-old boy during the American Civil War. In the intervening fifty-six years, he has written of pioneering men and women, of Civil War actions, of the construction of the transcontinental railroad, of cattle drives, and of beleaguered Native Americans. His style is engaging; his narratives entertaining as well as educational. Even in his fiction he attempts to stick as closely as possible to the historical record. Brown reaches a wide audience with his novels and nonfiction; he has broadened that readership by writing for juveniles and abridging some of his histories, including *Bury My Heart at Wounded Knee* and *Hear That Lonesome Whistle Blow,* for younger readers.

An Arkansas Childhood

Born in Louisiana in 1908, Brown moved with his widowed mother at an early age to nearby Stephens, Arkansas, to be near relatives. While his mother labored by day at a local dry-goods store, his grandmother took care of him and his younger sister. This grandmother had been a schoolteacher most of her life and still kept a shelf full of school readers. One day she sat the pre-school Brown on her lap and introduced him to the marvels of printed words. Suddenly these little marks that he had previously only barely noticed beneath pictures in magazines and on the pages of newspapers sprang to life. "It was the most startling event of my childhood," Brown recalled in *Contemporary Authors Autobiography Series (CAAS).* "From that moment I was an addict of the printed word, and addicts of the printed word, I eventually discovered, are almost certain to become compulsive writers, hooked on pencils and pens, and

typewriters, and nowadays marvelous contrivances called word processors."

Brown's reading addiction had expanded to Robert Louis Stevenson and Mark Twain by the time he entered first grade; he was also an avid magazine reader. Soon he also discovered the local printing plant in Stephens, and its owners introduced him to the wonderful world of type setting using a composing stick. Reading material as well as local characters increased in number and variety with the discovery of oil nearby; the small town of Stephens was inundated by the assorted panoply of actors in such a financial drama, and Brown's own stock increased as well. His mother having just been made the postmistress, he was

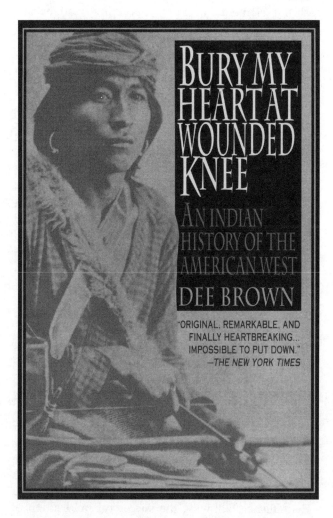

Brown's powerful 1970 book about the systematic destruction of Native American tribes as told through the eyes of the chiefs and warriors themselves has won wide critical acclaim.

pressed into service for special delivery letters, earning a dime for each successful delivery.

Brown left Stephens behind for high school, his family moving to Little Rock. "I do not know whether the schooling was any better or not," he noted in *CAAS*, "but downtown there was a splendid public library that in those more literate times was warmly supported by a majority of the citizens and their elected officials." This library soon became Brown's second home. A school librarian also influenced Brown's life in ways she could never have imagined. Introducing him to the three-volume history of the Lewis and Clark Expedition, this librarian "started me upon a course that I was to follow into my career as a writer," he commented in *CAAS*. This narrative history of the adventures of a journey involved all the elements of fine storytelling: danger, intrigue, romance and heroic lead characters. It was a formula that would inform all that Brown subsequently wrote.

Other early influences included the works of Sherwood Anderson, especially his *Winesburg, Ohio*, and that of John Dos Passos, such as *Manhattan Transfer* and the *U.S.A.* trilogy. Later these writers were joined by William Faulkner and Joseph Conrad to help round out Brown's artistic antecedents. By high school he was already writing his own short stories, winning $100 for an adventure story submitted to a contest in the pulp magazine *Blue Book*. In the next years he sold two more stories to the same magazine; he was encouraged to believe that he could actually earn a living from doing something he loved.

During his youth, Brown also made the acquaintance of many Indians from the region and slowly began to learn that the old myths about Indians had no validity. He had a best friend for a time who was Native American, and a pitcher for a local minor league team who helped him get free entry to baseball games also made him wonder about "all the blood-and-thunder tales of frontier Indian savagery." Increasingly when he went to the Saturday matinees featuring Westerns, he "cheered the warriors who were always cast as villains." In a *Publishers Weekly* interview with Lila P. Freilicher following the successful publication of *Bury My Heart at Wounded Knee*, Brown enlarged on this. "I grew up around the oil fields of Oklahoma where many of the workers were Oklahoma Indians," Brown told Freilicher. "All my buddies

"This tale of America's Gilded Age is told with a vigor and irony that do full justice to its excesses, energies, venalities, and dreams." —*Newsweek*

Hear That Lonesome Whistle Blow

RAILROADS IN THE WEST

DEE BROWN   author of BURY MY HEART AT WOUNDED KNEE

Continuing his interest in the American West, Brown's history of the expansion of railroads across the continent includes fascinating stories of the famous, the infamous, and even the common laborer.

were Indians. We would go to the Western movies together and it was then that I had my first real revelation about Indians. My buddy said to me, 'You know those aren't real Indians.'" This started Brown reading, and began in him a lifelong quest to show what Native Americans actually were and are like and what happened to them with the advent of the European in the Americas.

Upon graduation from high school, Brown worked for a time as a printer and reporter on a small newspaper in the heart of the Ozarks. He began his career humbly enough setting type for Christmas cards, then slowly graduated to the news end of the business when serendipity put him at the scene of a hurricane. His newspaper took advantage of his firsthand account, written directly onto the linotype machine so as to make that day's deadline. The brothers who owned the newspaper would sometimes give Brown hints on improving his writing style, teaching him about clarity and conciseness. "When I left their employment to go to college," Brown recalled in *CAAS*, "they probably soon forgot me, but I have never forgotten Tom and John Newman for the parts they played in helping me learn the skills I would use the remainder of my days."

From Librarian to Author

Brown slowly realized that there was a bigger world out there that he did not know about. College seemed a good place to start learning. He enrolled at Arkansas State Teachers College, intending to become a teacher, but later changed his major to library science. While there, he studied history with Dean McBrien, a professor fresh out of school himself and fired with an ambition to teach. McBrien not only enthused his students with his narrative reconstructions of history and his emphasis on the fascinating details of personal biographies to enliven such reconstructions, but also inspired select students each summer by taking them on road trips into and across the Old West. "These journeys and others that crisscrossed the West formed a basis for most of the books I would later write," Brown commented in *CAAS*.

Brown moved on to Washington, D.C., for graduate school in library science, attending George Washington University and working in filling stations, fast food restaurants, and as a repairman to put himself through school. This was the height of the Great Depression, the end of Hoover's presidency and the beginning of Roosevelt's New Deal. Washington was a vital city to be living in at the time. Brown had artist friends in the Federal Writers Project and soon began submitting his own work to small magazines. Finally Brown secured daytime employment with the Food and Drug Administration while continuing classes at night. He also married his college sweetheart, Sally Stroud, and set up a home.

One of his story submissions was published shortly thereafter, and Brown was approached by a New York agent to see if he had a novel in the works. He didn't, but soon wrote one for her,

a satire on the New Deal and Washington that was quickly sold. Then came the attack on Pearl Harbor and America's entry into the Second World War. Brown's publisher backed out of the deal on his satire, requesting something more patriotic. Brown had long wanted to write a biography of the frontiersman, Davy Crockett, but figured there was no time for such a venture now that he might be called up for service any day. In the event, he turned to a fictional account, writing his first novel, *Wave High the Banner*, in a matter of a few months. Published in 1942 shortly before Brown went into the Army, this novel was called "an exceptionally shrewd and just evaluation of a picturesque frontiersman" by Margaret Wallace writing in the *New York Times Book Review*. "'Wave High the Banner' is a sound and

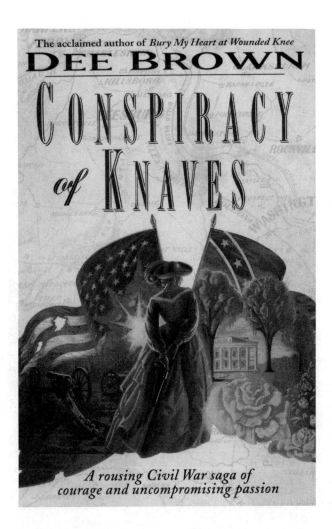

The acclaimed author of *Bury My Heart at Wounded Knee*

DEE BROWN

CONSPIRACY of KNAVES

A rousing Civil War saga of courage and uncompromising passion

Brown uses his extensive knowledge of the Civil War as the backdrop for this romantic tale of a female double agent.

honest and well-considered piece of work, entirely worthy of its subject," Wallace concluded.

Meanwhile, Brown was in basic training, one of millions of others called up to serve their country. He survived the war without firing a single shot at the enemy. Much of this time was spent lost in a bureaucratic muddle in Alabama, Philadelphia, Iowa, and finally back in Washington at the Army Ground Forces Headquarters. Here he met Martin Schmitt, and as the war came to an end and they were waiting for their discharges, they began collaboration on a pictorial history of the Indian wars. After considerable difficulties finding a publisher, they finally saw their book, *Fighting Indians of the West*, brought out by Scribner in 1948. Shortly after publication, Brown

AN ASTONISHING EPIC OF AMERICAN HISTORY BY THE RENOWNED
AUTHOR OF BURY MY HEART AT WOUNDED KNEE

The Way to
BRIGHT STAR

DEE BROWN

Still writing at the age of ninety, Brown won praise yet again with his picaresque adventure novel about a fifteen-year-old boy's life during the Civil War.

accepted a library position at the University of Illinois in Urbana where he remained until 1975, ultimately teaching in the library science program.

Bury My Heart at Wounded Knee

During the 1950s and 1960s Brown wore many hats. He was a father of two children, an academic librarian, and a part-time writer. During these years he published seventeen books, mostly in the field of nonfiction history, but also historical fiction. He compiled two more pictorial histories with Schmitt before moving on to solo efforts on the Civil War, including *Grierson's Raid*, *The Bold Cavaliers*, and *The Galvanized Yankees*. A western novel, *Yellowhorse*, was written to finance the purchase of a new car. "At this period in my life I thought I knew the different kinds of books I could write, and those I wanted to write," Brown observed in *CAAS*. "Yet writing was still an avocation, something I did partly for pleasure, especially for the pleasure of research."

One of the more powerful early histories from Brown is *The Gentle Tamers*, "an entertaining and factual introduction to the part women played in the shaping of the American West," according to Bevilacqua. Long before such feminist histories were popular, Brown tipped the historical hat to the women who had taken part in the westward migrations with every bit as much spirit and contempt for danger as did the men. Here were gathered women from missionaries such as Narcissa Whitman to the notorious such as Lola Montez. Stewart Holbrook, writing in the *New York Herald Tribune Book Review*, called Brown's assemblage of notable women an "excellent book," while Marshall Sprague noted "a sociological overtone" to "the book's fascinating comedy and pathos and terror" in the *New York Times Book Review*. Sprague concluded that "Brown . . . has produced an entertaining as well as instructive work. . . ."

Nothing, however, quite prepared the reviewers and the reading public alike for his 1970 publication, *Bury My Heart at Wounded Knee*. "By this time I did not know it," Brown wrote in *CAAS*, "but I was ready to write *Bury My Heart at Wounded Knee*." This book began life as a projected juvenile work on the Indian wars. But once Brown delivered an outline to his agent, Peter Matson, the idea was met with such enthusiasm that Brown turned the project into a larger and more comprehensive affair. For years he had been saving speeches and comments from Native Americans that he had culled from the archives. Once the project was sold to Holt, Brown took two years in the writing of it, maintaining a consistently Native American point of view throughout the writing, detailing the results of the philosophy of Manifest Destiny from the standpoint of the victims. "I collected so much information," Brown told Freilicher in *Publishers Weekly*, "that I thought it would drive me out of the house." The cartons of photocopies of treaties, photos, and other records took up half of a room, stacked floor to ceiling. After a full day of working at the library, Brown would come home and imagine himself an Indian elder in the nineteenth century relating the events of the thirty years from 1860 to 1890 in which the last of the Native Americans were driven from their land.

"Meticulously researched, original in its approach, and ardently told, *Bury My Heart at Wounded Knee: An Indian History of the American West*, deservedly received both popular and critical acclaim," Bevilacqua noted. Its structure was straightforward: Brown recounted the final destruction of Native American culture—the remaining 300,000 Indian survivors of European onslaught since the time of Columbus—which began with a fervor starting in 1860. "This is not a cheerful book," Brown wrote in his introduction, "but history has a way of intruding upon the present, and perhaps those who read it will have a clearer understanding of what the American Indian is, by knowing what he was. They may be surprised to hear words of gentle reasonableness coming from the mouths of Indians stereotyped in the American myth as ruthless savages."

Unashamedly revisionist, *Bury My Heart at Wounded Knee* provides an alternate history of the West and the frontier; it is one told unremittingly from the perspective of the Indian. Major white actors in the drama are always referred to by their Native American sobriquet. Thus General George Armstrong Custer, for example, is called Hard Backsides in the book. Brown chronicles the Indian struggle to protect the last of the their lands from the ever expanding white population in the late nineteenth century. Each chapter focuses on a different tribe—Navaho, Nez Perce, Kiowas, Sioux, and many more—and on the major historical events that ultimately drove that group from their ancestral lands. Here are the conflicts, treaties, and

betrayals all laid out in chronological order, interspersed with firsthand reports from the Indians themselves. Crazy Horse, Chief Joseph, Geronimo, and Sitting Bull are all allowed to speak for themselves, and most eloquently at that. A final chapter works as a symbolic conclusion to the business of colonization. Over two hundred representatives of various tribes who had gathered at Wounded Knee in South Dakota to take part in a ghost dance were slaughtered by soldiers who believed they had gathered to foment another uprising. From this "battle," the book takes its name.

Critical reaction to *Bury My Heart at Wounded Knee* was overwhelmingly positive. N. Scott Momaday, writing in the *New York Times Book Review*, called it an "extraordinary" book and "a compelling history of the American West" because of its depth of research and its Native American point of view. Helen McNeil, writing in *New Statesman* saw the book in political terms as a "scholarly and passionate chronicle" that was able to reach "bestsellerdom" because of the changed mood of the American public as a result of the Vietnam War. That war made it possible for the country to accept communal guilt for historical actions such as "the extermination of the American Indian." But McNeil also noted Brown's objectivity. "For a study whose proximity to national illusions would seem to make stereotypes inevitable, *Bury My Heart* is amazingly myth-free." Part of the power of the book, according to McNeil and other reviewers, is the consistently employed Native American perspective, so that even the Battle of the Little Big Horn, far from being Custer's Last Stand, "is shown to be the Cheyennes and Oglala Sioux making a last stand against invaders of sacred land traditionally theirs and specifically promised them by the Treaty of 1868."

Other critics also pointed out the revisionist implications of Brown's work. Cecil Eby, writing in *Washington Post Book World*, called *Bury My Heart at Wounded Knee* "a painful, shocking book which conveys not how the West was won, but how it was lost. . . ." Peter Farb, in the *New York Review of Books*, commented that "Brown dispels any illusions that may still exist that the Indian wars were civilization's mission or manifest destiny; the Indian wars are shown to be the dirty murders they were. . . . *Bury My Heart* is an attempt to write a different kind of history of white conquest of the West."

If you enjoy the works of Dee Brown, you may also want to check out the following books and films:

Sherman Alexie, *Smoke Signals,* 1998.
Scott O'Dell, *Thunder Rolling in the Mountains,* 1992.
Dances with Wolves, a film directed by Kevin Costner, 1990.

When *Bury My Heart at Wounded Knee* soared to the top of the bestseller lists and stayed there for a year, Brown became something of a talking head, appearing on television shows and touring the country. It took him over a year to find time to get back to his writing. "I'm sure glad this didn't happen to me 20 years ago," Brown told Freilicher in *Publishers Weekly.* "I would have thought myself a great author and I would have been insufferable."

More Tales of the Old West

With *Hear That Lonesome Whistle Blow,* Brown did for the construction of the transcontinental railroad what he had done for the doctrine of Manifest Destiny in *Bury My Heart.* His account took the glamour out of the building of that railway, showing the treacherous dealings the railroad companies engaged in to accomplish it. Writing in the *Washington Post Book World,* Peter J. Ognibene observed that "Brown has an impressive grasp of the political and economic dynamics which turned the building of the western railroads from an initially noble enterprise into a national disgrace." Ognibene went on to conclude that "It is a fascinating story, but at another level it is a cautionary tale." Bevilacqua called Brown's history "an engaging reconstruction of the drama surrounding the advent of the iron horse and a case against the railroads."

Brown's achievements in fiction also are notable in their reconstruction of events in the Old West. In *Creek Mary's Blood,* "his most ambitious novel," according to Bevilacqua, Brown tells the story of a Native American family from the time of the Revolution to the beginning of the twentieth century. Writing in *School Library Journal,* Cathy Clancy observed that "Dee Brown communicates

well the past sufferings and the present resentments of Native Americans, and his tale will enhance readers' concern." A critic in *Publishers Weekly* said that the work was "history cast in very human terms," while Joseph McLellan noted in *Washington Post Book World* that by "Using fictional characters against a carefully researched historical background, [Brown] combines the attractions of both genres." Mary Silva Cosgrave, writing in *Horn Book,* dubbed this 1980 novel "an inspired, brilliantly conceived" account of the efforts of the descendants of one American Indian family to preserve tribal lands "doomed by the white man's treachery, power, and greed."

More Western action was served up in *Killdeer Mountain,* the reconstruction of the life of an Indian fighter, Major Charles Rawley, as told by various people who knew Rawley during his career. These conflicting stories are tracked down by a newspaperman, Samuel Morrison, who is trying to make some sense of the major's life. *Horn Book*'s Cosgrave called *Killdeer Mountain* "a novel of high suspense and drama" placed against the backdrop of the struggle between the United States government and the American Indians, and Lois A. Strell noted in *School Library Journal* that Brown "has written a sophisticated yarn for good readers."

In 1998, at age ninety, Brown brought out a coming-of-age novel entitled *The Way to Bright Star,* the saga of fifteen-year-old Ben Butterfield. In 1862, young Ben leaves an Arkansas torn by the Civil War to help bring a pair of camels to the farm of a Union officer in Indiana. The animals had been seized as war contraband, but en route Ben is faced with a myriad of adventures and dangers, including being captured by Union troops, being robbed, and even falling in love. *Booklist*'s Brad Hooper called the work a "compelling narrative" and a "picaresque yarn whose main strength rests in its cast of colorful characters." These are people, Hooper felt, "with whom [the readers] will want to spend time." A critic *Kirkus Reviews* stated that *The Way to Bright Star* was "a sweet-natured, vigorous, colorful entertainment, and a compelling portrait of the frontier" by a "prolific western historian."

"Prolific" is a word often used to describe Dee Brown. But for Brown, it is doing what he loves. As he concluded in *CAAS,* there is a balance to be maintained between simply writing a book and writing one that is necessary. "Because far too many books are published, we writers should give more deliberation to what we are about to create. Is it entertaining, is it informative, is it unique? Can the world get along without it?" Throughout the course of his long writing career, Brown has produced books that answer his own criteria, creating a body of work that, in his own humble words, "contain[s] at least some small kernel that the world is in need of."

■ Works Cited

Bevilacqua, Winifred Farrant, "Dee Brown," *Dictionary of Literary Biography Yearbook, 1980*, Gale, 1981, pp. 143-47.

Brown, Dee, "Introduction," *Bury My Heart at Wounded Knee*, Holt, 1970, pp. xvi-xvii.

Brown, Dee, essay in *Contemporary Authors Autobiography Series*, Volume 6, Gale, 1988, pp. 45-59.

Clancy, Cathy, review of *Creek Mary's Blood*, School Library Journal, March, 1980, p. 146.

Cosgrave, Mary Silva, review of *Creek Mary's Blood*, Horn Book, August, 1980, p. 446.

Cosgrave, Mary Silva, review of *Killdeer Mountain*, Horn Book, June, 1983, pp. 336-37.

Review of *Creek Mary's Blood*, Publishers Weekly, February 8, 1980, p. 65.

Eby, Cecil, "How the West Was Lost," *Washington Post Book World*, February 28, 1971, p. 3.

Espey, John, "Memoirs of an Arkansas Traveler," *Washington Post Book World*, September 12, 1993, pp. 3, 7.

Farb, Peter, "Indian Corn," *New York Review of Books*, December 16, 1971, p. 36.

Freilicher, Lila P., "The Story Behind the Book: 'Bury My Heart at Wounded Knee'," *Publishers Weekly*, April 19, 1971, pp. 34-35.

Holbrook, Stewart, "A Gallery of Women, Very Few with Sunbonnets," *New York Herald Tribune Book Review*, April 13, 1958, p. 3.

Hooper, Brad, review of *The Way to Bright Star*, Booklist, May 15, 1998, p. 1563.

McLellan, Joseph, "Following the Trail of Tears," *Washington Post Book World*, March 16, 1980, pp. 4-5.

McNeil, Helen, "Savage," *New Statesman*, October 1, 1971, pp. 444-45.

Momaday, N. Scott, "When the West Was Won and Civilization Lost," *New York Times Book Review*, March 7, 1971, pp. 46-47.

Ognibene, Peter J., "How the West Was Overrun," *Washington Post Book World*, May 15, 1977, p. H7.

Sprague, Marshall, "On the Western Trail There Was Nobody Like a Dame," *New York Times Book Review*, April 20, 1958, pp. 6, 37.

Strell, Lois A., review of *Killdeer Mountain*, School Library Journal, March, 1983, pp. 199-200.

Wallace, Margaret, review of *Wave High the Banner*, New York Times Book Review, May 3, 1942, p. 16.

Review of *The Way to Bright Star*, Kirkus Reviews, May 1, 1998.

■ For More Information See

BOOKS

Contemporary Literary Criticism, Gale, Volume 18, 1981, Volume 47, 1988.

Snodgrass, Mary Ellen, *Encyclopedia of Frontier Literature*, ABC-Clio (Santa Barbara, CA), 1997.

Twentieth-Century Western Writers, St. James Press, 1991.

PERIODICALS

American Historical Review, April, 1955.
American West, March, 1975.
Atlantic Monthly, February, 1971.
Best Sellers, March 1, 1971.
Booklist, September 1, 1993, p. 27; October 15, 1994, p. 397; January 15, 1995, p. 855.
Book World, February 28, 1971, p. 3.
Catholic World, August, 1971.
Chicago Tribune Book World, March 2, 1980; March 13, 1983.
Christian Century, February 3, 1971.
Christian Science Monitor, June 21, 1977.
Detroit News, July 13, 1983.
Economist, October 2, 1971; September 10, 1977.
Globe and Mail (Toronto), February 14, 1987.
Guardian, September 21, 1974.
Journal of American History, November, 1966.
Library Journal, December 15, 1970, p. 4257; October 15, 1994, p. 73.
Life, April 2, 1971.
Lone Star Book Review, April, 1980, pp. 11, 24-25.
Los Angeles Times, July 1, 1987.
Los Angeles Times Book Review, April 3, 1983, pp. 2, 9; January 25, 1987, p. 2; August 9, 1987, p. 4; October 2, 1988, p. 14; December 18, 1994, p. 2.
National Review, March 9, 1971.
New Republic, December 14, 1974, p. 28.

New Statesman, September 20, 1977, pp. 451-52.

Newsweek, February 1, 1971; May 23, 1977; March 28, 1983, p. 71.

New York, April 7, 1980, pp. 76-77.

New Yorker, February 13, 1971.

New York Post, April 22, 1971.

New York Times, December 3, 1976; April 13, 1980.

New York Times Book Review, May 15, 1977, p. 15; April 13, 1980; April 27, 1980, p. 50; May 25, 1980, pp. 10, 22; April 26, 1981; June 5, 1983, pp. 15, 21; June 17, 1984, p. 20; January 11, 1987, pp. 12-13; April 21, 1991, p. 32; February 2, 1992, p. 11; January 29, 1995, p. 16; June 14, 1998, p. 20.

Pacific Historical Review, November, 1972.

Publishers Weekly, March 21, 1980; October 4, 1991, p. 73; October 24, 1994, pp. 47-48; January 20, 1997, p. 388.

Time, February 1, 1971, p. K8.

Times Literary Supplement, December 16, 1977.

Tribune Books (Chicago), January 25, 1987, p. 5.

Village Voice, August 5, 1971; June 27, 1977.

Voice Literary Supplement, November, 1991, p. 13.

Washington Post Book World, March 14, 1983; January 18, 1987, p. 7; March 3, 1991; January 5, 1992, pp. 6-7; December 27, 1992; January 8, 1995, p. 9.

Wilson Library Bulletin, March, 1978.*

—Sketch by J. Sydney Jones

Judith Ortiz Cofer

■ Personal

Born February 24, 1952, in Hormigueros, Puerto Rico; immigrated to United States, 1956; daughter of J. M. (in U.S. Navy) and Fanny (Morot) Ortiz; married Charles John Cofer (in business), November 13, 1971; children: Tanya. *Education:* Augusta College, B.A., 1974; Florida Atlantic University, M.A., 1977; attended Oxford University, 1977.

■ Addresses

Home—P.O. Box 938, Louisville, GA 30434. *Office*—Mercer University College, Forsyth, GA 31029. *Agent*—Berenice Hoffman Literary Agency, 215 West 75th St., New York, NY 10023.

■ Career

Bilingual teacher at public schools in Palm Beach County, FL, 1974-75; Broward Community College, Fort Lauderdale, FL, adjunct instructor in English, 1978-80, instructor in Spanish, 1979; University of Miami, Coral Gables, FL, lecturer in English, 1980-84; University of Georgia, Athens, instructor in English, 1984-87, Georgia Center for Continuing Education, instructor in English, 1987-88; Macon College, instructor in English, 1988-89; Mercer University College, Forsyth, GA, special programs coordinator, 1990; professor of English and Creative Writing, University of Georgia, 1994—. Adjunct instructor at Palm Beach Junior College, 1978-80. Conducts poetry workshops and gives poetry readings. Member of regular staff of International Conference on the Fantastic in Literature, 1979-82; member of literature panel of Fine Arts Council of Florida, 1982; member of administrative staff of Bread Loaf Writers' Conference, 1983 and 1984. *Member:* Poetry Society of America, Poets and Writers, Associated Writing Programs.

■ Awards, Honors

Scholar of English Speaking Union at Oxford University, 1977; fellow of Fine Arts Council of Florida, 1980; Bread Loaf Writers' Conference, scholar, 1981, John Atherton Scholar in Poetry, 1982; grant from Witter Bynner Foundation for Poetry, 1988, for *Letters From a Caribbean Island;* National Endowment for the Arts fellowship in poetry, 1989; nominee, Pulitzer Prize, 1990, for *The Line of the Sun;* PEN/Martha Albrand Special Citation, for *Silent Dancing;* Anisfield-Wolf Book Award, for *The Latin Deli;* O. Henry Award, 1994, for "Nada," a short story from *The Latin Deli;* Best

Book of the Year citation, American Library Association (ALA), 1996, for *An Island Like You: Stories of the Barrio;* awarded the first Pura Belpre medal by REFORM of ALA, 1996.

■ Writings

Latin Women Pray (chapbook), Florida Arts Gazette Press, 1980.

The Native Dancer (chapbook), Pteranodon Press, 1981.

Among the Ancestors (chapbook), Louisville News Press, 1981.

Latin Women Pray (three-act play), first produced in Atlanta at Georgia State University, June, 1984.

Peregrina (poems), Riverstone Press, 1986.

Terms of Survival (poems), Arte Publico, 1987.

(Contributor) *Triple Crown: Chicano, Puerto Rican and Cuban American Poetry* (trilogy; contains Ortiz Cofer's poetry collection *Reaching for the Mainland*), Bilingual Press, 1987.

The Line of the Sun (novel), University of Georgia Press, 1989, published in Spanish translation as *La linea del sol,* University of Puerto Rico Press, 1997.

Silent Dancing (personal essays), Arte Publico, 1990, published in Spanish translation as *Bailando en silencio,* Arte Publico, 1999.

The Latin Deli: Prose and Poetry, University of Georgia Press, 1993.

An Island Like You: Stories of the Barrio (short stories), Orchard Books, 1995.

Reaching for the Mainland and Selected New Poems, Bilingual Press, 1995.

The Year of Our Revolution: Selected and New Stories and Poems, Piñata Books, 1998.

Also author of the poetry collection *Letters From a Caribbean Island.* Work represented in anthologies, including *Hispanics in the U.S.,* Bilingual Review/Press, 1982; *Latina Writers; Revista Chicano-Riquena;* and *Heath Anthology of Modern American Literature.* Contributor of poems and articles to magazines, including *Glamour, The Georgia Review, Kenyon Review, Southern Humanities Review, Poem, Prairie Schooner, Apalachee Quarterly, Kansas Quarterly,* and *Kalliope.* Poetry editor of *Florida Arts Gazette,* 1978-81; member of editorial board of *Waves.* Ortiz Cofer has been anthologized in *The Best American Essays, The Norton Book of Women's Lives, The Pushcart Prize,* and the *O. Henry Prize Stories.*

■ Sidelights

"People ask me: If I am a Puerto Rican writer, why don't I write in Spanish?" the poet, essayist, and author Judith Ortiz Cofer wrote in the online publication, *The Global Education Project.* "Isn't writing in English a sellout? I respond that English is my literary language. The language of the country my parents brought me to. Spanish is my familial language, that lies between the lines of my English language. Because I am a daughter of the Puerto Rican diaspora, English gives life to my writing."

Such bilingual concerns are part of the territory for Cofer, born in Puerto Rico and raised in the U.S. A member of the Puerto Rican "diaspora," she however differs from other well-known writers of that experience in that she is a woman writing in standard American English, and she writes not of immigrant life in New York, but of life on the home island and in Paterson, New Jersey, where Cofer herself grew up. Roberto Márquez, writing in a *New York Times Book Review* article on Cofer's *The Line of the Sun,* declared that "Judith Ortiz Cofer's first novel confirms the continuing efflorescence and enlarges the resonance and reach of this [immigrant] literature." In her first novel, as well as in her collections of poetry and prose for adults such as *Silent Dancing* and *The Latin Deli,* and in collections intended for the young adult market, *An Island Like You* and *The Year of Our Revolution,* Cofer has made the bicultural experience understandable and approachable.

"I Am a Latina Wherever I Am"

Born in Puerto Rico in 1952, Cofer was brought to the United States at the age of two. Her mother and father married as teenagers, and her father was stationed with the military in Panama when Cofer was born. "He didn't come back home until I was two years old, and I had to get used to him at that time," Cofer told Rafael Ocasio in an interview in *The Americas Review.* Out of the army, her father tried to make a go of it in civilian life, but for financial reasons he again joined the armed forces, this time in the U.S. Navy. "That's when our back-and-forth travels began," Cofer told Ocasio. The family moved to Paterson, New Jersey, but would migrate back and forth between there and Puerto Rico every six months when her father sailed with the cargo fleet to Europe. They would stay with Cofer's maternal grandmother when in Puerto Rico, and it was during these periods that Cofer internalized the life, language, and culture of her homeland.

"Spanish was my home language, and it still is my family language, but that vocabulary has to do mainly with family matters," Cofer told Ocasio in her interview. Though she sometimes still dreams in Spanish, her broader linguistic experience is in the language of her adopted country, American English. Those years of traveling back and forth between Paterson and Puerto Rico provided Cofer with a fund of stories and experiences she still draws upon. The contrast between

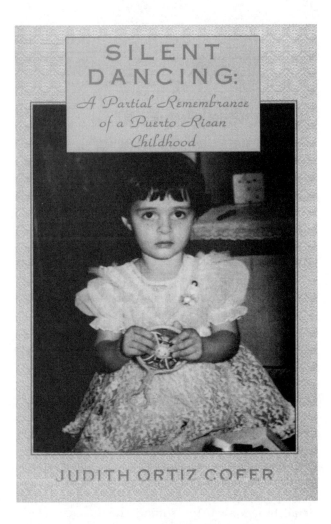

In her award-winning memoir of her early life in Puerto Rico, Cofer combines poetry with prose to explain her feelings about growing up experiencing two very different cultures.

America and her native island was sharp and deep—from the urban environment of Paterson to the rural and tradition-bound life in the village in Puerto Rico.

"The main contrast had to do, of course, with culture and language, as well as climate," Cofer told Ocasio. Her mother felt more secure on the island, for she could communicate better and was more at home in the small town environment provided there: "The shifts were abrupt and always traumatic, going back and forth." On the island, the children attended Catholic school taught by American nuns so that they would keep up their English skills. Cofer was the eternal new kid at school with these semi-annual moves. In the midst of such constant moving, she found one constant: books. The Paterson Public Library became her refuge in North America, and one year she went right through the entire fairy and folktale section, discovering that the Cinderella story was extant in cultures from Scandinavia to Africa.

"I think that I educated myself from the oral traditions of my grandmother's house and from all of those folktales and fairy tales that I absorbed growing up," Cofer noted in *The Americas Review*. In *The Global Education Project* Cofer wrote of these early years that "I absorbed literature, both spoken *cuentos* and books, as a creature who breathed ink. Each writer provided poems, novels, taught me that language could be tamed. I realized that I could make it perform. I had to believe the work was important to my being: To use my art as a bridge between my cultures. Unlike my parents, I was not always straddling. I began crossing the bridge, traveling back and forth without fear and confusion."

Like her parents, Cofer married young, at 19, but went on to earn an M.A. at Florida Atlantic University and attend Oxford University in 1977. During her postgraduate years she also was a bilingual teacher in the Florida public schools, as well as an adjunct professor and lecturer in English at University of Miami. Moving to Georgia, Cofer became a professor at the University of Georgia and set up home in Louisville, Georgia, with her husband and daughter. Her move to the South gave Cofer a further take on the multicultural experience, yet often confuses critics. As she noted in *The Global Education Project*, people often ask her what she is doing in the

South when the barrio is her proper subject. "My isolation from others, my living and teaching in the piney woods of Georgia has not dissipated my passion," she commented. "I write anywhere I can find 'a room of my own.' My psyche is that of 'immigrant writer.'"

An Oral Tradition

"In an extended family, the family story, gossip, or myth becomes something that is repeated so often and used in so many ways to teach lessons or to make a point that I couldn't help but be trained in that as I grew up," Cofer told Ocasio in *The Americas Review.* "When I became a writer [the oral tradition] became such a natural form of communication for me." Cofer's first literary efforts were in poetry, a form she still writes in. "Nothing contains the truth I know like poetry," Cofer wrote in *The Global Education Project.* "A poem is a sacred thing in that it connects a person in a very real way not through magic, but in a very natural process of association and chemistry to the unconscious." Early chapbooks led to her first volumes of poetry, *Peregrina, Terms of Survival,* and *Reaching for the Mainland.* Present in these poems already was the theme of a life in two worlds, of the immigrant experience. Of *Reaching for the Mainland,* a critic in *Library Journal* commented that "Cofer's warm, intimate use of language is always inviting and appealing." As a poet, Cofer has earned honors and critical acclaim.

In 1989, Cofer published her first novel, *The Line of the Sun,* and the first novel ever published by the University of Georgia Press. A Pulitzer Prize nominee, *The Line of the Sun* tells the story of a wild young boy born in the village of Salud in Puerto Rico. Guzmán is ungovernable as a child, even worse as a young man. He falls in love with the village prostitute and soothsayer, La Cabra, a woman twice his age. Ultimately he flees the island for New York, and is not heard of again for fifteen years. In the meantime, Guzmán's sister marries his best friend and the family moves to Paterson, New Jersey, taking up residence there in a Puerto Rican community, in El Building, along with their daughter and son. Marisol, the daughter, is thirteen, and has always been attracted to the myth of her lost uncle Guzmán. When he shows up one Christmas Eve, she becomes his closest attendant, nursing him when he

Cofer once again draws on her life experiences to relate tales about the struggles of Puerto Rican women living in New Jersey while still longing for their homeland.

is stabbed, spying for him, even enabling him at the end of the story to play the part of the mythic hero he has always desired.

Marisol is the narrator of the novel, and it is told in two parts: Marisol's mythic tales of the Salud, the Puerto Rican village she left when a baby, and in a more realistic tone set in the present in Paterson, New Jersey. "Cofer is a poet," noted Sonja Bolle in the *Los Angeles Times Book Review,* "and in her descriptions of the small town, her eye for detail brings alive the stifling and magical world of village life. . . ." Bolle concluded that the "lasting impression from Cofer's novel is the gulf that separates poverty-stricken life on the island and the trapped, tenement life on the Mainland." A reviewer for *Publishers Weekly*, while finding fault with Cofer's plotting and "arbitrary shifts in points of view," concluded that the novel "paints a colorful, revealing portrait of Puerto Rican culture and domestic relationships." Writing in *Wilson Library Bulletin*, Ellen Donohue Warwick called *The Line of the Sun* a "fine first novel" and noted also that "Much of the book's appeal springs from the choice of Marisol as narrator." Starr E. Smith observed in *Library Journal* that the "U.S. immigrant experience" was flavored with "a hint of magical realism" in Cofer's novel, and lauded the author's "well-realized characters and vibrant depictions of Puerto Rican folk culture." And in the *New York Times Book Review*, Márquez called Cofer "a prose writer of evocatively lyric authority, a novelist of historical compass and sensitivity," and one "from whom we may well look forward to hearing more."

If Cofer dealt with her Puerto Rican and New Jersey roots in a fictional format in her first novel, her next book, a collection of poetry and essays, dealt with this same experience more directly as autobiography. *Silent Dancing* "bridges the gap between autobiography and fiction. . . ." and between memories and social commentary, noted a reviewer for *Publishers Weekly*. In this book she deals with her early years, shuttling back and forth between Puerto Rico and the high-rise, urban life of Paterson. Cofer "recovers the warp and weft of her experience in stellar stories. . .," a *Publishers Weekly* reviewer concluded. Writing in *Library Journal*, Mary Margaret Benson observed that these "eminently readable memoirs are a delightful introduction to Puerto Rican culture." In this book, Cofer first experimented with combining essays and poems. The essays are not explanations of the poems, but are inspired by them and perhaps provide background to them.

In 1993, Cofer came out with *The Latin Deli*, "a delicious smorgasbord of the sights, smells, tastes, and sounds recalled from a cross-cultural girlhood," according to *Booklist*'s Whitney Scott. In this collection of poetry and short stories, Cofer presents universal coming-of-age concerns as well as young protagonists alternately baffled by prejudice against Hispanics by both blacks and whites, and by the battle of flesh and spirit as played out in the Catholic church. A critic writing in *Kirkus Reviews* deemed the collection a "compassionate, delicate rendering of Puerto Rican life in America. . . ." Cofer places her stories in a simu-

If you enjoy the works of Judith Ortiz Cofer, you may also want to check out the following books:

Lori M. Carlson, *Where Angels Glide at Dawn: New Stories from Latin America*, 1990.
Francisco Jiménez, *The Circuit*, 1997.
Piri Thomas, *Stories from El Barrio*, 1980.

lation of the barrio tenement, El Building, where she grew up in Paterson and where "the joys and tragedies of childhood, adolescence, and adulthood unfold," according to the *Kirkus Reviews* critic. Stories deal with real pain, as well, as in "Nada," in which a mother loses her only son in Vietnam not long after the death of her husband. This double loss drives her to suicide. "Nada" won the prestigious O. Henry Award in 1994 and the entire collection received the Anisfield-Wolf Book Award for its celebration of diversity.

Turning to a Young Adult Audience

"I believe there are many paths for my creative drive to take," Cofer told Ocasio in *The Americas Review*. One of those paths emerged in the mid-1990s when she realized that many of her stories were being anthologized for high school students; that her stories, poems, and essays spoke to that readership as directly as they do to older readers. Working with an editor at Orchard, Cofer wrote a series of short stories with young adults as central characters living in a multicultural world. The result was *An Island Like You: Stories of the Barrio*. Again set in and around Paterson's Puerto Rican barrio, El Building, these twelve "interrelated and emotionally varied stories" are told "with sensitivity, insight, and humor," according to Lauren Mayer in *School Library Journal*. Mayer concluded that the stories were so compelling because "these teens are doubly caught between two worlds—not only between childhood and adulthood, but also between their parents' culture and heritage and their own. . . ." In a starred *Booklist* review, Hazel Rochman noted that the teenage protagonists' voices are "funny, weary, and irreverent," and that Cofer "depicts a diverse neighborhood that's warm, vital, and nurturing, and that can be hell if you don't fit in."

The Year of Our
REVOLUTION
Judith Ortiz Cofer

Journeying back to Paterson, New Jersey, in the 1960s, Cofer relates the story of Maria Elenita's coming of age as she falls in love, becomes affected by the Vietnam War, and slowly breaks away from her parents.

Different teens are the focus in each of the linked tales: Yolanda watches her mom stumble toward a new relationship in "Don José of La Mancha" and then appears again in "The One Who Watches" as a shoplifting friend of the narrator, Doris. A reviewer in *Publishers Weekly* commented that the theme representing a "struggle to transcend one's roots but never succeeding (nor really wanting to)—is explored with enormous humanity and humor." The same reviewer forecast that this "fine collection" would help to shed light on an "underserved" young adult group. In an extensive *Horn Book* review, Rudine Sims Bishop observed that the collection "benefits from the consistency of quality that comes from a single talented writer." Bishop went on to note that

"Cofer's writing is lively, and the characters memorable. . . . The characters, their voices, and their experiences will seem familiar to many adolescents." Concluding the review, Bishop wrote, "I hope Cofer continues to write for young people."

Cofer has continued writing for the young adult audience, publishing a second collection of stories and poems, *The Year of Our Revolution*, in 1998. These stories about growing up during the turbulent sixties, once again are set in the Paterson barrio, and most of them are narrated in hindsight by Mary Ellen, also known as Maria Elenita. "Caught between Hispanic and American lifestyles, and eager to break free of traditional Hispanic values, Mary Ellen is strongly attracted to things that are alien to her parents," observed a reviewer for *Publishers Weekly.* The same reviewer went on to note that "Cofer's lyrical descriptions of how music and the Vietnam War fired Mary Ellen's youthful passions are affecting . . . for mature teenagers, there is wisdom aplenty in this radiant collection." Focusing on the verse in the collection, *Booklist*'s Debbie Carton wrote that the "poems highlight the conflicts, principles, and themes of the collection." Carton concluded that the book would be a tremendous "resource" for studies about ethnicity and also an invaluable experience for teens "able to savor" her "use of language."

Cofer maintains that her writing—poetry, essays, and short stories—has kept her connected to her island home even as she goes about her life as a college professor in the United States. "I would say that ninety per cent of what I write is about being Puerto Rican," Cofer told Rafael Ocasio, "even though I live in rural Georgia, my husband is North American and my daughter was born here. . . . You sit down at a table and call back the spirits of your ancestors. Poetry is my emotional and intellectual connection to my heritage."

■ Works Cited

Benson, Mary Margaret, review of *Silent Dancing*, *Library Journal*, July, 1990, pp. 96-97.

Bishop, Rudine Sims, review of *An Island Like You*, *Horn Book*, September-October, 1995, p. 581.

Bolle, Sonja, review of *The Line of the Sun*, *Los Angeles Times Book Review*, August 6, 1989, p. 6.

Carton, Debbie, review of *The Year of Our Revolution, Booklist*, July 19, 1998, p. 1870.

Cofer, Judith Ortiz, "Judith Ortiz Cofer," *The Global Education Project*, located at http://ultrix.rampo.edu/global/cofer.html.

Review of *An Island Like You, Publishers Weekly*, April 17, 1995, p. 61.

Review of *The Latin Deli, Kirkus Reviews*, October 1, 1993.

Review of *The Line of the Sun, Publishers Weekly*, April, 28, 1989, p. 61.

Márquez, Roberto, "Island Heritage," *New York Times Book Review*, September 24, 1989, p. 46.

Mayer, Lauren, review of *An Island Like You, School Library Journal*, July, 1995, pp. 92-93.

Ocasio, Rafael, "An Interview with Judith Ortiz Cofer," *The Americas Review*, Fall-Winter, 1994, pp. 84-90.

Review of *Reaching for the Mainland, Library Journal*, February 15, 1996, p. 154.

Rochman, Hazel, review of *An Island Like You, Booklist*, February 15, 1995, p. 1082.

Scott, Whitney, review of *The Latin Deli, Booklist*, November 15, 1993, p. 609.

Review of *Silent Dancing, Publishers Weekly*, June 8, 1990, p. 609.

Smith, Starr E., review of *The Line of the Sun, Library Journal*, May 15, 1989, p. 88.

Warwick, Ellen Donohue, review of *The Line of the Sun, Wilson Library Bulletin*, October, 1989, p. 123.

Review of *The Year of Our Revolution, Publishers Weekly*, July 27, 1998, p. 78.

■ For More Information See

BOOKS

American Women Writers, Volume 5, supplement, Continuum Publishing, 1994.

The Oxford Companion to Women's Writing in the United States, Oxford University Press, 1995.

PERIODICALS

Bulletin of the Center for Children's Books, April, 1995, p. 267.

Kirkus Reviews, June 15, 1998, p. 892.

Kliatt, September, 1991, p. 5; September, 1996, p. 3.

Library Journal, November 1, 1993, p. 93; July, 1998, p. 76.

Publishers Weekly, April 10, 1995, p. 60; December 2, 1996, p. 62.

Voice of Youth Advocates, August, 1995, p. 155.*

—Sketch by J. Sydney Jones

Diane Duane

76; writer's assistant, 1976-78; freelance writer, 1978—; Filmation Studios, Reseda, CA, staff writer, 1983-84. *Member:* Writers Guild of America East.

■ Personal

Born May 18, 1952, in New York, NY; daughter of Edward David (an aircraft engineer) and Elizabeth Kathryn (Burke) Duane; married Robert Peter Smyth (a writer under pseudonym Peter Norwood), February 15, 1987.

■ Addresses

Home—c/o Sloane Club, 52 Lower Sloane St., London SW1W 8BS, England. *Agent*—Donald Maass Literary Agency, 64 West 84th St., Apt. 3-A, New York, NY 10024; Meg Davis, MBA Agency, 45 Fitzroy St., London W1P 5HR, England.

■ Career

Novelist and television writer. Pilgrim State Hospital, Brentwood, NY, registered nurse, 1974; Payne Whitney Clinic, Cornell/New York Hospital Medical Center, New York City, psychiatric nurse, 1974-

■ Awards, Honors

Deep Wizardry was named one of *School Library Journal*'s Best Books, 1985, and was on *Voice of Youth Advocates*' list of best science fiction and fantasy titles for young adults, 1986; *The Door into Shadow* was on *Voice of Youth Advocates*' list of best science fiction and fantasy titles for young adults, 1986.

■ Writings

FOR YOUNG PEOPLE; "WIZARDRY" SERIES

So You Want to Be a Wizard, Delacorte, 1983.
Deep Wizardry, Delacorte, 1985.
High Wizardry, Delacorte, 1990.
Support Your Local Wizard, Guild American (New York City), 1990.
A Wizard Abroad, Corgi (London), 1993.

Also author of *Wizards at Large.*

FANTASY NOVELS; "EPIC TALES OF THE FIVE" SERIES

The Door into Fire, Dell, 1979.

The Door into Shadow, Bluejay Books (New York City), 1984.

The Door into Sunset, Tor Books (New York City), 1993.

SCIENCE FICTION NOVELS; BASED ON "STAR TREK" TELE-VISION SERIES

The Wounded Sky, Pocket, 1983.

My Enemy, My Ally, Pocket, 1984.

(With Peter Norwood) *The Romulan Way,* Pocket, 1987.

Spock's World, Pocket, 1988.

Doctor's Orders, Pocket, 1990.

The Next Generation: Dark Mirror, Pocket, 1993.

The Next Generation: Intellivore, Pocket, 1997.

Also author of "Star Trek" novels *Swordhunt* and *Birthright,* both published by Pocket Books. Coauthor, with Peter David, Tony Isabella, and Dan Jurgens, *The Best of Star Trek,* published by DC Comics. *Spock's World* also was released on audio cassette in 1989.

SCIENCE FICTION NOVELS; "SPACE COPS" SERIES; WITH PETER NORWOOD

Mindblast, Avon, 1991.

Kill Station, Avon, 1992.

High Moon, Avon, 1992.

SCIENCE FICTION NOVELS; MARVEL COMICS' "SPIDER-MAN" SERIES

The Venom Factor, illustrated by Ron Lim, Byron Preiss Multimedia, 1994.

The Lizard Sanction, illustrated by Darick Robertson and Scott Koblish, Byron Preiss Multimedia, 1995.

The Octopus Agenda, illustrated by Darick Robertson, Byron Preiss Multimedia, 1996.

"HARBINGER" TRILOGY

Starrise at Corrivale, TSR, 1998.

Storm at Eldala, TSR, 1999.

Nightfall at Alderon, TSR, 1999.

OTHER

(Story editor) *Dinosaucers* (syndicated animated television series), DIC Enterprises, 1986-87.

X-Com UFO Defense (science-fiction novel), Prima, 1995.

It Crawled Out of the Woodwork, Boxtree (London), 1996.

The Cats of Grand Central, Warner, 1997.

The Book of Night with Moon, Hodder & Stoughton, 1997.

Marvel Comics' X-Men: Empire's End, Byron Preiss Multimedia, 1997.

To Visit the Queen, Aspect/Warner, 1999.

Also author, with Norwood, of *Keeper of the City* (fantasy), Bantam. Coauthor, with Michael Reaves, of a screenplay for the syndicated television series *Star Trek: The Next Generation.*

Work represented in anthologies, including *Flashing Swords! 5,* edited by Lin Carter, Dell, 1981; *Sixteen: Short Stories by Outstanding Young Adult Writers,* edited by Donald R. Gallo, Delacorte, 1984; and *Dragons and Dreams: A Collection of New Fantasy and Science Fiction Stories,* edited by Jane Yolen and others, Harper, 1986. Contributor to periodicals, including *Fantasy Book.*

■ **Sidelights**

Since her first novel in 1979, Diane Duane has penned a variety of science fiction and fantasy novels for both adults and children. A prolific author, she plans each of her books far in advance, and dedicates a great deal of time to researching her science-based plots. Called "not only highly talented but highly unpredictable" by Jessica Yates in *Twentieth-Century Young Adult Writers,* Duane's diverse output is characterized by imaginative plots, strong, well-rounded male and female characters, and a firm grounding in such time-honored virtues as beauty, heroism, and loyalty.

"My childhood was essentially quite boring and sometimes rather unhappy," Duane once commented, "but the unhappiness was tempered with a great love of books and writing in general. I have been writing for almost as long as I've been reading. This started out as an expression of discontent . . . the library simply didn't stock enough of the kinds of books that I wanted to read, so I began to write my own, occasionally illustrating them (usually in crayon). When I left high school, I went on to study astronomy (something else I had loved greatly from a young age), didn't do too well at that, and then on a friend's recommendation went on to study nursing, which I did

Frelorn s'Ferrant in his attempt to regain the throne of the kingdom of Arlen against the usurpation of his greedy half-brother, Cillmod, whose rule is guided by the ancient Shadow. In opposition to the Shadow's evil powers stands the Goddess, the creator of life in Duane's mythical world. In *The Door into Sunset,* still supported by Segnbora, who has focused her magic powers and now rallies dragons to Frelorn's cause, and Queen Eftgan d'Arienn and her troops from the neighboring kingdom of Darthan, the Prince engages in a war of absolutes in a novel that a *Publishers*

"Enormous fun."—*Kirkus Reviews*

High WIZARDRY
DIANE DUANE

Combining magic with technology, Duane creates a tale about a young girl who uses a computer to travel across the universe, where she must become a wizard and confront the evil Lone One.

much better at. But the writing, for my own enjoyment, went on all the time."

Duane's first book, *The Door into Fire,* introduces five characters, some human, some not, whose adventures span several volumes in the "Epic Tales of the Five" series. These adult fantasies, which include *The Door into Shadow* and *The Door into Sunset,* encompass an epic battle between good and evil hinging on the paranormal abilities and growth of each character. In *The Door into Shadow,* for instance, a young woman named Segnbora vows to support the fugitive Prince

"For a Spidey-fan like yours truly, this book was like coming home again."
—*Comics Buyer's Guide*

SPIDER-MAN
THE VENOM FACTOR

A NOVEL BY *NEW YORK TIMES* BESTSELLING AUTHOR
DIANE DUANE

In addition to her original fantasy tales, Duane has penned books based on the "Star Trek" series and on the Marvel comic book character Spider-Man, the latter being praised for its adept mix of modern-day reality and superhero fantasy.

Weekly reviewer deemed an "intelligent and exhilarating Swords and Sorcery adventure."

Despite the fact that their settings are products of the author's vivid imagination, Duane's fantasy books require extensive background research—"a great deal of reading in myths and legends of all countries, comparative religions, folklore, fairy tales, and (every now and then) other people's fantasy novels," she once explained. "One wants to see what the colleagues are up to! But I find the oldest material the most useful for my purposes. Fraser's *Golden Bough* and the *Larousse Encyclopedia of Mythology* have been two major helps to my fantasy work: the old themes, the Jungian 'archetypes,' are what makes fantasy work best in

Four unlikely heroes in feline form are the main characters in this 1997 book about magical cats who have to defend the Gates between their world and another dimension.

any time and place it's set—ancient Greece or modern Manhattan."

"Wizardry" Series

With her book *So You Want to Be a Wizard*, Duane began her popular series of teen novels about the fantastic exploits of two modern teenagers in an alternate Earth. From reading a book in the local library, twelve-year-old Kit Rodriguez and thirteen-year-old Nita Callahan learn to harness the powers of magic as a defense against several neighborhood bullies. However, instead of simplifying their lives, the magic complicates things, as they suddenly find themselves in an alien city inhabited by machines that attack living creatures. Given the task of rescuing a magical book from a dragon's lair, the children incur the wrath of the evil Starsnuffer, who follows them back into their own world and snuffs out the light of the Sun. Using their powers and magical incantations from the book to vanquish their foe, the children are also aided by Fred, a "white hole" from the edge of the galaxy. Praising *So You Want to Be a Wizard* as "outstanding" and "original," *Horn Book* reviewer Ann A. Flowers added that the novel "stands between the works of Diane Wynne Jones, in its wizardry and spells, and those of Madeleine L'Engle, in its scientific concepts and titanic battles between good and evil."

Further novels in the "Wizardry" series have included *Deep Wizardry*, *High Wizardry*, and *A Wizard Abroad*. In *Deep Wizardry*, Nita and Kit must come to the rescue again, this time to help an injured Whale wizard named S'reee prevent the evil Lone Power from coaxing a dormant volcano beneath Manhattan into unleashing its power and destroying the city. Nita's eleven-year-old sister Dairine, a sprouting computer hacker, finds a way to incorporate the ancient laws of wizardry with modern technology in *High Wizardry*. Programming the family's laptop computer to transport her across the Universe, Dairine is followed by caretakers Nita and Kit as she is initiated into wizardom by confronting the malevolent Lone One. *A Wizard Abroad* finds the teens in Ireland where they rally the country's wizards to help battle the ghostly Fomori, an army of ancient invaders that are the pawns of the Lone One. Of the "Wizardry" series, Jessica Yates commented in *School Librarian* that Duane "has succeeded in writing exciting and moral fantasy which doesn't

STAR•DRIVE NOVELS

DIANE DUANE

STARRISE AT CORRIVALE
Volume One of the HARBINGER TRILOGY

In this first installment of the "Harbinger Trilogy," disgraced Marine Gabriel Connor must redeem himself in the eyes of the authorities by accepting a deadly mission.

preach, and her style . . . lives up to the challenge of her cosmic theme."

Something for the Trekkies

In 1983 Duane published the first of her "Star Trek" novels. Based on the characters from the original television series, *The Wounded Sky* would be followed by many more books, including several, such as *Dark Mirror*, based on the cast of characters familiar to viewers of television's *Star Trek: The Next Generation*. In *My Enemy, My Ally*,

Captain Kirk and the crew of the starship *Enterprise* join a Romulan commander in a brief peace, during which time the two commanders team up to stop Romulan scientists from channeling Vulcan mind powers into weaponry. A political debate on whether the planet Vulcan should secede from the Federation is the subject of *Spock's World*, while "Bones" McCoy becomes the central character in *Doctor's Orders*. With Kirk gone on a routine mission to a newly discovered planet, Dr. McCoy is left as acting captain and must confront an aggressive attack by a Klingon spaceship with designs on the unclaimed planet. Praising Duane for staying close to the facts set out in the original series, a *School Library Journal* reviewer dubbed *Doctor's Orders* "a fast-paced, well-written adventure."

About writing science fiction, Duane once explained, "I would say that nearly half the time I spend in 'writing' a book is spent in research—especially in the sciences. Science fiction is worthless without a good solid grounding in the sciences that underlie it, though you would be surprised how many people try to write it without studying, and then fail miserably, and don't understand why. These people typically think that writing science fiction should be easy 'because you're making it all up.' Nothing could be further from the truth. I spend at least one day a week rummaging in the local library, or reading *New Scientist* or *Science News* to keep up on the latest developments. So many of these have suggested ideas for new projects that it seems unlikely I'll run out of ideas for novels before the middle of the next century or so . . . since any new discovery brings with it the question, 'How will people react to this?' And people are the heart of good science fiction."

While many of her books are suitable for a teen audience, Duane never consciously decided to write with that age group in mind. "I always wrote what pleased me," Duane once admitted, "and was rather shocked when it began to sell (though the shock was very pleasant). Occasionally I find I'm writing a story which younger readers would probably appreciate more thoroughly than older ones, or rather, it would take older readers of taste and discernment to have fun with a story that younger readers would have no problem with at all. I let my publishers label or target the markets for my books, and I myself sit home and get on with the storytelling.

If you enjoy the works of Diane Duane, you may also want to check out the following books and films:

Katherine Kurtz, *The Quest for Saint Camber*, 1986.
Joan D. Vinge, *The Snow Queen*, 1980.
Labyrinth, a film starring David Bowie, 1986.

"It took several years of uneven output to get used to the fact that I was going to be able to make my living as a writer," Duane previously noted, ". . . for it's hard to go smoothly from a job where you 'punch the clock' to one where you are the only judge of how much work you do each day. I don't consider writing 'work'—at least not when it's coming easily. When I'm having to write something I don't care for (or don't care for at the moment), the situation sometimes looks different. But this rarely lasts."

In addition to her popular "Wizards" and "Star Trek" books for young adult readers, Duane is the author of several novels featuring the Marvel comic book character Spider-Man. These books have been praised for mixing modern-day reality with super hero fantasy in an entertaining and believable fashion. Along with her husband, a writer under the name Peter Norwood, she has also written several books featuring the pair's Space Cop heroes. Despite her continued versatility of subject, Duane retains similar themes in all her books. "But they're subject to change without notice," she once noted, "and in any case I don't care to spell them out. I prefer to let the reader find them, if he or she cares to. If the themes aren't obvious, so much the better—a book made primarily for entertainment purposes is not the place for a writer to shout. People who are listening hard enough will hear even the whispers, the rest shouldn't be distracted from being entertained, which in itself is a noble thing, in this busy, crazy world. My only and daily hope is that my readers feel they're getting their money's worth."

■ Works Cited

Review of *Doctor's Orders, School Library Journal*, December, 1990, p. 140.

Review of *The Door into Sunset, Publishers Weekly*, January 4, 1993, p. 62.

Flowers, Ann A., review of *So You Want to Be a Wizard, Horn Book*, December, 1983, p. 716.

Yates, Jessica, review of *So You Want to Be a Wizard; Deep Wizardry; High Wizardry, School Librarian*, August, 1992, p. 113.

Yates, Jessica, *Twentieth-Century Young Adult Writers*, St. James Press, 1994, pp. 191-92.

■ For More Information See

PERIODICALS

Analog, October, 1984, pp. 146-47.

Booklist, August, 1984, pp. 1596-97; February 15, 1993, p. 10; October 15, 1993, p. 195; October 15, 1994, p. 405.

Horn Book, May-June, 1985, p. 311.

Kirkus Reviews, October 15, 1993, p. 1297; February 1, 1999.

New York Times Book Review, November 6, 1988.

Publishers Weekly, March 9, 1984, p. 111; April 13, 1990, p. 67; September 22, 1997, p. 74.

School Librarian, February, 1994.

School Library Journal, March, 1985, p. 176; March, 1990, pp. 216-17.

Voice of Youth Advocates, February, 1984, p. 342; February, 1990, p. 371; December, 1990, p. 296; April, 1992, p. 42; October, 1993, pp. 225-26; October, 1995, pp. 207-8.

Washington Post Book World, May 12, 1985, p. 8.*

Jack Finney

■ Personal

Born Walter Braden Finney, October 2, 1911, in Milwaukee, WI; died of pneumonia, November 14, 1995, in Greenbrae, CA; married G. Marguerite Guest; children: Margie, Kenneth. *Education:* Attended Knox College, Galesburg, IL.

■ Career

Writer.

■ Awards, Honors

Special Prize, *Ellery Queen's Mystery Magazine* contest, c. 1946, for "The Widow's Walk"; best short story collection, *Infinity Science Fiction*, 1958, for *The Third Level;* World Fantasy life achievement award, 1987.

■ Writings

Five Against the House (novel), Doubleday, 1954.

The Body Snatchers (novel), Dell, 1955, reprinted as *Invasion of the Body Snatchers,* Dell, 1961, revised edition published as *The Invasion of the Body Snatchers,* Award, 1973.

Telephone Roulette (play), Dramatic Publishing, 1956.

The Third Level (short stories; includes "The Third Level," "Such Interesting Neighbors," and "Second Chance"), Rinehart, 1957 (published in England as *The Clock of Time,* Eyre & Spottiswoode, 1958).

The House of Numbers (novel), Dell, 1957.

Assault on a Queen (novel), Simon & Schuster, 1959.

I Love Galesburg in the Springtime (short stories), Simon & Schuster, 1963.

Good Neighbor Sam (novel), Simon & Schuster, 1963.

This Winter's Hobby (play), first produced in New Haven, CT, 1966.

The Woodrow Wilson Dime (novel), Simon & Schuster, 1968.

Time and Again (novel), Simon & Schuster, 1970, Scribner Paperback Editions, 1995.

Marion's Wall (novel), Simon & Schuster, 1973.

The Night People (novel), Doubleday, 1977.

Forgotten News: The Crime of the Century, and Other Lost Stories (nonfiction), Doubleday, 1983.

About Time (short stories), Simon & Schuster, 1986.

Three by Finney (contains *The Woodrow Wilson Dime, The Night People,* and *Marion's Wall*), Simon & Schuster, 1987.

From Time to Time: A Novel, Simon and Schuster, 1995.

Contributor to periodicals, including *Collier's, Cosmopolitan, Good Housekeeping, Ladies' Home Journal, McCall's,* and *Saturday Evening Post.*

■ Adaptations

Five against the House was adapted for a movie of the same name in 1955; *The Body Snatchers* was filmed as *Invasion of the Body Snatchers* in 1956, again in 1979, and as *Body Snatchers* in 1993 by Warner Bros.; *House of Numbers* was filmed in 1957; *Good Neighbor Sam* was filmed in 1964, starring Jack Lemmon; *Assault on a Queen* was filmed in 1966; *Marion's Wall* was filmed as *Maxie,* 1985; the short story, "The Love Letter," was filmed for a TV movie, 1998.

■ Sidelights

American author Jack Finney announced his major thematic material early in his career, in the short story "I'm Scared": "Haven't you noticed," the narrator comments, ". . . on the part of nearly everyone you know, a growing rebellion against the *present*?"

Indeed, Finney carried out something of a one-man crusade against the present in many of his novels and numerous short stories and in their movie adaptations, and won a cult following for his novels *The Body Snatchers* and *Time and Again.* Finney's narrator in "I'm Scared" goes on to remark: "Man is disturbing the clock of time, and I am afraid it will break. When it does, I leave to your imagination the last few hours of madness that will be left to us all; all the countless moments that now make up our lives suddenly ripped apart and chaotically tangled in time." For Finney, however, the breaking apart of time was usually an experience to be treasured; sipped like fine old wine. The past was, for him, another country that afforded a more casual pace of life, a time when faces carried less anxiety, more cheerful optimism.

Michael Beard noted in *Dictionary of Literary Biography* that "the portrait of an entire society straining semiconsciously to escape the present is a compact argument for the sensibility behind most of [Finney's] writings." But Beard also pointed out that Finney was not a writer to be categorized simply as someone working in science fiction because of the tendency on the part of many of his protagonists toward time travel. "The premise that time is malleable and subject to change through human emotions is not a common science-fiction theme," Beard wrote. "The science that underlies Finney's time-travel is often, properly speaking, not science, but sympathetic magic." Far from being a science fiction writer, or thriller writer as other critics have labeled him, or a mystery writer as still others have written, Finney was, at heart a romantic. "Finney creates ingenious, suspenseful narratives, treats regretfully, though sometimes humorously, the tensions and conflicts in mid-20th-century America," Seymour Rudin noted in *St. James Guide to Crime and Mystery Writers,* "and contrasts the latter, though not always explicitly, with a romantic imagined pre-modern age."

In his best known works, such as *The Body Snatchers, Time and Again,* and the latter's sequel, *From Time to Time,* Finney casts a critical eye on the present. Time travel—a literal escape from the present—informs those last two works while the power of love and a rootedness in the past empowers us to transcend the soulless, all-conforming present as in *The Body Snatchers.* Over and again this theme of alienation from current time and a return to the past or an alternate time is announced in Finney's short stories, especially those collected in *The Third Level;* it is also a recurrent motif in his lesser novel-length fiction, including *The Woodrow Wilson Dime* and in *Marion's Wall,* in which reincarnation is the engine of time travel. Even in his crime and suspense fiction such as *Assault on a Queen* and *The Night People,* there is a touch of the sentimentalized past or a jaundiced view of the present that helps to fuel the engine of the plot.

The Man with No Past

For a man like Finney, who could so lovingly recreate the New York of the 1880s or the early twentieth century, it is a curiosity that so little is known of his own past. As Beard noted, "Finney is a writer who values his privacy." Born in Milwaukee, Wisconsin in 1911, he was brought up in Chicago. He attended Knox College and worked for a time in New York City as an advertising copywriter, the profession of his best loved protagonist, Simon Morley from the novels *Time and Again* and *From Time to Time.* By the 1950s he had settled in California, in Mill Valley,

The 1956 sci-fi film *Invasion of the Body Snatchers*—adapted from Finney's book *The Body Snatchers*—stars Kevin McCarthy and Dana Wynter as they fight against the alien pod people who are slowly replacing mankind with duplicates.

north of San Francisco. Here, Finney would continue to make his home with his family until his death in 1995.

Finney began publishing short stories in 1946, winning an award from *Ellery Queen's Mystery Magazine* for such early efforts as "The Widow's Walk." These first stories were mostly suspense, published in the pages of *Collier's*. Finney continued to write for such slick magazines rather than the pulps that were the home of mystery and science fiction writers. In 1954 he published his first novel, *Five Against the House,* a tale of college students who are out for excitement to enhance their dull academic lives. They create an elaborate plan to rob a nightclub in Reno in this story which, according to Beard, "sets the pattern for [Finney's] suspense stories," such as *Assault on a Queen,* in which thieves target the *Queen Mary* steamship. In *Assault on a Queen*, the thieves, older

and more professional adventurers, plan to refloat a sunken World War I U-Boat as part of their scheme to rob the passenger liner. Both of these mystery-suspense novels were turned into films.

In late 1954, Finney published a serialized story in *Collier's* that changed everything for the 43-year-old writer and that allowed him to support his family solely on his writing.

The Body Snatchers and Beyond

The story in question dealt with an alien invasion of Earth and showed similarities to earlier science fiction works, such as *The Puppet Masters* by Robert Heinlein, and the short story, "The Father Thing," by Philip K. Dick. Finney's story presented non-specific aliens: there were no green-skinned creatures with antennae-eyes. Instead, Finney, in his story and in the subsequent novel, *The Body Snatchers*, deals with these aliens only in the human forms that they inhabit. It is the aliens' plan to take over Earth by physically duplicating actual earthlings, who are then destroyed. These mindless, zombie-like replicas of humans are born out of giant seed pods, which the aliens produce in a large nursery. Though most of the inhabitants of the small town of Santa Mira (called Mill Valley in later editions of the book) do not see anything bizarre happening, one earthling does. Dr. Miles Bennell is pitted against this invasion, a man who is "a representative of specific values," according to Beard in *Dictionary of Literary Biography*. Bennell is loyal to the past—to the home he still lives in which once belonged to his parents, and to the medical practice that he has inherited from his father. The aliens, in this context, can be read as symbolic of the present and future: the world of boring conformity and mindless obedience.

Bennell slowly comes to discover that several people in his community are complaining of loved ones and close relations who do not seem to be themselves—quite literally. There is an uncle who "looks, sounds, acts and remembers exactly" like the real uncle. "On the outside," wails his suspicious niece. "But *inside* he's different. His responses . . . aren't *emotionally* right . . . that look, way in back of the eyes is gone." A young son fears his mother; mysterious green pods turn up in people's houses and begin to grow human replications. Bennell comes to learn that these life forms have come from another planet and are intent on becoming an opportunistic parasite here on Earth; to take over the human inhabitants and turn them all into willing, emotionless, slaves.

In the novel, the conflict between Bennell and the aliens is countered by the love story between the doctor and Becky Driscoll, a subplot that at times overshadows the suspenseful plot. So intrusive was the romantic element, that when the book was filmed, Bennell's love interest was destroyed by the aliens. "Finney's emphasis on the love relationship suggests that romantic love of the naïve, traditional kind lines up most effectively against the forces of conformity and eroded individuality which the pods represent," concluded Beard. Eventually, with the help of Becky, Bennell is able to defeat the aliens in the book: burning the main nursery of the seed pods sends these creatures hurtling off into space, in search of some other planet to populate.

The issue of modern-day conformity raised by the novel has led many critics to view Finney's book and subsequent film adaptations (there have been three movies made thus far, though most viewers agree the first is still the best) as an allegory on life in the 1950s. Whether this allegory stands for the follow-the-leader anti-communism and McCarthyism rampant at the time, or is representative of mindless post-industrial material culture, is a debating point among critics and readers alike. In the end, Finney was not interested in presenting moral lessons, but in giving readers a

Unlike most sci-fi writers, Finney takes a subtle approach to time travel as Si Morley uses his mind and a dose of hypnotism to travel back to the year 1882 in a secret government experiment to influence the course of history.

good yarn to sink their mental teeth into. When Bennell finally succeeds in driving the aliens away by burning their pod nursery, this is not part of some message; rather it is the denouement of the action. Movie versions have been less kind to the human victims, but Finney, as in most of his fiction, enjoyed the traditional happy ending. E. Barbara Boatner, reviewing in *Kliatt* an expanded, 1973 version of the novel entitled *The Invasion of the Body Snatchers*, declared that "High suspense and low-profile aliens are the key to the success of the book."

Finney returned to the short story for his next publication, *The Third Level*, stories that deal almost exclusively with time travel. Though Finney was still operating only marginally in the bounds of science fiction with such stories, P. Schuyler Miller, writing in *Astounding Science-Fiction* noted that "If you want to know the kind of SF the general public wants, this [volume of short stories] is as good a sample as you're likely to get." Collected here are stories such as "I'm Scared," "Such Interesting Neighbors," "Of Missing Persons," "Second Chance," and the title story of the volume, "The Third Level." Here are all manner of time travel adventures, both forward and backward in time, as well as space travel. All of these stories provide escapist reading in the most literal of its meanings: Finney's characters are escaping from their present predicaments. A commuter discovers a third level in Grand Central station from which trains run back in time to America of the 1890s; neighbors in California turn out to be refugees from the future, seeking a world free of the fear of the hydrogen bomb; a vintage car is the vehicle of time travel back to the 1920s in yet another story. More nostalgia for the past is found in a further short story collection, *I Love Galesburg in the Springtime*, with its title story and "The Love Letter" both providing fond glimpses of an earlier, more pristine America.

Time and Again and Its Sequel

Two more novels followed these short stories; both the humorous *Good Neighbor Sam*, turned into a movie starring Jack Lemmon, and the alternate-time book, *The Woodrow Wilson Dime*, in which the eponymous coin serves as the catalyst for time travel. But by far Finney's most popular novel, *Time and Again*, was published in 1970 when the

Finney explores the possibilities of time travel again in this 1986 collection featuring likeable characters who sometimes find their dreams—and sometimes don't—in the past.

author had honed his time-travel devices over decades of writing. Beard noted in *Dictionary of Literary Biography* that this book "is the most solid and consequential of Finney's novels and the one in which his characteristic stratagems and complex turns of plot work out in the most satisfying manner."

Simon Morley, called Si by his friends, is busy at his drawing board at a New York ad agency when he is offered a seductive proposition by one Rube Prien—he has been chosen to take part in a top-secret government project that could make an enormous change in the history of mankind. Morley, suitably skeptical yet also full of curiosity and good will, accepts the challenge and discovers that the project is one of time travel. But in this project, directed by Dr. E. E. Danziger, there are no science fiction contraptions to take one into the past; instead one wills oneself backward in time, prompted by appropriate atmosphere. Morley takes up residence in New York's famous Dakota building overlooking Central Park, in a room which was uninhabited during the time to which Morley has chosen to return: New York City of the 1880s. Morley steeps himself in the period, studying dress, daily events, and moments of historical import. The past slowly becomes alive for him, and aided by hypnosis, he is able to make trial runs back in time, initially to sort out an old family problem for his twentieth-century girlfriend, Katie. Soon, however, the past has Morley in its grip; he takes a room at a boarding house on Gramercy Park, and there meets the daughter of the house, Julia, a woman who is actually some 80 years his senior. The real intentions of Danziger and Prien soon become clear to Morley: they hope that he will help to change government policy of the time making Cuba an American possession, thereby diverting twentieth-century difficulties with that island.

However, such plot twists are secondary to this novel in which "the real fascination . . . lies in Morley's discovery of the New York" of the 1880s, according to a reviewer in *Publishers Weekly*. Finney included actual photos and engravings from the time as illustrations to his book to give it an added touch of reality. Finney's talent for "making his time travel perfectly believable," concluded *Publishers Weekly*, is achieved by "the smooth use of authentic details." Morley falls in love not only with the past, but also with Julia, and soon he must choose both between worlds and between loves. He ultimately opts for the past and for Julia, but only after contriving to thwart Danziger's attempts at controlling history. Morley destroys the future possibility of the time-travel project by diverting—in the past—a meeting between the young woman and man who would be Danziger's father and mother. Morley is left in the past with his beloved Julia. He looks around at his nineteenth-century world: "At the gaslighted brownstones beside me. At the nighttime winter sky. This too was an imperfect world, but—I drew a deep breath, sharply chill in my lungs—the air was still clean. The rivers flowed fresh as they had since time began." He goes to his new home, at Gramercy Park 19. According to Beard, it is just such a fascination with the New York of the past

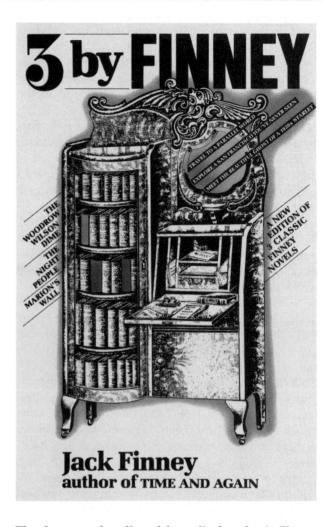

Jack Finney
author of TIME AND AGAIN

The three novels collected here display classic Finney style, including a story of time travel, one about a movie star ghost from the 1920s, and a third about four San Francisco well-to-dos whose pranks have serious consequences.

that has made Finney's novel "a minor cult book among New York enthusiasts."

Writing in the *New York Times Book Review,* W. G. Rogers called Finney's novel "a most ingenious confection of time now and time then," and concluded that in the pages of this book "you go back to a wonderful world and have a wonderful time doing it." A writer for *Booklist* called the novel "a scrupulously controlled, painstakingly researched entertainment," while *Horn Book*'s Mary Silva Cosgrave called *Time and Again* "cleverly conceived" and concluded that the results of Morley's time travel "are as comical and thrilling as an old Keystone Cops silent movie, with an old-fashioned romance thrown in for good measure." So popular has the book been, that it has stayed in print since its publication in 1970, has been twice optioned for movies, and has had a Broadway musical treatment.

Devoted fans had to wait a quarter of a century for a sequel to the book. In 1995 Finney published *From Time to Time,* in which Morley makes a return to the present only to be recruited for yet another mission in time. On this occasion Morley's job is to stop World War I from happening, and he is dispatched to 1912 for said mission. Part of his small task is to keep the fated passenger liner *Titanic* from sinking. After all the action, Morley once again returns to his wife and child in nineteenth-century New York. Finney was undaunted by the rigors of such a plot device. As Frank Rich noted in the *New York Times Book Review,* "Mr. Finney barely pretends to meet the obligations of fiction, science or otherwise, as he takes us on an ebulliently guided tour of old New York." Rich noted that "The glories of 'From Time to Time' are set pieces that could be pulled out of its story entirely and read in any sequence," and that lovers of New York would "exult once more in [Finney's] sweet articulation of a fine romance." Most reviewers felt that this sequel lacked the plot coherence of the original, but that Finney's evocation of a past time, especially his description of theatrical New York of the day, provided offsetting pleasure for the reader. *Publishers Weekly* concluded that "this mind-stretching escapist adventure is studded with period photos and news clippings that function as an integral part of the story," while Linda Vretos, writing in *School Library Journal,* called the novel "a real page-turner, loaded with nostalgia, detail, suspense, and a mind-boggling ending. . . ." And writing in the *Magazine of Fantasy and Science Fiction,* Robert K. J. Killheffer provided a fine summation of Finney's final work, noting that "he offers a smart, snappy yarn, enlivened by the inherent thrill of time travel and the particular excitement of old New York—not serious literature, perhaps, but serious fun."

Finney wrote two other novels, *Marion's Wall* and *The Night People,* as well as a collection of essays and one of stories between these two time-travel novels featuring Si Morley, but his lasting popularity lies with *Time and Again.* Talking with Vickie Sheff-Cahan of *People* magazine shortly after publication of his last book, Finney told her that as

If you enjoy the works of Jack Finney, you may also want to check out the following books and films:

E. L. Doctorow, *The Waterworks,* 1994.
Whitley Strieber, *The Forbidden Zone,* 1993.
Time after Time, a film starring Malcolm McDowell, 1979.

a child, he "would read about people who would get in a box that a mad professor invented. . . . Bells would ring, sparks would fly, and they would step out at the Battle of Waterloo." He also told Maria Ricapito of *Entertainment Weekly* that "There's no past time I'd like to stay in. I want to stay here permanently." But in the event, Finney died not long after publication of *From Time to Time,* succumbing to pneumonia on November 14, 1995 at age 84.

■ Works Cited

Beard, Michael, "Jack Finney," *Dictionary of Literary Biography,* Volume 8: *Twentieth-Century American Science Fiction Writers,* Gale, 1981, pp. 182-85.

Boatner, E. Barbara, review of *The Invasion of the Body Snatchers, Kliatt,* spring, 1979, p. 17.

Cosgrave, Mary Silva, review of *Time and Again, Horn Book,* October, 1970, p. 502.

Finney, Jack, "I'm Scared," in *The Third Level,* Rinehart, 1957.

Finney, Jack, *Time and Again,* Simon and Schuster, 1970, p. 398.

Finney, Jack, *Invasion of the Body Snatchers,* Simon and Schuster, 1998, p. 21.

Review of *From Time to Time, Publishers Weekly,* November 28, 1994, p. 42.

Killheffer, Robert K. J., review of *From Time to Time, Magazine of Fantasy and Science Fiction,* September, 1995, pp. 19-25.

Miller, P. Schuyler, review of *The Third Level, Astounding Science-Fiction,* May, 1958.

Ricapito, Maria, "Time Passages," *Entertainment Weekly,* February 24, 1995, p. 109.

Rich, Frank, "The 20th Century Should Have Been the Best," *New York Times Book Review,* February 19, 1995, p. 10.

Rogers, W. G., review of *Time and Again, New York Times Book Review,* August 2, 1970, p. 24.

Rudin, Seymour, "Finney, Jack," *St. James Guide to Crime and Mystery Writers,* St. James Press, 1996, pp. 361-62.

Sheff-Cahan, Vickie, "Talking With Jack Finney," *People,* April 10, 1995, p. 30.

Review of *Time and Again, Publishers Weekly,* March 9, 1970, p. 81.

Review of *Time and Again, Booklist,* September 1, 1970, p. 36.

Vretos, Linda, review of *From Time to Time, School Library Journal,* August, 1995, p. 171.

■ **For More Information See**

PERIODICALS

American Spectator, December, 1987.
Astounding Science Fiction, September, 1955.
Atlantic, May, 1983.
Kliatt, May, 1995, p. 52; September, 1996, p. 53.
Listener, April 3, 1980.
Los Angeles Times Book Review, May 29, 1983; March 26, 1995, p. 11.

New York Times, July 25, 1970; May 25, 1990.
New York Times Book Review, April 14, 1968; April 15, 1973, p. 34; January 19, 1986, p. 32; April 28, 1996, p. 36.
Observer, June 15, 1980.
Saturday Review, October 23, 1971; November 27, 1971.
School Library Journal, September, 1992, p. 158.
Time, July 20, 1970.
Times Literary Supplement, June 10, 1965.
Vanity Fair, February, 1995, pp. 60, 62.
Voice of Youth Advocates, April, 1990, p. 19.
Washington Post, March 2, 1983.
Wilson Library Bulletin, December, 1994, p. 29.

■ **Obituaries**

PERIODICALS

Los Angeles Times, November 17, 1995, p. A32.
New York Times, November 17, 1995, p. B15.
Times (London), November 27, 1995, p. 21.
Washington Post, November 17, 1995, p. B4.*

—Sketch by J. Sydney Jones

Stanley Kubrick

■ Personal

Born July 26, 1928, in Bronx, NY; died March 7, 1999, at home near St. Alban's, Hertfordshire, England; son of Jacques L. (a doctor) and Gertrude (Perveler) Kubrick; married Toba Metz, 1947 (divorced, 1952); married Ruth Sobotka (a dancer), 1952 (later divorced); married Suzanne Christiane Harlan (a painter), April, 1958; children: (second marriage) Katharine; (third marriage) Anya, Vivian. *Education:* Attended City College (now the City University of New York). *Hobbies and other interests:* Reading, listening to classical music, chess.

■ Addresses

Office—c/o Louis C. Blau, 10100 Santa Monica Blvd., Los Angeles, CA 90067. *Agent*—CAA, 9830 Wilshire Blvd., Beverly Hills, CA 90212.

■ Career

Look magazine, New York City, staff photographer, 1946-50; screenwriter, producer, and director of motion pictures, 1951-99.

■ Awards, Honors

New York Film Critics Award for Best Director, and Best Written American Comedy Award, Writers Guild of America, and Academy of Motion Picture Arts and Sciences (Oscar) Award nominations for best picture, best director, and best screenplay, all 1964, all for *Dr. Strangelove; or, How I Learned to Stop Worrying and Love the Bomb*; Academy of Motion Picture Arts and Sciences Award for special visual effects, and nominations for best director and best screenplay, 1968, all for *2001: A Space Odyssey*.

New York Film Critics Awards for best director award and best film, and Academy of Motion Picture Arts and Sciences Award nominations for best picture, best director, and best screenplay, all 1971, all for *A Clockwork Orange*; National Board of Review of Motion Pictures Awards for best director and best English language film, and Academy of Motion Picture Arts and Sciences Award nominations for best picture, best director, and best screenplay, all 1975, all for *Barry Lyndon*.

Academy of Motion Picture Arts and Sciences Award nomination for best screenplay, 1987, for *Full Metal Jacket*; Luchino Visconti Award, 1988; D. W. Griffith Award, Directors Guild of America, 1997, for lifetime achievement; Golden Lion, Venice International Film Festival, 1997, for lifetime achievement.

■ Credits

WRITER AND DIRECTOR

Day of the Fight (one-reel short documentary), RKO, 1951.

Flying Padre (documentary), RKO, 1952.

(With Howard O. Sackler) *Killer's Kiss,* United Artists, 1955.

The Killing (adapted from the novel *Clean Break* by Lionel White), Harris-Kubrick, 1956.

(With Calder Willingham and Jim Thompson) *Paths of Glory* (adapted from the novel by Humphrey Cobb), United Artists, 1957.

(With James Harris and Vladimir Nabokov) *Lolita* (adapted from Nabokov's novel), Metro-Goldwyn-Mayer, 1962.

(With Peter George and Terry Southern) *Dr. Strangelove; or, How I Learned to Stop Worrying and Love the Bomb* (adapted from George's novel *Red Alert*), Columbia, 1964.

(With Arthur C. Clarke) *2001: A Space Odyssey* (based on Clarke's short story "The Sentinel"), Metro-Goldwyn-Mayer, 1968.

A Clockwork Orange (adapted from the novel by Anthony Burgess; produced by Warner Brothers, 1971), Abelard, 1972.

Barry Lyndon (adapted from the novel by William Makepeace Thackeray), Warner Brothers, 1975.

(With Diane Johnson) *The Shining* (based on the novel by Stephen King), Warner Brothers, 1980.

(With Gustav Hasford and Michael Herr) *Full Metal Jacket* (based on Hasford's novel *The Short-Timers*), Warner Brothers, 1987.

(With Frederic Raphael) *Eyes Wide Shut* (based on the novel *Traumnovelle* ["Dream Story"] by Arthur Schnitzler), Warner Brothers, 1999.

DIRECTOR

The Seafarers (documentary), Seafarers International Union, 1953.

Fear and Desire, J. Burstyn, 1953.

Spartacus, Universal, 1960.

■ Sidelights

In a career spanning nearly half a century, a director might be expected to create one or perhaps two memorable films. However, by the time of his death in 1999, screenwriter-director Stanley Kubrick was credited with at least half a dozen groundbreaking and thought-provoking movies whose cinematic impact is timeless. Whether forg-

ing new styles of cinema, as he did with *Dr. Strangelove, 2001: A Space Odyssey,* and *A Clockwork Orange,* or reinventing old genres, as he did with *Paths of Glory, Barry Lyndon,* and *Full Metal Jacket,* Kubrick brought a unique style and sensibility to his work. In an industry where so many films are made by committee, Kubrick established an unparalleled degree of independence that allowed him to bring his visions to the screen without outside interference. As a result, "Stanley Kubrick's unique contribution to film—what makes him loom larger than other directors who may make more 'perfect' films—is [his] capacity to tackle essential and awesome questions that intimidate filmmakers of lesser nerve and intellect," Paul D. Zimmerman stated in a 1972 *Newsweek* article. In dealing with those "questions" Kubrick often stirred debate and controversy.

Although he never won an Oscar for Best Director or Best Picture and none of his films ever took top prize at a major film festival, few could deny the singular impact Kubrick had on modern cinema. Upon honoring him with a lifetime achievement award in 1997, organizers of the Venice International Film Festival remarked that "[he] is one of the greatest living filmmakers, along with [Italian director Michelangelo] Antonioni and [Japanese director Akira] Kurosawa," as Robert Koehler reported in *Variety,* "and the only living film master capable of delivering masterpieces in nearly every film genre."

Kubrick was born in the Bronx, New York, in 1928, the son of a doctor. He showed an early interest in film and photography, and was so skilled at chess that by age twelve he was playing the game for money. He was bored with school, however, and although he served as class photographer, he fared less well in his academic studies. After graduating in 1945, he found a position as a staff photographer for *Look* magazine. He continued in that job for four years, all the while maintaining an interest in film. He regularly attended various cinemas and arthouses around New York, and visited the city's Museum of Modern Art for screenings of classic films by world-renowned directors such as Akira Kurosawa, D. W. Griffith, and Erich von Stroheim. "I was star-struck by these fantastic movies," Kubrick told reporter Lloyd Grove of the *Washington Post* in a 1987 interview. "I was never star-struck in the sense of saying, 'Gee, I'm going to go to Hollywood and make $5,000 a week and live in a great

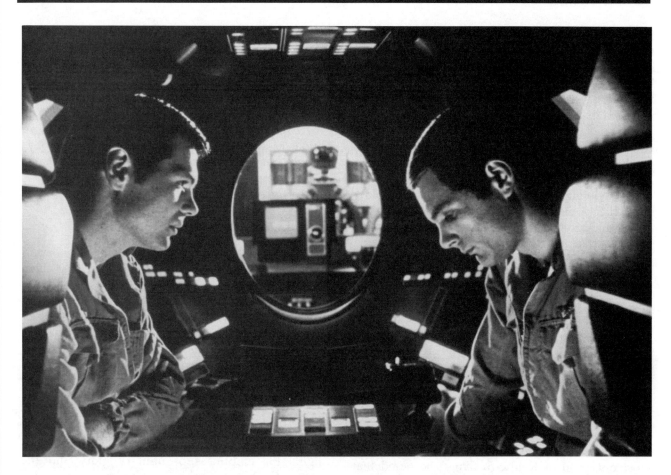

Kubrick's tour de force adaptation of the Arthur C. Clarke story *2001: A Space Odyssey* was light years ahead of its time with its stunning visual imagery, sound, and thought-provoking plotline that has boggled audiences since its 1968 debut.

place and have a sports car.' I was really in love with movies." The director also found inspiration in the lesser films he saw: "I'd seen so many movies that were bad, I thought, `Even though I don't know anything, I can't believe I can't make a movie at least as good as this.' And that's why I started, why I tried."

In 1951 Kubrick created his first film, a one-reel documentary called *Day of the Fight,* which he based on a photo study he had done for *Look.* Not only did he write and direct the film, he also did the editing and producing. Kubrick sold *Day of the Fight* to RKO Radio Pictures, which also picked up his next film, the 1952 documentary *Flying Padre.* By this time, he was a full-time film-maker and was financing his career by making documentaries for various sponsors, one such work being the 1953 film *The Seafarers,* made for the Seafarers International Union. Kubrick's earn-

ings from these early documentaries allowed him to independently produce and direct his first feature film, 1953's *Fear and Desire.* Based on a screenplay by Howard O. Sackler, the film follows the activities of a unit of soldiers on patrol. As the four soldiers become trapped behind enemy lines, they find themselves examining what is of most importance to them: the things they fear and desire. The film was distributed in limited circulation to the arthouse circuit, but later critics have found it an interesting indicator of the director's future career. While Kubrick did not write the script for this first feature, the film is nonetheless "a fascinating effort containing a host of ideas, images, and themes which continue to appear in Kubrick's later films," Norman Kagan stated in *The Cinema of Stanley Kubrick.* As *Film Quarterly* contributor Jackson Burgess described it, in *Fear and Desire* "a powerful and complex emotion is conveyed, and a vision of the vexing conflicts of virtue and authority and the uncertainty which swathes every moral choice." As a result, "considering [Kubrick's] youth and experience, the film has surprising coherence," John Russell Taylor wrote in an essay that appeared in his 1975 book *Directors and Directions.*

Kubrick engaged in some creative financing to produce his next film: he borrowed money from friends and relatives, deferred salaries and lab fees while shooting the film, and lived on unemployment checks. Based on a screenplay he wrote with Howard O. Sackler, *Killer's Kiss* was picked up by United Artists in 1955 and was shown worldwide as a second feature on double bills. In this *film noir,* boxer Davy Gordon attempts to save dancer Gloria Price from her relationship with a mob boss. While *Sight and Sound* reviewer Gavin Lambert found the film "a melodrama too full of familiar and not always skilful contrivances," he added that "it has a simplicity of outline, an atmospheric power, a directness in its characterisation, that suggests a maturing and distinctive personality." The critic particularly praised the director's "approach to characterisation and atmosphere," an assessment which later critics echoed. While Norman Kagan considered *Killer's Kiss* "the most untypical of Kubrick's films," he noted that the thriller "is most successful at creating the ambiance of lower-class New York life, realistic touches and urban types." The film found favor with contemporary audiences, and proved so profitable for United Artists that the studio offered Kubrick a contract to produce further low-budget pictures. But he had little interest in giving up any control in his work, and so he refused.

Instead, Kubrick began work on a second *film noir,* this one about a team of thieves trying to heist two million dollars from a racetrack. *The Killing* appeared in 1956, and is the film the director considered his first "finished" work. Several critics compared *The Killing* to John Huston's 1950 classic *The Asphalt Jungle.* Like that work, "the action is thickly and informatively plotted, possessed of that classic fatality that ensures retribution," Arlene Croce wrote in the journal *Film Culture.* She went on to praise the director's "visual authority," which "consistently dominates a flawed script." In reviewing Kubrick's early films, *American Scholar* contributor Charles Thomas Samuels described *The Killing* as "a tightly plotted action movie that nevertheless subverts some of the genre's basic assumptions." Instead of showing the

theft as a display of human skill, "*The Killing* reveals how poignant an error it is to neglect needs and feelings in one's dependence on technique," thus creating "a modest critique of faceless organizational efficiency." The film was successful enough to turn a profit, and prompted a *Time* reviewer to declare that Kubrick "has shown more audacity with dialogue and camera than Hollywood has seen since the obstreperous Orson Welles went riding out of town."

Pitfalls of Love and War

Kubrick selected a novel he had read in his youth as his next film. Humphrey Cobb's *Paths of Glory* was a fictional treatment of a true incident from World War I. Like the novel, the screenplay by Kubrick and his coauthors follows the results of a failed French attack on the German lines. When one company of French soldiers refuses to leave their trenches, the general in charge orders his men to fire upon them. After that order is also refused, three men are randomly chosen to be court-martialed for cowardice. The ensuing trial, which pits infantry commander Colonel Dax against the commanding General Broulard, highlights the emptiness of military glory and the clash of values between the men who direct wars and the men who actually fight them. Despite the bleak subject matter and ending, Kubrick was able to secure studio financing for the project because actor Kirk Douglas agreed to star in the picture. With Douglas's support, Kubrick kept the studio from meddling with the film's somber ending, and *Paths of Glory* was completed as originally scripted. The result, according to *Dictionary of Literary Biography* contributor Joseph Adamson III, is that "the terrible inevitability of the final execution is now one of *Paths of Glory*'s most powerful moments, as well as a necessary realization of the tragic vision of Cobb's novel."

When *Paths of Glory* appeared in 1957, it was immediately hailed as an unusual and powerful movie. *Sight and Sound* critic Lambert praised it as "meaningful as well as brilliant," and added that "this is not only a film of unusual substance but a powerfully realised and gripping work of art." Jonathan Baumbach similarly noted in *Film Culture* that the movie is "directed with obvious sincerity and restraint" and termed it "a dedicated, passionately honest, angry film told with great visual eloquence." The director uses "black and whites, light and darkness in the film" and reverses the usual correspondence of white to good and black to evil to illustrate the class conflict between officers and enlisted men, as Harriet Deer and Irving Deer noted in the *Journal of Popular Film.* While this allowed Kubrick "to make his visual content express his theme," the Deers added, it also meant that he "has had to rob [his characters] of complexity." Despite this sometimes "heavy-handed" message, David Denby stated in a 1991 *Premiere* article, *Paths of Glory* is also "a great, bitter intelligent movie, made in a spirit of sustained anger that is virtually unheard-of in the American cinema. It is *the* American anti-war movie, in comparison to which all others look soft, morally evasive, or just plain goody-goody."

> "Kubrick has made his life into an artist's odyssey, a search for new freedoms and powers with which to illuminate the world."
>
> —Norman Kagan

Although *Paths of Glory* proved a critical success, Kubrick encountered career difficulties after its release. His sometime scriptwriting collaborator, novelist Jim Thompson, was unable to complete a script for Kubrick due to illness. Kubrick himself wrote two screenplays but could find no backers to finance their production. He then spent six months with Marlon Brando preparing for the film *One-Eyed Jacks,* only to have the star fire him at the last minute so he could direct the film himself. Thus when Kirk Douglas asked him to take over the direction of a project he was both starring in and producing, Kubrick agreed. The result was the 1960 film *Spartacus,* based on Howard Fast's novel of a slave revolt in ancient Rome. While the film was a huge popular success (and was reissued in a restored version in 1991), Kubrick has preferred not to count it as one of his films because he did not have total control over the project. At the same time, with its unambiguous, upbeat ending, the film did not fit into Kubrick's vision as expressed in *Killer's Kiss, The Killing,* and *Paths of Glory.* "For each of these films," Adamson explained, "the setting is violent

and hostile to romantic or optimistic visions, and the stories all concern plans that go wrong."

For his next project, Kubrick again turned to literature for inspiration. Instead of using a tragic setting involving the criminal underworld or the battlefield, however, this time the director found a more comic vision in Vladimir Nabokov's complex and controversial masterpiece *Lolita.* Because of its subject matter—a middle-aged European becomes erotically obsessed with an American thirteen-year-old and ends up murdering his rival for her affections—Kubrick was able to option the best-selling novel himself; no Hollywood studio wanted to risk the controversy involved in bringing such a book to the screen. Kubrick hired Nabokov to write a screenplay adaptation and then reworked most of it (although the novelist was given sole screen credit to ward off complaints from critics about deviations from the novel).

Nevertheless, when the film of *Lolita* appeared in 1962, it provoked a wide range of responses. Conservative groups objected to the subject matter, while some reviewers felt the blackly satirical movie was not particularly faithful to the novel. "Most of what made the novel fun cannot be translated into film," Norman N. Holland observed in the *Hudson Review,* although he acknowledged that "the strength of the novel was its deft, swift satire of Americana, and this Nabokov and Kubrick do translate—no mean trick in film, where the slight exaggeration into satirical absurdity when rendered forty feet across can easily become too broad." However, Pauline Kael remarked in *Partisan Review* that "if you can get over the reviewers' preoccupation with the sacredness of the novel . . . you'll probably find that even the characters that *are* different . . . are successful in terms of the film." As a result, Kael concluded, "the surprise of *Lolita* is how enjoyable it is: it's the first *new* American comedy since those great days in the forties when Preston Sturges recreated comedy with a verbal slapstick. *Lolita* is black slapstick and at times it's so far out that you gasp as you laugh."

Later critics have also debated the worth of Kubrick's version of *Lolita.* Charles Samuels found it weakened by a "timidity" that results in neither "pathetic May-December romance . . . nor Nabokovian satire, but an incompatible mixture of the two." Kubrick himself acknowledged that he had to tone down the sexual content of the film to avoid protests and banning attempts by interest groups, and admitted that "this cripples the film's final scene, when Humbert should realize for the first time that he is in love with Lolita," as Joseph Adamson III explained. Nevertheless, other reviewers have found *Lolita* a successful expression of Kubrick's usual themes; Tom Milne wrote in *Sight and Sound* that the lack of erotic content was appropriate since "what Kubrick was after was not an evocation of Humbert's sensuous joy in his nymphet, but of his obsessive fear of what his tabooed love will bring." It was with *Lolita*, the critic added, "that Kubrick demonstrated . . . it was possible to adapt his style to both complexity *and* blockbuster length." John Russell Taylor argued that *Lolita* "stands up as the first full, mature expression of Kubrick's personality and point of view," and that "it enables us to appreciate fully for the first time the comic aspects of Kubrick's vision." Writer-director Paul Schrader asserted in a 1989 *American Film* article that "Kubrick, collaborating with Nabokov, wrote a script worthy of the twentieth century's greatest novel—no mean accomplishment." He concluded that "Kubrick's adaptation is a delight to the eye, ear and brain."

Visions Strange and Wonderful

If *Lolita* was the first of Kubrick's films to show a humorous side, his next effort made it clear the director had a definite flair for comedy. While the subject of nuclear annihilation may not seem like a good subject for farce, Kubrick's *Dr. Strangelove; or, How I Learned to Stop Worrying and Love the Bomb* proved otherwise. Working from Peter George's novel *Red Alert*, Kubrick and his cowriters created a darkly satirical look at how man's inability to control the machines he has built leads to the destruction of the world. When General Jack D. Ripper barricades himself in his office and initiates an attack against Russia, it sets off a chain of catastrophic events that no one— not President Merkin Muffley, Premier Dmitri Kissoff, or weapons scientist Dr. Strangelove—can stop. "The only way to tell the story," Kubrick was quoted as saying in the *Dictionary of Literary Biography*, "was as a black comedy, or better, a nightmare comedy, where the things you laugh at most are really the heart of the paradoxical postures that make a nuclear war possible." Thus General Ripper is obsessed with the purity of his

bodily fluids; Premier Kissoff is a womanizing drunkard; and Dr. Strangelove is possessed by a Nazi spirit.

Critics and audiences alike applauded the movie, which earned Kubrick his first Academy Award nominations, for best film, director, and screenplay. Calling *Dr. Strangelove* a "masterpiece" and "certainly one of the funniest" movies ever made, *New York Review of Books* contributor Robert Brustein hailed "the way it exploits the exciting narrative conventions of the Hollywood war movie . . . and even more, for the way it turns these conventions upside down, and cruelly scourges them." Milne also praised Kubrick's direction for "a style which allows him to range with perfect freedom from utter seriousness to the wildest slapstick, without ever loosening the film's claw-like grip on the audience." While *Village Voice* critic Andrew Sarris considered *Dr. Strangelove* "grossly overrated" even if "not a bad movie by any standards," later critics have identified it as a milestone in both Kubrick's career and American cinema. Samuels considered it "a film consolidating all the best in its predecessors," and explained that "while exposing the ultimate destructiveness of a culture perversely in love with machines, the film itself avoids mechanical flourishes, making direction reticently serve the content." "*Dr. Strangelove*'s reputation has solidified over the years," Adamson stated, "as time has revealed it to be a landmark film, one of the most important of its decade."

With the critical and popular success of *Dr. Strangelove*, Kubrick was able to obtain financial backing for his next project, what he hoped would become the "proverbial good science fiction movie," as he frequently described it. Reading several novels and finding none to suit his purpose, he began collaborating with noted science fiction (SF) author Arthur C. Clarke. Over a period of two years, the two men developed a script while Clarke simultaneously worked on a novel version. Kubrick brought in concept designers from the aerospace industry and convinced several scientific corporations to assist in developing the picture. While this helped create one of the most realistic portrayals of life in space ever put on film, *2001: A Space Odyssey* was more than a mechanical space epic, focusing instead on the evolution of humanity. The film opens during the "dawn of man" some four million years ago, as a large black monolith marks the moment in time when man's ancestors become tool-users. The film then jumps to the year 2001, where man uncovers a second monolith on the moon, thus setting off a strong radio signal toward the outer solar system. The spaceship *Discovery*, guided by the intelligent HAL 9000 computer, is sent to investigate the signal. When the HAL 9000 begins to see the human crew—who know nothing of the ship's true purpose—as obstacles to the mission, it begins to eliminate them. However, crewman Dave Bowman survives, and upon arriving at a moon of Jupiter, he encounters a third monolith. The object precipitates the beginning of the ultimate journey for Bowman, at the end of which he is transformed into the Star Child, the next—and possibly final—stage of human evolution.

Kubrick's visualization of this story, filled with innovative and eye-popping special effects, was nonetheless a puzzlement to many critics. Less than one-third of the film's two-plus hours contained dialogue; combined with the spare plot, this led several critics to pan the film as a bore. *New Republic* critic Stanley Kauffmann, for instance, remarked that "the gadgets are there for themselves, not for use in an artwork," and added that the emphasis on the mechanical creates "a film that is so dull, it even dulls our interest in the technical ingenuity for the sake of which Kubrick has allowed it to become dull." However, other critics hailed the film as a cinematic masterpiece, a visually rich intellectual examination of humanity's future. "Kubrick's *2001*," said Elie Flatto in *Film Comment*, "is one of the most entertaining as well as insightful films ever to have appeared on screen." Moviegoers made the film a hit, with many fans returning for repeated viewings, and the phenomenon led some critics to reassess the film. Joseph Gelmis of *Newsday*, for instance, originally found the film slow and lacking drama; but after a second viewing, he wrote that *2001* "is a masterwork. . . . This awesome film is light-years ahead of any science fiction you have ever seen."

"Here's Johnny!" Jack Nicholson creeped out audiences in Kubrick's 1980 adaptation of the Stephen King novel *The Shining*.

Tim Hunter perhaps summed up the initial critical reaction to *2001* in his *Film Heritage* review by writing that "*2001: A Space Odyssey* cannot be easily judged if only because of its dazzling technical perfection. To be able to see beyond that may take a few years."

On the whole, subsequent critical assessment of *2001* has confirmed it as one of the most groundbreaking films ever made. While Kubrick's Oscar-winning special effects did set the stage for *Star Wars, Alien,* and other popular science fiction successes of the late 1970s and early 1980s, it was the film's exploration of ideas that made it truly innovative. "What is wrong with most science fiction stories is that they content themselves with external discovery or, at most, with a mere moral lesson," Harriet and Irving Deer explained. "Kubrick, on the other hand, compels us in *2001* to desert the mechanistic, supposedly objective order of the world and to create our own subjective reality." In a twenty-fifth anniversary retrospective of the film, *Omni* contributor Piers Bizony noted that *2001* "still looks surprisingly fresh in 1993: it's not just about spaceships, about *how* we will get into space; it's also about *why*." This is why, the critic added, "*2001* stands as the epitome of SF filmmaking." A "witty, mind-bending science fiction classic," as Vincent Canby similarly described it in the *New York Times*, *2001* is "forever separate . . . from all [science fiction films] that came before and all that have come after."

Alienation Past and Future

Although he had two financially successful, Oscar-nominated films behind him, Kubrick was unable to secure financing for an epic biography of Napoleon; instead he turned to another novel for inspiration. Working from Anthony Burgess's novel *A Clockwork Orange*, Kubrick created his most controversial work. Set in the near future, the film follows the punishment and eventual liberation of a violent, Beethoven-loving punk named Alex. Whereas *2001* showed a machine trying to duplicate humanity, in *A Clockwork Orange* man is transformed into a machine: the murderous Alex is brainwashed into becoming a model citizen. "The film intentionally raises many issues viewers could conceivably feel disturbed about and then flashes vivid pictures of the issues' furthest extremes on the screen in nightmare images," Adamson summarized. "Not only the usual

sources of controversy—sex and violence—but also political domination, technological manipulation, religious sanctimony, and ideological hysteria are hyperbolized and thrust in front of viewers." Kubrick's use of savagely violent images was not as new or disturbing as the inventive way in which he filmed them: accompanied by strains of lofty classical music and often set among beautifully elaborate scenery.

The film's violent scenes and conclusion—when Alex breaks free of his brainwashing and begins his brutality again without society's interference—made *A Clockwork Orange* a hotly debated film among critics and viewers. The portrayal of Alex's character as charming if brutal led some observers to charge that the film romanticized violent crime, and even legitimized it. In Britain, after several supposed "copycat" crimes were reported, *A Clockwork Orange* was subjected to censorship attempts; Kubrick and the film's distributor then pulled the film from circulation, even though it had been playing to sellout crowds in London. "In truth, the film, like the book, goes to great pains to discourage full identification with the character and strives to portray Alex as a beast to be feared as well as a prodigy to be ambivalently admired," Adamson noted. Nevertheless, some critics found fault with the film for failing to capture the wit of the original novel. The *New Republic*'s Kauffmann, for instance, believed that "the modest moral resonance of the book is reduced . . . mostly because Kubrick has to replace Burgess's linguistic ingenuity with cinematic ingenuity, and he doesn't." Samuels, on the other hand, stated that "Kubrick finds brilliant cinematic equivalents for Burgess' gimmicks," but added that the director is "limited by the original's intellectual and emotional thinness."

But other reviewers asserted that Kubrick had created yet another groundbreaking film, and moviegoers agreed by making the movie one of the box office successes of 1971. *A Clockwork Orange* received four Oscar nominations, including Best Picture and Best Director, and later assessments have reflected its critical acceptance. John Russell Taylor lauded Kubrick as a "popular artist," and praised the film as his best to date; Taylor wrote that *A Clockwork Orange* proved that the director is "skilled in adapting the latest techniques to the task of communicating complicated ideas to the largest possible audience." According to Harriet and Irving Deer, the film forces its audience to confront the idea that man cannot be completely separated from his primitive impulses without losing his humanity. "When we discover that a thief, rapist and murderer is more human than the supposedly sane and moral society in which he lives," the critics explained, "we must become imaginatively engaged in making sense of the situation." Kubrick's complex exploration of the social and human issues surrounding violence has led to an enduring popularity. "The film's place in the pantheon of cult classics has become so secure that seeing *Clockwork* is a cinematic initiation ritual for each new generation of thrill-seeking teen audiences," Chris Nashawaty wrote in *Entertainment Weekly*, adding that decades later "the debate [over the film] still resonates."

2001 "is a masterwork. . . . This awesome film is light-years ahead of any science fiction you have ever seen."

—Joseph Gelmis

In 1975, Kubrick stepped away from the future visions of his two previous works with his next effort, an historical costume drama called *Barry Lyndon*. Adapted from the novel by nineteenth-century British author William Makepeace Thackeray, the film is a portrayal of the title character's journey from poverty to nobility. As the naive commoner Redmond Barry transforms himself through marriage into the sophisticated Lord Barry Lyndon, he discovers the high cost of gaining all he thought that he desired. For this costume drama, Kubrick used elaborate sets and clothing to re-create the beautiful yet corrupt society of the European aristocracy.

While a few critics faulted the film for appearing "more concerned with landscapes, architecture, period interiors, costumes, etc., than with what happens to the people in them," as John Simon wrote in *New York*, the majority hailed *Barry Lyndon* as yet another success for the versatile Kubrick. Harold Rosenberg praised the film's "faultless aesthetic package" and added in his *New York Times* review that "I could have watched *Barry Lyndon* for another two hours without the

slightest interest in what was happening to its hero." Lauding "the originality of the [film's] achievement," *Salmagundi* contributor Alan Spiegel explained that in *Barry Lyndon* "the fusion of art and human suffering . . . has become a structural concept that both determines and permeates the emotional ambience of an entire film."

Other reviewers likewise observed that the visual opulence of the film helped to reinforce its themes. Gene Youngblood noted in *Take One* that "the fops and fools in the movie play out their follies against an earth so resplendent, in rooms so overarching and vaulted, that anything they do becomes ludicrous, utterly insignificant." As a result, the critic added, "I think *Barry Lyndon* is the most intelligent, most amazing, most radical movie Stanley Kubrick has made—which is to say it's among the great achievements of contemporary cinema." Hans Feldmann considered the film, following *2001* and *A Clockwork Orange*, as completing "a trilogy on the moral and psychological nature of Western man and on the destiny of his civilization." The critic explained in *Film Quarterly* that "Redmond Barry's failure to achieve selfhood in the terms prescribed by his society is his tragedy, and by extension the tragedy of Western man." Adamson observed a similar correlation between the three films, writing that *Barry Lyndon* "implies Kubrick's view that man was just as deluded and corrupted a creature in the romantic past as he is in the degenerate present and will be in the apocalyptic future." While the film received several Oscar nominations, including Best Picture and Best Director, it was not as popular as Kubrick's previous films, a fact Adamson attributed to a lack of the "surface sensationalism that had made Kubrick's past intellectual constructs more palatable to the mass audience." Nevertheless, Feldmann concluded, *Barry Lyndon* helps support "the claim that [Kubrick] is one of America's top film directors. He is more than that. Stanley Kubrick is a critic of his age, one of its interpreters and one of its artists."

Horrors Real and Imaginary

Having reimagined film genres from science fiction to costume drama to black comedy, for his next movie Kubrick turned to yet another genre: horror. The director brought his distinctive style to popular novelist Stephen King's *The Shining*, a tale of a ghostly hotel that drives its caretaker to

Full Metal Jacket, **based on Gustav Hasford's novel** *The Short-Timers,* **follows young soldiers through basic training and into urban warfare during the Vietnam Tet offensive.**

violence. Aspiring writer Jack Torrance has brought his wife and son to an isolated Colorado hotel, the Overlook; while they maintain the building during the empty winter season, Jack hopes the solitude will allow him to finally complete the novel he has been working on. However, Jack's son Danny has premonitions that something evil lurks at the hotel, perhaps the same thing that caused the previous caretaker to butcher his family and commit suicide. As the winter progresses, sinister apparitions begin to manifest themselves and Jack becomes increasingly unstable, leading to the inevitable result.

Because Kubrick's version of *The Shining* deviated both from King's original story and the conventions of horror films, it received a considerable amount of negative criticism. *New Yorker* writer Pauline Kael suggested that Kubrick's "absorption in film technology distances us," such that "though we may admire the effects, we're never

drawn in by them. . . . We wait for revelations—the events that will connect the different types of parapsychological phenomena we've been observing—and since we don't get those revelations, the picture seems not to make any sense." "Kubrick simply makes Jack crazy, or crazy-seeming," Henry Bromell stated in the *Atlantic,* "an exaggerated, highly stylized bogeyman rising from the shadows to frighten children." As a result, the critic felt that Kubrick's version lost much of the underlying emotional horror surrounding Jack's transformation that had made King's novel so terrifying.

However, other reviewers felt Kubrick's version of *The Shining* was effective, if considered on its own terms. The director "has tried for the ultimate horror film—and almost achieved it," a *People* critic noted, for "he proves a master at creating a sense of impending dread through music, shadow and startling camera angles." Richard T. Jameson attributed negative criticism of the film to mistaken expectations of a typical horror film, and remarked in *Film Comment* that "*The Shining* is a horror movie only in the sense that all Kubrick's mature work has been horror movies." The director again uses visuals to reflect his theme, according to Jameson: "The Overlook's spaces mirror Jack's bankruptcy. The sterility of its vastness, the spaces that proliferate yet really connect with each other is a continuum that encloses rather than releases, frustrates rather than liberates—all this becomes an extension of his own barrenness of mind and spirit." Flo Leibowitz and Lynn Jeffress similarly found deeper levels to the film: "Kubrick builds his world carefully and it soon becomes clear that the Overlook is much more than it seems," they wrote in *Film Quarterly*. "At one very important level it is a symbol of America, haunted by a murderous past that has made it what it is: a showy display of affluence and excess. . ., built at the expense of innocent victims."

Innocent and not-so-innocent victims figure in Kubrick's next work, *Full Metal Jacket*. While several American films in the late 1970s and 1980s had dealt with the painful subject of the Vietnam War, Kubrick's 1987 film was the first to portray urban rather than jungle warfare. Working with Michael Herr and Gustav Hasford from Hasford's novel *The Short-Timers*, the director showed two aspects of soldiering during that conflict: first, the exacting and brutal basic training that transforms young men into killing machines; and second, the disorienting, random nature of the fighting as experienced by the Marines during the Tet offensive of 1968. Even more than Kubrick's other films, *Full Metal Jacket* received drastically differing reviews upon its release, many of which compared it with Oliver Stone's *Platoon*, which had received a best picture Oscar the previous year. Critics of Kubrick's film faulted it both for its episodic nature and what *National Review* writer John Simon called a lack of "a human center." "This is Kubrick's fatal flaw," the critic explained: "He is a master technician, but at a loss when it comes to people." While Tom O'Brien admitted the movie "has some good moments," he found it "too abstract, uneven, and fractured to work as compelling drama." The director, he suggested in *Commonweal*, "is not interested in character, or continuity, but idea. This is inconvenient in a narrative medium like film, although Kubrick at times has gotten the better of the problem." *New Yorker* film critic Pauline Kael panned the film, writing

that "this may be [Kubrick's] worst movie. He probably believes he's numbing us by the power of his vision, but he's actually numbing us by its emptiness."

Washington Post critic Desson Howe disagreed, hailing *Full Metal Jacket* as "the most eloquent and exacting vision of the [Vietnam] war to date" and praising Kubrick's direction as "inspired with technique rather than overblown with it." *Time*'s Richard Corliss similarly admired the "Olympian elegance and precision of Kubrick's filmmaking," and noted that unlike *Platoon*, "Kubrick's film does not want to say every last word about Viet Nam. It wants to isolate a time, a place and a disease." Rita Kempley asserted in the *Washington Post* that *Full Metal Jacket* "should not be compared with Oliver Stone's sweaty, cathartic *Platoon*, the moral surrealism of *Apocalypse Now* or even the emotional romance of *Coming Home*." Instead, she wrote, "it's a cynical statement that recreates the wahoo war-movie structure, then crumbles it to undermine idealized carnage, even as the moviegoing public is swept with 'Nam nostalgia." Writing in *Newsweek*, critic Jack Kroll expressed similar sentiments. "Kubrick's film scorches you with the absolute chill of its depiction of the war as a plague of corruption and dehumanization," he said.

A Lasting Legacy

As Kubrick brought his complex cinematic vision to the screen, he became known for his meticulous approach to filmmaking. He often required numerous takes until a scene was exactly as he wanted it; he often did his own lighting, camerawork, and editing, and he insisted on retaining strict control over the marketing and distribution of his films. A resident of England since the early 1960s, Kubrick refused to fly, and so after *Lolita* all his films were shot on location in England. While filming, he surrounded his projects with a strict veil of secrecy, forbidding actors and crew from making any comments about a film until its release. He shunned publicity and was termed a recluse by some media-watchers—even though he was constantly in touch with the outside world through satellite television, telephone, fax, and e-mail. The resulting mystique surrounding the director, when combined with his considerable track record in producing distinguished films, meant that each new Kubrick work was eagerly anticipated by audiences and critics alike.

If you enjoy the works of Stanley Kubrick, you may also want to check out the following films:

Being There, starring Peter Sellers, 1979.
THX 1138, directed by George Lucas, 1971.
Saving Private Ryan, directed by Steven Spielberg, 1998.

So when, nearly a decade after making *Full Metal Jacket*, rumors spread that the director was finally beginning a new film, anticipation was high. But Kubrick's control over information was so absolute, little was known about the picture besides its title—*Eyes Wide Shut*—and its stars: Hollywood power couple Tom Cruise and Nicole Kidman. Kubrick had just presented his completed version of the film to studio heads in March, 1999, when word came that the director had died unexpectedly at his home outside London. His last film, it was finally revealed, would venture into yet another genre: the intimate, psychological study of human relationships. The director was confident this film, an examination of the marriage of two psychiatrists, would be his best yet.

As news of Kubrick's death spread, testimonials to the director's enduring legacy poured in. "The loss to the world of cinema is incalculable," director Michael Winner told London *Times* correspondent Carol Midgley. "He will be remembered as one of the greatest geniuses since cinema evolved," Michael Wilmington wrote in the *Chicago Tribune*. "His work was marked by cinematic brilliance, consummate cinematography, intense acting, highly literate screenplays . . . and daring subject matter." Throughout the director's "selective but magnificent career," Wilmington continued, "Kubrick's great subjects were usually the nightmarish traps that afflict humankind: war, crime, obsession, mortality and madness." "Few directors have ever divided critical opinion like Stanley Kubrick," James Christopher noted in the London *Times*. "His critics called him pretentious, fussy, intractable. But to many others he is a unique artist with a personal vision matched only by his brilliant way with a camera." As Derek Malcolm similarly observed in the *Guardian*, "many of his films are already on the lists of cinema classics not just because they are brilliantly

made but because they had something pertinent to say." "Some myopic viewers only saw Mr. Kubrick as a technocrat, more concerned with the special lenses he had ground for particular shots than in developing dramatic themes," *Boston Globe* writer Michael Blowen concluded. "Nothing could be farther from the truth. Mr. Kubrick developed the technology only to actualize the humanity of his films."

Nevertheless, as the creator of several indelible screen images—Slim Pickens riding a bomb to the world's destruction in *Dr. Strangelove*; the black monolith and Star Child of *2001*; Jack Nicholson crowing "He-e-re's Johnny!" in *The Shining*—Kubrick will ultimately be remembered for his extraordinary ability to create a complete visual experience. "Kubrick is, among other things, a true screen poet," Daniel De Vries said in his *Films of Stanley Kubrick*. The critic explained that "what is wonderful about Kubrick's imagistic skill is that theme and image conjoin so naturally in his movies. . . . This is one facet of Kubrick's genius—his ability to project theme without using symbols, by creating visual images which *are* the themes of his films." "[It] is not alone the size and seriousness and complexity of Kubrick's moral vision which makes him the finest of . . . directors," author Anthony Burgess stated, "but his ability to express his vision in a coherent structure of images." As Jack Kroll of *Time* noted in his assessment of *Full Metal Jacket*, "no living director matches Kubrick in his ability to create a physical world that transmits a film's emotional frequency," often making his settings contain as much personality as his characters. Writing in the introduction to his book *The Films of Stanley Kubrick*, Daniel De Vries commented, "One might often disagree with Kubrick's ideas . . . but none of that detracts from the fact that Kubrick puts together picture shows which are entertaining, aesthetically pleasing, and provoking, all at the same time."

"Kubrick has made his life into an artist's odyssey, a search for new freedoms and powers with which to illuminate the world," Norman Kagan asserted. "It is clear . . . that Kubrick can make any source material fit comfortably into the fabric of his work as a whole," Gene D. Phillips observed in the *St. James Film Directors Encyclopedia*, adding that "it is equally evident that Kubrick wants to continue to create films that will stimulate his audience to think about serious human problems, as his films have done from the beginning."

■ Works Cited

Adamson, Joseph III, "Stanley Kubrick," *Dictionary of Literary Biography*, Volume 26: *American Screenwriters*, Gale, 1984, pp. 191-98.

Baumbach, Jonathan, review of *Paths of Glory, Film Culture*, February, 1958, p. 15.

Bizony, Piers, "2001 at 25," *Omni*, May, 1993, pp. 42-46, 50.

Blowen, Michael, "Stanley Kubrick, Master Filmmaker, Is Dead at 70," *Boston Globe*, March 8, 1999, p. A1.

Bromell, Henry, "The Dimming of Stanley Kubrick," *Atlantic*, August, 1980, pp. 80-83.

Brustein, Robert, "Out of This World," *New York Review of Books*, February 6, 1964, pp. 3-4.

Burgess, Jackson, "The `Anti-Militarism' of Stanley Kubrick," *Film Quarterly*, Fall, 1964, pp. 4-11.

Canby, Vincent, "`2010' Pursues the Mystery of `2001,'" *New York Times*, December 7, 1984, p. C15.

Christopher, James, "Kubrick: A Cinematic Odyssey," *Times* (London), March 8, 1999, p. 3.

Corliss, Richard, "Welcome to Viet Nam, the Movie: II," *Time*, June 29, 1987, p. 66.

Croce, Arlene, review of *The Killing, Film Culture*, Volume 2, Number 3, 1956, pp. 30-31.

Deer, Harriet, and Irving Deer, "Kubrick and the Structures of Popular Culture," *Journal of Popular Film*, Volume 3, Number 3, 1974, pp. 232-44.

Denby, David, "Voyage of the Damned," *Premiere*, July, 1991, pp. 22, 26.

De Vries, Daniel, introduction to his *The Films of Stanley Kubrick*, Eerdmans, 1973, pp. 5-7.

Feldmann, Hans, "Kubrick and His Discontents," *Film Quarterly*, Fall, 1976, pp. 12-19.

Flatto, Elie, "`2001: A Space Odyssey': The Eternal Renewal," *Film Comment*, Winter, 1969, pp. 7-8.

Gelmis, Joseph, review of *2001: A Space Odyssey, Newsday*, April 20, 1968.

Grove, Lloyd, "Stanley Kubrick, At a Distance," *Washington Post*, June 28, 1987, p. F1.

Holland, Norman N., "Film, Metafilm, and Unfilm," *Hudson Review*, Autumn, 1962, pp. 406-12.

Howe, Desson, review of *Full Metal Jacket, Washington Post*, June 26, 1987.

Hunter, Tim, review of *2001: A Space Odyssey, Film Heritage*, Summer, 1968, pp. 12-20.

Jameson, Richard T., "Kubrick's Shining," *Film Comment*, July-August, 1980, pp. 28-32.

Kael, Pauline, review of *Lolita, Partisan Review*, Fall, 1962.

Kael, Pauline, "Devolution," *New Yorker*, June 9, 1980, pp. 130-47.

Kael, Pauline, "Ponderoso," *New Yorker*, July 13, 1987, pp. 75-76.

Kagan, Norman, *The Cinema of Stanley Kubrick*, Holt, 1972.

Kauffmann, Stanley, "Lost in the Stars," *New Republic*, May 4, 1968, pp. 24, 41.

Kauffmann, Stanley, review of *A Clockwork Orange, New Republic*, January 1-8, 1972.

Kempley, Rita, review of *Full Metal Jacket, Washington Post*, June 26, 1987.

Review of *The Killing, Time*, June 4, 1956, p. 106.

Koehler, Robert, "Kubrick's Path of Glory to Venice," *Variety*, August 25-31, 1997, p. 42.

Kroll, Jack, "1968: Kubrick's Vietnam Odyssey," *Newsweek*, June 29, 1987, pp. 64-65.

Lambert, Gavin, review of *Killer's Kiss, Sight and Sound*, Spring, 1956, p. 198.

Lambert, Gavin, review of *Paths of Glory, Sight and Sound*, Winter, 1957-58, pp. 144-45.

Leibowitz, Flo, and Lynn Jeffress, review of *The Shining, Film Quarterly*, spring, 1981, pp. 45-51.

Malcolm, Derek, "The Genius Who Outdid Hollywood," *Guardian*, March 8, 1999, p. 3.

Midgley, Carol, "Film Director Stanley Kubrick Dies Aged 70," *Times* (London), March 8, 1999, p. 1.

Milne, Tom, "How I Learned to Stop Worrying and Love Stanley Kubrick," *Sight and Sound*, Spring, 1964, pp. 64-72.

Nashawaty, Chris, "`The Old Ultraviolence,'" *Entertainment Weekly*, December 15, 1995, p. 92.

O'Brien, Tom, "Satired Out," *Commonweal*, August 14, 1987, pp. 457-58.

Phillips, Gene D., "Stanley Kubrick," *St. James Film Directors Encyclopedia*, St. James Press, 1998, pp. 249-51.

Rosenberg, Harold, "Notes on Seeing `Barry Lyndon,'" *New York Times*, February 29, 1976.

Samuels, Charles Thomas, "The Context of `A Clockwork Orange,'" *American Scholar*, Summer, 1972, pp. 439-43.

Sarris, Andrew, review of *Dr. Strangelove, Village Voice*, February 13, 1964.

Schrader, Paul, "`Lolita': Rapier Innuendos and Roman Ping-Pong," *American Film*, October, 1989, pp. 18-22.

Review of *The Shining, People*, June 30, 1980, pp. 14, 16.

Simon, John, "Million-Dollar Blimps," *New York*, December 29-January 5, 1975-76, pp. 84-87.

Simon, John, "Twice-Bitten Bullet," *National Review*, August 14, 1987, pp. 52-53.

Spiegel, Alan, "Kubrick's `Barry Lyndon,'" *Salmagundi*, Summer-Fall, 1977, pp. 194-208.

Taylor, John Russell, "Stanley Kubrick," *Directors and Directions: Cinema for the Seventies*, Hill & Wang, 1975, pp. 100-35.

Wilmington, Michael, "Director of `Dr. Strangelove,' `2001,'" *Chicago Tribune*, March 8, 1999.

Youngblood, Gene, "Flamingo Hours: Luminous Machines," *Take One*, January, 1977, p. 27.

Zimmerman, Paul D., "Kubrick's Brilliant Vision," *Newsweek*, January 3, 1972, pp. 28-33.

■ For More Information See

BOOKS

Agel, Jerome, *The Making of Kubrick's 2001*, New American Library, 1970.

Baxter, John, *Stanley Kubrick: A Biography*, Carroll & Graf, 1997.

Clarke, Arthur C., *The Lost Worlds of 2001*, New American Library, 1972.

Falsetto, Mario, *Stanley Kubrick: A Narrative and Stylistic Analysis*, Greenwood Press, 1994.

Falsetto, Mario, editor, *Perspectives on Stanley Kubrick*, G. K. Hall, 1996.

Garcia Mainar, Luis M., *Narrative and Stylistic Patterns in the Films of Stanley Kubrick*, Camden House, 1999.

Geduld, Carolyn, *Filmguide to 2001: A Space Odyssey*, Indiana University Press, 1973.

Gelmis, Joseph, *The Film Director as Superstar*, Doubleday, 1970.

Kauffmann, Stanley, *Living Images: Film Comment and Criticism*, Harper, 1975.

LoBrutto, Vincent, *Stanley Kubrick: A Biography*, D. I. Fine, 1997.

Phillips, Gene D., *Stanley Kubrick: A Film Odyssey*, Popular Library, 1975, revised edition, 1977.

Walker, Alexander, *Stanley Kubrick Directs*, Harcourt, 1971, new edition, 1999.

PERIODICALS

American Film, June, 1980, p. 49; October, 1983, pp. 90-91; June, 1987, p. 11; September, 1987, p. 20; April, 1990, p. 56.

Artforum, February, 1969.

Christian Science Monitor, May 10, 1968.

Cinema, winter, 1972-73.

Commentary, January, 1988, p. 48.

Entertainment Weekly, October 2, 1998, p. 18.

Esquire, July, 1958.

Eye, August, 1968.

Film Comment, summer, 1965; March-April, 1994, p. 4; September-October, 1996, p. 81+.

Film Culture, spring, 1970.

Film Quarterly, fall, 1968; summer, 1983, p. 48; winter, 1988, p. 24.

Guardian, May 3, 1996.

Life, March 13, 1964.

Los Angeles Times, June 26, 1987; July 7, 1987; July 26, 1987; January 28, 1988; June 21, 1989.

Maclean's, June 16, 1980.

Nation, June 3, 1968; June 14, 1980, p. 732.

New Leader, July 14, 1980; October 10, 1994.

New Republic, June 14, 1980, p. 26; July 27, 1987, pp. 28-29.

Newsweek, December 2, 1957; December 22, 1975; May 26, 1980, p. 96.

New York, June 9, 1980, pp. 60-64; May 13, 1991, pp. 95-96; January 24, 1994, p. 56.

New Yorker, November 12, 1966.

New York Times, April 4, 1968; April 14, 1968; December 20, 1971; January 4, 1972; December 31, 1972; May 23, 1980; June 21, 1987; June 26, 1987; September 15, 1998.

New York Times Magazine, October 12, 1958; January 6, 1966; August 15, 1993, p. 66.

People, May 13, 1991, p. 20; June 9, 1997; May 18, 1998.

Playboy, September, 1968.

Premiere, November, 1991, p. 126.

Rolling Stone, May 16, 1991, p. 118.

Saturday Review, April 20, 1968; December 25, 1971.

Sight and Sound, summer, 1968.

Time, December 20, 1971; December 15, 1975; June 2, 1980, p. 69.

Variety, October 6, 1997.

Washington Post, July 12, 1987.

■ Obituaries

PERIODICALS

Guardian, March 8, 1999, pp. 1, 15.

Los Angeles Times, March 8, 1999, p. 1.

Newsweek, March 22, 1999, pp. 96-98.

New York Times, March 8, 1999, p. 1.
Telegraph (London), March 8, 1999.
Times (London), March 8, 1999, p. 23.
Washington Post, March 8, 1999, p. A1.*

—Sketch by Diane Telgen

Christa Laird

■ Personal

Born December, 1944, in London, England; married Nigel Laird (an educator), 1968; children: Julian, Adam. *Education:* University of Bristol, degree in social work, 1966; University of Exeter, qualification in social work, 1968; University of Oxford, B.Litt.

■ Addresses

Home—82 Lonsdale Rd., Oxford OX2 7ER, England.

■ Career

Author, social worker, and educator. Has worked for the Training Section of the British Social Services Department as a specialist on child abuse and child protectiton; has also worked in management as a locum training officer, and as a teacher of literature at Oxford University. *Member:* Amnesty International.

■ Awards, Honors

Janusz Korczak Literary Award, 1992, for *Shadow of the Wall.*

■ Writings

HISTORICAL FICTION

Shadow of the Wall, Julia Macrae (London), 1989, Greenwillow (New York), 1990.
The Forgotten Son, Julia Macrae, 1990.
But Can the Phoenix Sing?, Julia Macrae, 1993, Greenwillow, 1995.

■ Sidelights

An English author of historical fiction for young people, Laird has been consistently praised for writing moving, thought-provoking works that successfully blend real facts, people, and events with invented characters and situations. Although she has written only three books, Laird is considered one of the most promising creators of young adult literature. The author has set two of her works, *Shadow of the Wall* and its sequel *But Can the Phoenix Sing?,* in the periods during and immediately following the Holocaust, while her third book, *The Forgotten Son,* takes place in twelfth-century France. All of Laird's stories feature young men who are searching for their identities during times of social repression, and her works explore sophisticated moral concepts such as the individual's capacity for good and evil and the emergence of courage from oppression.

Recognized for her thorough research, Laird is noted for including an abundance of accurate information about the periods she depicts as well as prefaces and postscripts that provide further resources. Although her books contain war, death, cruelty, abandonment, and other difficult issues, Laird is also acknowledged for underscoring the humanity and universality of the situations she describes, and her books are often viewed as testimonies to the indomitability of the human spirit. In a 1998 autobiographical essay for *Something about the Author Autobiography Series (SAAS)*, Laird wrote that her "inclination to write was a maternal legacy; the subject matter, on the other hand, rather persistently paternal." She continued, "They say that all works of fiction are essentially autobiographical, and my sons tease me that my three books are all about searching for a lost father, which I suppose, in a way, they are."

Born in London, Laird arrived in the world less than three months after the 1944 death of her father at the Battle of Arnhem, the first attempt by the Allies to free Holland from Nazi occupation. "Perhaps the most poignant aspect of my father's death," Laird said, "is the fact that it was, in a very particular sense, unnecessary." Laird's father was born in Cologne, Germany, to a successful Jewish architect and his gentile wife. Shortly after Hitler's rise to power, the couple left Germany, making their way to England via Holland. Laird's father obtained a law degree from Oxford University, then volunteered for the armed forces, which as an alien he was not required to do. Later, he joined a parachute regiment. That led to his involvement in the Battle of Arnhem, where he was killed at age twenty-four.

Laird wrote in *SAAS*, "Overshadowed though it was by my father's death, my childhood, like most, contained both joys and miseries, and in my case there were definitely more of the former." Devoted to her mother, a writer who published magazine articles and short stories (several of which were broadcast on BBC radio), five-year-old Christa was upset and resentful when her mother remarried. "At that time, and for several years afterwards," Laird noted, "the secret that I hated my stepfather was one I chose to share, like a

sacrificial offering, with only the most special or coveted of friends." She added, "Not that my stepfather was cruel or abusive in any way; distant, certainly, and unsure how to relate to children, with other more pressing things on his mind than how to win over a resentful and probably rather self-opinionated little girl." As an adult, Laird's attitude toward her stepfather mellowed; when he died, she remembered, "I was genuinely sad."

Many of Laird's happiest childhood memories are associated with her maternal grandparents: her grandfather, as Laird described him in *SAAS*, "was a dear and endlessly patient man," while her grandmother "was a more irascible, indeed fiery, character." Laird's grandfather took her to the London Zoo and played cards and board games with her, while her grandmother kept a jar of sweets in a secret place in the corner of her cupboard for Christa and her younger brother Paul. When she was eight, Laird's grandparents booked expensive seats outside the Savoy Hotel for Coronation Day—the celebration of Queen Elizabeth II's ascension to the throne. Christa boasted to her mother afterwards that she "had been close enough to see the Queen's blue eyes as she passed in her golden coach!"

Her grandparents also owned a cottage in North Devon on England's southwestern coast. As Laird noted in her *SAAS* essay, until her early teens she spent all of her holidays here, "when the days were always long and sunny and the hydrangea bushes in the cottage garden always in full bloom." On several occasions, Laird's mother took her and her brother to nearby Lundy Island. Laird has special memories of that lonely, windswept place. She recalled in her *SAAS* essay a particular adventure that occurred when the family stayed on Lundy for two nights: "The best moment then was when we stood watching the steamer depart with its cargo of day trippers, and we could begin to pretend that we had been shipwrecked and marooned, with only seabirds and wild deer and the ghosts in the ruined castle for company."

When Laird was about twelve, she was sent to the same boarding school her mother had attended; Laird wrote that they even shared the same math teacher, "who," the author noted, "could never decide which one of us was the less numerate." After a few days of homesickness,

Laird adjusted well to her new school. She recalled, "I enjoyed both sports and academic work, so on the whole school was a positive experience; and several of the friends I made then are still my friends today." At fifteen, she made what she described as "probably the first major mistake in my life." Although she was considered an apt pupil with a particular talent for languages, Laird decided that she did not want to go to college—"I had enough of school and discipline," she remembered. Her mother and stepfather sent Laird to a school in Switzerland where she could study French and German seriously; her experience in Switzerland, which she described in *SAAS* as "not much more than an enjoyable and fattening diversion," led her to change her mind about university.

Returning to England, Laird crammed two years of study into one year at a London tutorial college. She wrote that "no less than three of my teachers in that year succumbed to nervous breakdowns or other health-related problems—coincidence rather than consequence, I hope." After passing her "A-level" exams, Laird was accepted by the University of Bristol. "I was to spend three of the happiest years of my life [there]," she wrote. Before starting college, Laird went to the United States for five months to get to know her father's twin sisters who had emigrated there in 1947. One of her aunts had married William Castle, the producer of *Rosemary's Baby* and other thrillers; staying in Beverly Hills with the Castles was, Laird acknowledged, "a dizzying experience" and "enough to spoil an impressionable eighteen-year-old for life!" Since her first visit, Laird has traveled elsewhere in America, including the Grand Canyon. "Few other places have made such a deep and lasting impression on me," she wrote.

In 1963, Laird began her course work at the University of Bristol. On her first day of classes, she met Nigel Laird, whom she would eventually marry. "Not that it was love at first sight, exactly," the author recalled in *SAAS*. "Love works in mysterious ways, and it took a good many shared classes, enough cups of coffee to float a battleship, and several months of sitting around in various bars for me to subtly persuade Nigel to persuade me that he was the man who should share my life." During her three years at university, Laird "lived in a constant state of exhilaration," she wrote in *SAAS*. She enjoyed her classes, had a rich social life, traveled extensively in France and Germany, and became one of the early members of Amnesty International. After graduation, Nigel Laird went to teach in Austria as preparation for a career as a specialist in modern languages, while Christa went to the University of Exeter in Devon—the county in which she had spent her blissful summer holidays—to earn her degree in social work. Laird wrote that she "never seriously considered any career other than social work. . . . I *do* regret not having better career advice at that point."

A story of courage in the desperate world of the Warsaw Ghetto

Beech TREE

A Beech Tree Paperback Book $4.95

SHADOW OF THE WALL

CHRISTA LAIRD

In her award-winning 1989 debut novel, Laird tells the story of fourteen-year-old Misha Edelman, who must get food to his mother in the war-torn Warsaw Ghetto and then help smuggle a young girl out to safety from the Nazis.

After completing her degree, Laird became a child care officer, a social worker who worked with families and children. For her first assignment, she returned to Bristol, where Nigel was earning his post-graduate teaching qualification. In 1968, they married and settled in Coventry, a city that Laird described in *SAAS* as "famous for its wholesale destruction in World War Two and for the remarkable new cathedral built, in the spirit of reconciliation, alongside the shattered ruins of the old." While living in Coventry, the Lairds had two sons, Julian and Adam. After Julian's birth, Laird found that she adored her son but, as she noted in her *SAAS* essay, "he was not quite articulate enough at age one and a half to satisfy even my admittedly modest intellectual requirements." She continued, "So it was to fill a certain void that while he was taking his morning nap, I started to write my first novel."

Directed to adults, the story describes a female terrorist, hospitalized after an injury, who develops a relationship with a social worker who has been assigned to protect her. "I expect," Laird offered, "the social worker was far too transparently 'me'"; the novel, she noted, "malingers to this day at the bottom of a drawer somewhere because last time I had a clear out I couldn't bring myself to throw it in the bin! I am mildly intrigued by this because I *have* succeeded in jettisoning manuscripts which have taken just as much time and effort to produce; perhaps it is because the idea of the 'good' terrorist is one which continues to fascinate me, both from an ethical and an aesthetic point of view. It makes one consider the gulf between public and private virtue, which has always struck me as one of *the* most interesting moral issues of our day."

Decides to Write

In 1972, Nigel Laird was accepted as an instructor at an independent school for boys in Oxford. Five years later, with her sons in nursery school, Christa was, as she wrote in *SAAS*, "ready to meet a fresh challenge." That, she decided, should be writing. "In a vague and visionless way . . . I had always wanted to write," she explained. Despite her training in the social sciences, Laird admitted that her heart "belongs much more to languages and literature." She decided to return to her degree subject, German, to do literary research.

In addition, as she noted in her essay, Laird was "fascinated by the subject of oppression and responses to it; the obvious solution seemed to be to combine these strands of interest and to write a thesis on a specific aspect of the German literary response to Nazism." Laird completed a thesis on fascist mentality in the works of German novelists Gunter Grass and Siegfried Lenz and received her B.Litt (now changed to M.Litt) from Oxford. She began teaching literature part-time at Oxford and also returned to social work. However, while she was working on her research degree, Laird came across a reference to Janusz Korczak, a heroic Polish Jew who was a pediatrician, writer, educator, broadcaster, and social worker. When the Nazis sealed off the Warsaw Ghetto in 1940, Korczak took two hundred children into its confines from an orphanage that he managed, and he tried to guarantee them safety as well as some quality of life. When the Nazis deported the children to the death camp of Treblinka, Korczak was offered the chance of a reprieve, but he is said to have replied, "Desertion is not in my vocabulary." Instead, he went with the children to his death. Laird realized that she needed to tell Korczak's story; in researching it, she discovered that "the sacrificial manner of Korczak's death was but an extension of his entire way of life."

Written while she worked full-time as a locum training officer, Laird's first book, *Shadow of the Wall*, was published in 1989. The novel is set in wartime Poland and tells the story of a fourteen-year-old Jewish boy, Misha Edelman, who lives with his two sisters in one of Janusz Korczak's orphanages in the Warsaw Ghetto. Misha, whose father is dead and whose mother is dying of tuberculosis, at great personal risk tries to bring food and medicine to his mother on the other side of the wall. In the streets, he sees shootings and beatings as well as the effects of disease and starvation. In the orphanage, he sees Korczak struggle to provide the children with a haven of love and support. When life at the orphanage becomes more difficult, Misha and Korczak smuggle the boy's infant sister to the home of a gentile family. Mrs. Edelman dies soon after, and Misha, who then joins a resistance group, watches as Korczak marches to the head of the line of children bound for Treblinka. Among this group is the boy's other sister. After the train departs, Misha escapes from the ghetto through a sewer. *Shadow of the Wall* was praised as a gripping, heart-rending book that

Another story of the Warsaw Ghetto and the Nazi menace, this 1993 novel is told in flashback as Misha recalls his escape from the Germans and his work to save other Jews from the Holocaust.

concluded that *Shadow of the Wall* "serves as bearable context for any young person exploring the important question of how the Holocaust could have happened." In 1992, Laird received the first Janus Korczak Literary Award for *Shadow of the Wall.*

Laird followed the success of *Shadow of the Wall* with a second novel, *The Forgotten Son.* Published in 1990 and set in the twelfth century, this work features Peter Astrolabe, the fourteen-year-old son of the famous French scholars Abelard and Heloise. The couple, forbidden by law to have a romantic relationship, married secretly after the birth of their son. When their union came to light, Abelard was emasculated and became a monk, while Heloise became a nun; their famous exchange of letters on love and suffering popularized their story as a romantic tragedy. Abandoned at four months, Peter searches to discover the facts about his childhood. His quest leads him to a new awareness, both about his identity and about the social forces that destroyed his parents.

Calling the book "warm-hearted and moving," Margery Fisher of *Growing Point* noted that the forgotten boy of eight hundred years ago "can be understood by young readers in the 'teens today because his problem is not unlike that of any youth caught in the complexities of a broken family." *School Librarian* contributor Frank Warren agreed, noting that *The Forgotten Son* will "perhaps have added cogency for any readers who feel parental neglect or who are experiencing some sort of crisis in relation to personal identity." L. Atterton of *Books for Your Children* called the work an "exquisitely detailed and moving emotional awakening" and concluded, "The heart breaks for Heloise, for the honesty, passion, and unselfishness of her love. . . ."

reflects Laird's smooth, skillful interweaving of true story and fictional narrative. Writing in *Horn Book*, Hanna B. Zeiger claimed that the interwoven stories are "a testament to the courage of those who survived as well as those who died," while Adrian Jackson of *Books for Keeps* declared, "The scene where the Doctor leads the children onto the train for Treblinka is etched in my mind." Writing in *Growing Point*, Margery Fisher commented, "A book like this can be an effective sermon against war and, more valuably, a proclamation of the strength of the human spirit." Betsy Hearne of *Bulletin of the Center for Children's Books*

Writing in *SAAS*, Laird noted, "The challenge for me was to find a fresh perspective on an ancient story, which has been retold by many writers and artists over the centuries, so the discovery that the lovers did actually have a son, about whom very little is known, was a gift." Laird enthused, "I loved writing *The Forgotten Son;* it is my favorite of the three books so far and, my family and I believe, the best, although it has done much less well in terms of sales than the others. Perhaps that is because the subject matter is less accessible or dramatic than the Holocaust—or perhaps our judgement is simply wrong."

If you enjoy the works of Christa Laird, you may also want to check out the following books and films:

Edith Baer, *A Frost in the Night*, 1988.
Aranka Siegel, *Grace in the Wilderness: After the Liberation, 1945-1948*, 1985.
Schindler's List, a film directed by Steven Spielberg, 1993.

Continues Misha's Story

After completing *The Forgotten Son*, Laird began writing a novel for adults about Misha, the protagonist of her first book, *Shadow of the Wall*. This sequel featured the character as a grown-up and contained little reference to its predecessor, except, the author wrote in *SAAS*, "through a few flashbacks, to his experiences after escaping from the ghetto." However, her publishers demanded a rewrite, so Laird focused on Misha's life after he left the Warsaw Ghetto. The result was *But Can the Phoenix Sing?*, a story for young people published in 1993. Laird takes Misha through experiences as a partisan in the forests of eastern Poland through his return to Warsaw, where he works as a courier for the underground resistance, to his capture by the Wehrmacht after in the Warsaw Uprising of 1944. The novel also describes Misha's experience as a POW in Germany—always hiding his identity as a Jew—as well as his liberation and relocation to England. *But Can the Phoenix Sing?* includes tragedy: Misha's lover, Eva, a girl who leads him to the partisan group in the Parczew forest, is killed, and so are her twin brother and the doctor who is their friend. Laird frames the story with Misha's relationship with his teenage stepson, Richard. Now a teacher, Misha writes his story in a letter to Richard, who by now is estranged from his stepfather and has been involved in an anti-Semitic prank. Richard comments on the main narrative in letters to his girlfriend. Through Misha's letter, Richard gains both an understanding of his stepfather and realizations about himself.

Writing in the *School Librarian*, Audrey Baker called *Phoenix* "much more than an adventure or war story," while Peter D. Sieruta of *Horn Book* predicted that "it is the intense, horrifying scenes of wartime struggle that will continue to burn in the reader's mind." Betsy Hearne of *Bulletin of the Center for Children's Books* also noted the intensity of the book, describing it as "undiluted by either the stepson's occasional outbursts in letters to a girlfriend . . . or by the kind of historical explanation that occasionally marked the previous book." Hearne concluded that it is "a tribute to Laird's research that she has so completely absorbed factual information into the depth of a story." Writing in *Booklist*, Hazel Rochman commented, "What's splendid about this story is the account of the partisans. . . . Teens will be held by Misha's haunting discovery that cruelty and tenderness can co-exist 'not just in one culture or country . . . but in one person even.'"

Writing in *SAAS*, Laird noted that both *Shadow of the Wall* and *But Can the Phoenix Sing?* are "about courageous responses to oppression, about human resilience and different sorts of courage, all themes which have fascinated me since my teens, perhaps because of my own pre-history." Two of the author's aunts were active in the Dutch Resistance in Amsterdam, and her grandparents concealed Allied airmen and weapons in their home, despite the fact that, as Laird commented, "my grandfather, archetypally Jewish to look at, lived in virtual seclusion at the top of the house and could ill-afford to run extra risks." She continued, "I remain fascinated by the quality of courage in its thousand manifestations, and haunted by the question of whether I could ever rise to the challenge, as my family did, of putting my own life at risk for the sake of others. At the end of *Shadow on the Wall*, I have written a brief outline of Korczak's life and have gone on to say: 'If these stories of love and horror have one message for those of us who live in happier circumstances, it is surely one of humility; for none of us knows the limits—good or evil, moral or physical—of which we are capable, until put to the test.'"

Laird mused that good and evil can be found "in lots of different packages, and sometimes the packaging obscures their true character, so that they are not always immediately recognizable. . . . [I]t is worth remembering that one person's terrorist is often another person's freedom fighter. If there are such things as moral absolutes, they are elusive creatures, and typically easier to identify on someone else's territory than on one's own. These are some of the questions that have preoccupied me over the years, and, having no answers which are remotely satisfactory, I have tried instead to work them in some way into my books."

■ Works Cited

Atterton, J., review of *The Forgotten Son, Books for Your Children,* summer, 1991, p. 24.

Baker, Audrey, review of *But Can the Phoenix Sing?, School Librarian,* February, 1994, p. 31.

Fisher, Margery, review of *The Forgotten Son, Growing Point,* March, 1991, pp. 5484-85.

Fisher, review of *Shadow of the Wall, Growing Point,* September, 1989, p. 5213.

Hearne, Betsy, review of *But Can the Phoenix Sing?, Bulletin of the Center for Children's Books,* November, 1995, pp. 96-97.

Hearne, review of *Shadow of the Wall, Bulletin of the Center for Children's Books,* May, 1990, p. 217.

Jackson, Adrian, review of *Shadow of the Wall, Books for Keeps,* March, 1991, p. 9.

Laird, Christa, essay in *Something about the Author Autobiography Series,* Volume 26, Gale, 1998, pp. 117-32.

Rochman, Hazel, review of *But Can the Phoenix Sing?, Booklist,* November 15, 1995, p. 548.

Sieruta, Peter D., review of *But Can the Phoenix Sing?, Horn Book,* March-April, 1996, p. 210.

Warren, Frank, review of *The Forgotten Son, School Librarian,* May, 1991, p. 72.

Zeiger, Hanna B., review of *Shadow of the Wall, Horn Book,* September-October, 1990, p. 604.

■ For More Information See

PERIODICALS

Booklist, May 15, 1990, p. 1801.

Books for Keeps, July, 1995, p. 13.

Junior Bookshelf, December, 1993, p. 247.

Publishers Weekly, April 27, 1990, p. 62.

School Library Journal, October, 1995, p. 155.

Times Educational Supplement, February 15, 1991, p. 30; November 12, 1993, p. 3.

Wilson Library Bulletin, January 1991, p. 14; March 1991, p. 110.

—Sketch by Gerard J. Senick

Jacob Lawrence

■ Personal

Born September 7, 1917, in Atlantic City, NJ; son of Jacob Armstead Lawrence (a railroad worker) and Rose Lee; married Gwendolyn Knight (an artist).

■ Career

Painter, printmaker, and muralist. Taught at Pratt Institute and at University of Washington, Seattle, 1971-83, retired as Professor Emeritus. *Wartime service:* Coast Guard, 1943-45. *Member:* American Academy and Institute of Arts and Letters; American Academy of Arts and Sciences.

■ Awards, Honors

First African American to have his work displayed in a major New York gallery and to be included in the permanent collection of the Museum of Modern Art, both 1941; elected into National Institute of Arts and Letters, 1965; Spingarn Medal, 1971, N.A.A.C.P.; inducted into American Academy of Arts and Letters 1983; National Medal of Arts, 1990. Lawrence has also received more than two dozen honorary degrees.

■ Sidelights

Jacob Lawrence was one of the first African American artists to rise to prominence in the mainstream American art world. He was encouraged by teachers and fellow artists during his teenage years to study both art and African American history. He combined these interests to produce works unique in both their subject and style. Many of these comprise series of panels that join together to create a narrative. Lawrence is also known as an illustrator of books for adults and children.

In the early part of the twentieth century, huge numbers of African Americans migrated from the rural South to the cities of the North. They hoped to find jobs in growing industries, particularly on the automobile assembly lines of Detroit, Michigan. Lawrence's parents, Jacob Armstead Lawrence and Rose Lee, were among these migrants. They met and married in Atlantic City, New Jersey. The oldest of their three children, Jacob, was born there on September 7, 1917. During Lawrence's childhood, his family was forced to relocate many times as his parents looked for work. Steady jobs were hard to find, especially for African Americans. Racial prejudice prevented them from pursuing certain jobs or professions. These many moves had a disruptive effect on Lawrence, who was a quiet and sensitive boy; he found it difficult to constantly adjust to new neighborhoods and schools.

The hardest adjustment of all came when he was thirteen. It was then that he went to live with his mother in Harlem, the mostly African American section of New York City. It was a crowded, teeming place, and the public school Lawrence attended was considered among the roughest in the area. But Harlem in the 1930s was also the center of what became known as the Harlem Renaissance. Many African American artists, writers, musicians, and scholars lived there. It was a time of great creativity and excitement. To keep her son out of trouble, Rose Lawrence enrolled him in an after-school arts and crafts program at a local community center. It was taught by a young African American artist named Charles Alston. Alston liked the serious, quiet Lawrence and made sure he had lots of materials for his efforts: soap to carve, reeds to make baskets, crayons and pencils for drawing, wood for construction. "I decided then that I wanted to be an artist," Lawrence later wrote. He found that drawing geometric designs in bright colors satisfied him greatly. He soon moved on to elaborate patterns and developed his own method of painting in which particular shapes were rendered in corresponding colors, one at a time; he would paint all the triangles in red, then do all the squares in yellow, and so on. Lawrence continued in this mode through much of his career. This notable consistency of color is apparent in the artist's later series of story panels.

In addition to his interest in slave history and Haitian heroes, Lawrence has chronicled the daily experience of the African American, as in 1952's "Christmas Pageant," which colorfully reflects the spiritual side of life.

Quickly Gained Notice among Artists

Alston recognized that the young Lawrence was a significant talent. He remarked in later years that Lawrence never asked like the other children, "What should I do next?" He always had a project in mind and simply needed information to help him complete it. Alston told many of his artist friends about this gifted young man. They frequently visited the class to see his work and encourage him. Lawrence quickly became known among the artistic circles of Harlem.

Lawrence got many of his ideas from the books and magazines he found at the center where the classes were held. He once came across an article about a famous artist who made papier-maché masks. Lawrence had Alston show him how to mix papier-maché, and he went on to create many colorful, life-size masks. He also used cardboard boxes to fashion three-sided scenes depicting locales in Harlem—stores, barbershops, houses, and newsstands. These were like miniature theater sets, though Lawrence had never been to the theater.

During the time he worked with Alston, Lawrence found little at school to interest him. After two years of high school he dropped out, despite his mother's protests. This was during the Great Depression, and jobs were extremely scarce. Lawrence was able to earn only meager funds by selling old bottles and running errands. He continued to paint whenever he could, but times were hard. Then, in 1936, Lawrence was accepted into the Civilian Conservation Corps (CCC), a government program designed to get young men out of the cities to work on projects such as planting trees and building roads and dams. Lawrence's CCC service taught him many new skills and made him think that perhaps painting should be only a hobby.

Enters Depression-era Funding Program

He returned to New York but still could find no work besides odd jobs. He again began attending art classes at various community centers, including one offered by the acclaimed sculptor Augusta Savage. Like Alston, Savage recognized Lawrence's talent and took him under her wing. She soon realized that Lawrence was having difficulty earning money. She took him to a government office

"Tombstones" is housed at the famous Whitney Museum of American Art in New York City.

to enroll him in a project that helped support artists. But Lawrence was not eligible because he was only twenty years old and not the required twenty-one. Lawrence was extremely disappointed and continued looking for other work. Savage did not give up, however. She waited a year and on Lawrence's twenty-first birthday, she took him back to the government office to sign him up. He was accepted and offered $25 a week, a comfortable living in those days. He was free to do what he wanted as long as he produced two paintings every six weeks. Lawrence later stated, "If Augusta Savage hadn't insisted on getting me on the project, I would never have become an artist. It was a real turning point for me."

For about a year and a half, Lawrence was able to take classes, hone his painting skills, and put concerns about money out of his mind. Through the funding project he met many other artists and writers. They gathered in each other's studios to exchange ideas about art, literature, and life in general. Lawrence's paintings from this period are mostly scenes of Harlem, among them *Clinic* and *Bar 'N Grill.* He was able to keenly illustrate how hard it was to survive during the Depression years. Through color, pattern, and exaggerated form, he expressed weariness and despair.

Studied Role of African Americans in American History

During these years Lawrence regularly attended a discussion group focusing on African and African American history held at the local public library. It was led by a prominent scholar, Charles Seifert. Seifert applauded Lawrence's interest and encouraged him to study American history in depth, especially the role of African Americans. The artist had never learned this history in school. Now he uncovered many critical events and heroes forgotten by the public school system. These discoveries provided him with subjects for many of his works.

Lawrence was particularly drawn to the life story of Francis Dominique Toussaint, known as Toussaint L'Ouverture, the military leader of eighteenth-century Haiti, who overthrew the slave system and liberated the Caribbean island nation from French domination. Lawrence read everything he could about Toussaint and decided to paint a record of his achievements. But one painting was not enough. Lawrence ultimately unveiled a series of forty-one panels, beginning with Christopher Columbus's "discovery" of Haiti and then

In his 1950 work "Depression," Lawrence reveals how his brief stay at a mental institution in Queens deeply affected his art.

outlining Toussaint's childhood, battles, and death in a French prison. The settings of the scenes employed a great measure of realism, but Lawrence used intense color and exaggeration to express the emotional power of this hero.

This series and later ones have been compared to movie stills or slides that narrate a story as the viewer progresses through them. Lawrence continued in this method, portraying the lives of several African American heroes, including Harriet Tubman, a leader of the Underground Railroad of antislavery forces who smuggled slaves North; writer and abolitionist Frederick Douglass; and John Brown, a white abolitionist who led a slave revolt in Virginia. In all of these works, he used his formidable artistic skills to conjure the struggle for freedom and justice, forcefully representing the strength of character of his subjects.

Exhibited L'Ouverture series

Lawrence was only twenty-two when he completed the Toussaint L'Ouverture series in 1938. It received much attention for its unusual subject matter and praise for its artistry. Two acquaintances of Lawrence prominent in the art world arranged for the panels to be included in an exhibition at the Baltimore Museum of Art. This was the first major museum to feature an exhibition by African American artists. An entire room was devoted to Lawrence's panels. The exhibition won him great recognition and several fellowships. Lawrence was encouraged by his success to begin work on still another series. This one told the story of the many African Americans who migrated to the cities of the North around World War I. The sixty panels were created from accounts he gathered from family members, his own childhood experiences, and exhaustive research. Painted in Lawrence's bold, geometric style, with many vivid colors, they depict the hard life of the migrants, but also their courage and dignity.

In 1992 Lawrence published a book, *The Great Migration,* using many panels from the series. In the introduction he wrote, "Uprooting yourself from one way of life to make your way in another involves conflict and struggle. But out of the struggle comes a kind of power, and even beauty. I tried to convey this in the rhythm of the pictures, and in the repetition of certain images." The Migration series was another triumph. About this

If you enjoy the works of Jacob Lawrence, you may also want to check out the following:

The paintings of visual artist Romare Bearden.
The story quilts of Faith Ringgold.
The sculptures of Augusta Savage.

time Lawrence married a young painter he had met through Savage named Gwendolyn Knight. She became indispensable to his career, frequently helping him prepare his panels. But more important, Knight offered unflagging support when Lawrence encountered various artistic and emotional obstacles in later years.

Lawrence served in the Coast Guard during World War II, from 1943 to 1945. He was a steward's mate, the only rating available to African Americans because the military was segregated by race in those days. Lawrence was lucky to be selected for the Coast Guard's first racially integrated crew. The crew commander knew of his artistic career and secured Lawrence a position as a public relations officer. He was assigned to paint a record of life in the Coast Guard. The troopship he served on sailed to Italy, Egypt, and India. Lawrence's Coast Guard paintings were shown at several museums after the war.

Doubts of America's "Number One" Black Painter

Lawrence's reputation grew quickly in the postwar years. He was called "America's number one black painter." But this phrase troubled him because it seemed to suggest two different criteria of value, one for black artists and a different one for "real" artists. During this time Lawrence also found it difficult locating new subjects for his paintings. Trends in art were changing, too. Abstract art, that which focused on the emotional rather than the physical realm, was beginning to dominate the art world.

These forces combined to create doubt in Lawrence's mind about his talents and abilities; he began to question his success and wonder if it were not just luck that got him where he was.

His anxiety became so severe that in 1949 he entered a hospital to seek treatment. Lawrence felt that his two years there greatly helped him reconcile his feelings and increase his understanding of his place in the world. His work of the 1950s reflects this new peace. Perhaps the most important series from these years is *Struggle: From the History of the American People.* These thirty paintings display key events in U.S. history, emphasizing the role of ordinary people of all races and heritages.

Received Numerous Awards

Despite Lawrence's doubts, the art world continued to honor him. In 1953 he was the first African American artist to receive a large grant from the National Institute of Arts and Letters and the first elected a member of the Institute in 1965. In 1983 he was only the second African American elected to the fifty-member American Academy of Arts and Letters. He also received the National Medal of Arts from President George Bush in 1990. These are just a few of the many awards Lawrence has received.

Since the 1960s Lawrence has spent much of his time teaching. He was a professor of art at the University of Washington in Seattle for many years. Most recently he has dedicated his talents to book illustration. His panels from the Harriet Tubman series were published in a volume called *Harriet and the Promised Land* in 1967. And in 1970 he lent his hand to an edition of Aesop's Fables

(a new edition of this work appeared in 1998). In addition to the publication of his book *The Great Migration,* the early 1990s saw his panels about abolitionist John Brown published in *John Brown: One Man against Slavery.* In all of these endeavors, Lawrence has labored to reveal the commitment to freedom and justice of people struggling for life's most basic needs and in so doing, miraculously maintaining their humanity and a sense of hope.

■ For More Information See

BOOKS

Duggleby, John, *Story Painter: The Life of Jacob Lawrence,* Chronicle, 1998.

Howard, Nancy Shroyer, *Jacob Lawrence: American Scenes, American Struggles,* Davis, 1996.

Lawrence, Jacob, *The Great Migration: An American Story,* HarperCollins, 1993.

Lawrence, Jacob, and Richard J. Powell, *Jacob Lawrence,* Rizzoli, 1992.

Wheat, Ellen, *Jacob Lawrence, American Painter,* University of Washington Press, 1986.

PERIODICALS

Art in America, February, 1988.
Booklist, February 15, 1994, p. 1048.
Christian Science Monitor, February 4, 1994, p. 12.
Ebony, September, 1992, pp. 62.

Joan Miró

■ Personal

Born April 20, 1893, in Barcelona, Spain; died of heart disease, December 25, 1983, in Palma, Majorca, Spain; son of Miguel Miró Adzerias (a goldsmith and watchmaker) and Dolores Ferra; married Pilar Juncosa, 1929; children: Dolores. *Education:* Attended Escuela Oficial de Bellas Artes de la Longa, Barcelona, 1907, commercial school in Barcelona, 1907, and Gali's Escuela d'Arte, 1912-15.

■ Career

Artist. Worked as bookkeeper, 1910. First exhibition, Barcelona, Spain, 1918. Paintings, sculpture, and miscellaneous works represented in permanent collections of museums throughout North America and Europe. Designer for Claca (street-theater group) in 1970s. *Exhibitions:* First solo exhibition at the Galeries Dalmau, Barcelona, 1918; first Paris exhibition at the Galerie La Licorne, 1921; first American exhibition at Curt Valentin Gallery, New York, 1930; numerous solo shows and exhibitions of Miró's work have been mounted at museums

around the world, including New York's Museum of Modern Art (1940, 1959, 1973, 1993), Musee National d'Art Moderne, Paris (1962, 1978, 1984), Tate Gallery, London (1964, 1974), Kunsthaus, Zurich (1964, 1986), Museum of Western Art, Tokyo (1966), Guggenheim Museum, New York (1972, 1983), Fundacio Joan Miró, Barcelona (1976, 1986), and Queen Sofia Museum, Madrid (1993). Miró's works are part of the collections of several museums and institutions, including Fundacio Joan Miró, Barcelona; Nationalgalerie, Berlin; Tate Gallery, London; Kunsthaus, Zurich; Foundation Maeght, St. Paul-de-Vence, France; Guggenheim Museum, New York; Museum of Modern Art, New York; Stedelijk Museum, Amsterdam; Centre Georges Pompidou, Paris; and Queen Sofia Museum, Madrid.

■ Awards, Honors

Grand Prix for Graphics, Venice Biennale, 1954; International Prize from Guggenheim Foundation, 1959, for mural *Night and Day* at UNESCO headquarters in Paris; received honorary doctorate from Harvard University, 1968; named commander of French Legion of Honor, 1974; Grand Cross of Isabel la Catolica, 1978.

■ Writings

Miró (catalog), Galerie Melki, 1974.

Catalan Notebooks: Unpublished Drawings and Writings, translated from the French by Dinah Harrison, Rizzoli, 1977.

Joan Miró: Selected Writings and Interviews, edited by Margit Rowell, G. K. Hall, 1986.

ILLUSTRATOR

Paul Eluard, *A toute epreuve* (verse), Gerald Cramer, 1958, Firefly, 1984.

OTHER

Miró's art works, notably paintings and sculpture, are represented in numerous volumes.

■ Sidelights

When Joan Miró died in 1983 at the age of ninety, his passing was cited as the end of an era, for Miró was considered the last of the great European modernists of the twentieth century. During a long and prolific career, Miró had shined alongside such luminaries as Pablo Picasso, Alexander Calder, René Magritte, and others of similar renown—"the artists born between 1880 and 1900 who reshaped both culture and consciousness," according to *Time* magazine art critic Robert Hughes. Miró's work blended many elements from the modern age's most daring artistic movements—Cubist painting, Surrealist poetry, and Dada doctrine—into a unique style that is familiar to the viewer, and yet instantly recognizable as his own. Miró became, as James Gardner declared in the *National Review,* "one of the visual giants of the century. His work is effortlessly and almost infallibly beautiful. His images have no message to them, yet they are living human documents of an almost unfathomable sensitivity."

Though Miró and his work are often grouped with currents in twentieth-century French art, his images were frequently inspired by recollections of his native Catalonia. This four-province area in Spain—running from the Pyrenees Mountains at the border of France down to the Mediterranean Sea and anchored by the majestic city of Barcelona—captivated Miró with its sunny clime, endless skies, and proud history reaching back to ancient times. The Catalonians traded with the ancient Greeks and Romans, rivaled the seagoing merchants of Venice in the Middle Ages, and even existed as a sovereign entity for a time in the

1930s. Even the Catalan language is a separate tongue, related to Provencal and Italian. Because of this history, Catalonian culture is older than that of the rest of Spain, but more importantly, Catalonia and especially Barcelona were quite receptive to the movements in avant-garde art that gave rise to Miró's own style.

Miró was born in Barcelona at home on the Pasaje del Credito in 1893, the first child of the goldsmith and watchmaker Miguel Miró Adzerias and his spouse Dolores. He was named "Joan" (the Catalan version of "Juan") after his paternal grandfather, who had been a blacksmith by trade. As a youngster, Miró loved to visit Barcelona's Museum of Romanesque Art and Architecture, and he grew up not far from the fantastical buildings of Antonio Gaudi, a renowned architect closely associated with Barcelona's skyline. But he was a poor student, nicknamed "Fathead" by his classmates, and seemed only to like his art classes. Around 1907, when he was about fourteen, Miró enrolled in courses at the La Longa School of Fine Arts in Barcelona. But his practical-minded parents discouraged him from pursuing art as a career, and pushed him instead toward business and finance. Few believed that young Miró possessed enough talent for a career as an artist, and accordingly his father found him a position as a bookkeeper around 1910.

The profession and its long hours—from eight in the morning until one in afternoon, then again from three until nine at night—crushed Miró, and in due time he suffered a breakdown and contracted typhoid fever. He spent three months in bed, and only then did his father rescind his decision about his son's vocation. Partly to recuperate, and also since he could not afford to rent studio space, Miró went off by himself to his family's farmhouse in Montroig ("red mountain"), in the Tarragona province. Though he was finally left alone to pursue his vocation, Miró initially found trouble with the process of putting his visions to canvas. "I had very great difficulties in expressing myself artistically. I just couldn't accomplish that," Miró recalled to *ArtNews* contributor Michael Gibson in 1980.

Develops His Own Style

Back in Barcelona, Miró slowly began to develop a unique style. "His sinuous and elastic line took

A native of Catalonia, Miró expressed his love of his homeland in a number of works, including "Catalan Landscape: The Hunter," painted from 1923-24.

part of its character from Art Nouveau calligraphy, the pervasive civic style of Barcelona in his boyhood," wrote Hughes in *Time*. Miró then took up study at another school of art, run by a well-known Barcelona artist named Francisco Gali. Gali expressed dismay that his student Miró could not, or perhaps would not, draw a straight line when an image called for it. Gali would force Miró to hold an object behind his back, and thus draw it from touch rather than sight. Here Miró also learned sculpture, a medium which gave free rein to his passion for curvilinear forms.

After Miró's first solo exhibition in Barcelona in 1918 was greeted somewhat coolly, he decided to move to Paris. Like many rising talents of his era, Miró longed to be part of what was then the great and heady nexus of the art world. Catalonia's most celebrated artist of all time, Picasso, was already there. The two had never met in Barcelona, though they lived there at the same time; Picasso—twelve years Miró's senior—was already so legendary that the younger painter was too intimidated to pay a call on Picasso's Barcelona studio. But their mothers knew one another, and when Miró decided to move to Paris he asked Senora Picasso if there was anything she would like him to bring to her son. She sent along a large cake, and Miró's delivery of the confection began a friendship that proved invaluable to Miró, who was overwhelmed and intimidated by Paris those first months in 1920. Picasso found Miró's work intriguing, and introduced him to many influential creative colleagues, such as Henri Matisse, the Cubist Georges Braque, and Andre Breton, the Surrealist and editor of the groundbreaking journal *La Revolution surrealiste*.

Miró's first major work was *The Farm*, painted in 1921-22 and first owned by the writer Ernest Hemingway, who had already come to love the Catalonian landscape. It depicts a scene very much like Montroig, displays Miró's uniquely flat spatial perspective, and is painted in hues designed to resemble the morning quiet in Tarragona. "It has in it all that you feel about Spain when you are there and all that you feel when you are away and cannot go there," Hemingway said of *The Farm.* "No one else has been able to paint these two very opposing things."

In Paris, Miró found a better reception among dealers and fellow artists for his art, though he still struggled financially. Both Calder and Max Ernst were fans of his from this early period, and by 1924 Miró had established close ties with the Surrealists. They adored his work, which had become almost as nonsensical and deliberately unrelated to reality as their poetry. Breton once called Miró "the most Surrealist among us." Surrealism believed that one should create from one's dreams, and Miró adjusted this idea and began painting his hunger-induced hallucinations, for he often went without food in these days. "This Is the Color of My Dreams," he wrote in French across a pool of blue in *Photo,* dating from 1925. Miró was also an avid reader of modern literature, and was particularly fond of the work of Guillaume Apollinaire, Paul Eluard, Charles Baudelaire, and Arthur Rimbaud. Contrasting with such cultured pursuits were the boxing lessons Miró took alongside Hemingway at Paris's American Center.

Miró left Paris and his studio on the Rue Blomet for Montroig every summer between 1919 and 1933. In 1929 he married Pilar Juncosa, and again, in contrast to the far more free-spirited creative circles to which he belonged, remained happily married for the next 54 years. Yet Miró's quiet demeanor and stable personal life belied his very radical ideas about art and inspiration. "The only thing that's clear to me is that I intend to destroy, destroy everything that exists in painting," the iconoclast said in a 1931 interview transcribed in Margit Rowell's *Joan Miró: Selected Writings and Interviews.* "I have an utter contempt for painting. The only thing that interests me is the spirit itself, and I only use the customary artist's tools—brushes, canvas, paints—in order to get the best results."

By this time Miró had a young daughter to support as well, and he remained an acclaimed, but not well remunerated, Spanish artist living in Paris. Consequently, he moved back to Barcelona with his family in 1932, coinciding with

Miró uses bright colors and asymmetric, two-dimensional shapes in a style shown clearly here in "The Port."

Catalonia's brief interim of self-rule. However, the Spanish civil war erupted while Miró and his family were visiting Paris in 1936. The war, launched against a leftist-governed Republic by Generalissimo Francisco Franco, ended with victory for Franco's fascists in 1939, and also coincided with the rise of fascist governments in Germany and Italy.

Art and Politics

Miró allowed his art to voice his political convictions, which were firmly on the side of the soon-to-be defeated Spanish Loyalists. In 1937 he did a poster for the group, Aidez l'Espagne, and that same year was commissioned by architect Josep Luis Sert to create a mural for the Spanish Pavilion at the 1937 World's Fair in Paris; Sert requested one of Picasso as well. Picasso sent *Guernica* as his entry. A massive tour de force commemorating the destruction of a Basque town of the same name by Nazi Germany's Luftwaffe planes, *Guernica* was a powerful criticism of Franco and fascism, and has since become Spain's most famous work of art. For the Pavilion Miró painted *El Segador* ("The Reaper"), "a portrait of an anguished but defiant farmer," wrote Stanley Meisler in *Smithsonian*. "After the fair closed, this symbol of oppression was dismantled and shipped to Valencia, the wartime capital of the Spanish Republic. It was never found again."

Despite the political crises, Miró continued to develop and maintain the vocabulary of shapes and images that would come to characterize his prolific body of work. "Tiny forms in vast empty spaces," is how the artist once summed up his work, reported Hughes in *Time*. The elements common to his paintings were a freewheeling asymmetry, use of vibrant, almost unnatural color combinations, flattened spatial relationships, and a whole new alphabet of exuberant symbols—stars, moons, suggestive commas, a ladder with bird, woman with bird's beak, Catalan earthen-

ware pottery, and the ubiquitous barretina hat worn by Catalonian men. The titles he gave his works were also similarly inspired: "Ciphers and Constellations in Love with a Woman," "People at Night, Guided by the Phosphorescent Tracks of Snails," and "The Red Sun Gnaws at the Spider" are but three examples.

Soon there was trouble across the European continent, and Miró deliberated on a course of action. He first went to a tranquil Normandy village called Varengeville, where his friends Braque and Calder were also ensconced. Here he began his *Constellation* series, the twenty-three paintings that would come to be considered the pinnacle of Miró's achievement. Because of wartime blackout restrictions in Varengeville—no lights could be visible at night, so that enemy bombers would not be able to detect towns below—windows had to be painted or heavily curtained. Miró painted his a dark blue, and he was astounded that the stars in the Normandy night sky were visible anyway.

Miró lived his final years in Majorca, while still actively painting and exhibiting his work around the world.

MIRÓ

Walter Erben

TASCHEN

This book by Walter Erben surveys the career of the great Surrealist painter.

So he put a piece of paper up to the window and began tracing them.

But Miró's sojourn in Varengeville was not to last long. The Luftwaffe began to bomb Normandy in May of 1940, and Miró decided to take his wife and daughter back to Paris, but they spent just a few days there before Nazi troops marched into the city. It was too dangerous for an avowed critic of Franco to be back in Barcelona, but Pilar's family was from the Mediterranean island of Majorca, off the coast of Spain, and so they made their way there and settled. The artist worked under an assumed name, however, since Majorca was still a possession of Spain.

Constellations Recognized as Signature Work

Miró continued with his *Constellations* over the course of the next year. "While the world outside generated an ever greater atmosphere of foreboding, he made what might well have been a last roundup of all the ideas and all the images that had been dearest to him," wrote Rosamond Bernier in *Smithsonian* in 1980. "They were multitudinous, those images, as if each painting were a refugee ship to be filled to the last inch of standing with birds, beasts, insects, stars, emblematic men and women, the sky, the sun and the moon."

After the war's end, some of Miró's *Constellations* were the first paintings from Europe to reach American shores. The war had put a stop to all transatlantic business, and there existed no other means to transmit images except by photograph. The art came in a diplomatic pouch, the clever ruse of well-connected art dealer Pierre Matisse, son of the artist Henri. The owner of a Manhattan gallery, for years the younger Matisse had ardently championed Miró's genius to American collectors, curators, and dealers, a devotion which eventually paid off: the Museum of Modern Art began to acquire many works by Miró, and built up an impressive collection over the years; they also staged Miró's first museum retrospective in 1940.

In contrast, no French museum would purchase any of Miró's works until relatively late in his long career. And the situation in his native Spain was of another world altogether: Miró and his family again returned to Barcelona after the war,

though Franco was still in power, but liked Majorca so much that in 1956 Miró had a studio by the architect Sert built for him in Palma, the island's capital. The still-fascist, repressive Franco government left the renowned artist more or less to himself, but at one point did offer him the position of national director of fine arts, which he declined. He also refused to cooperate in government-sponsored attempts to mount exhibitions of his work in Spain.

> *"The only thing that's clear to me is that I intend to destroy, destroy everything that exists in painting. I have an utter contempt for painting. The only thing that interests me is the spirit itself, and I only use the customary artist's tools—brushes, canvas, paints—in order to get the best results."*
>
> —Joan Miró

Miró first traveled to the United States in 1947, accepting mural commissions for a building at Harvard University Law School and another inside a hotel in Cincinnati—"but we all knew it would wind up in the Cincinnati Museum; otherwise I would not have done it," he told Gibson in *ArtNews*. This marked a new phase of Miró's work: the large-scale pieces and ceramic works such as *Wall of the Sun* and *Wall of the Moon*, both completed in 1957 and installed in the UNESCO Building in Paris. Many of these works—for which museums, universities, and other civic institutions paid dearly—are considered somewhat less than exemplary by art critics otherwise inclined to lavish praise on Miró. While not as intimate as his poem-paintings or works on paper, the larger creations nevertheless are characteristic of Miró's exuberant, elegant style. But the artist considered their long-term impact, knowing that they would be viewed by thousands of passers-by for years, and not just the minority of people who visit museums. "It's the young people who matter to me," Miró told Bernier in the *Smithsonian* in 1980, "not the old dodoes. I'm working for the year 2000, and the people of tomorrow."

Miró died in Palma on Christmas Day of 1983. His death was mourned by the art world as the

If you enjoy the works of Joan Miró, you may also want to check out the following:

The works of French painters Henri Matisse and Georges Braque, and Spanish cubist Pablo Picasso.

The paintings of "naturalistic" surrealists like Spanish artist Salvador Dali and Belgian artist René Magritte.

The work of "organic" surrealists like French painter André Masson.

end of an era, his impact on the art of the century acknowledged by all. "When one looks at those now nostalgic household objects of the 1950s, the kidney coffee table and the ball-on-wire chair leg, one realizes that they owe their existence to the flat, floating shapes and springy calligraphy of Miró's *Constellations* in the 1940s," wrote Hughes in *Time*. Even more ubiquitous has been Miró's stamp upon Spain's graphic arts in the decades after his death, much of which has a decidedly Miró-esque presence. Freed from fascism by the Franco's 1975 death, by the 1990s Spain was considered one of the most vibrant cultural stages in all of Europe. "In Barcelona, almost every bank uses a logo that either derives from a Miró design or imitates one," wrote Meisler in *Smithsonian*. Advertising images on Barcelona billboards, and in the subway caverns of Madrid, mimic this style with their curvilinear black shapes against bold primary colors that recall Catalonian earth and sky.

Hemingway's beloved *Farm* would eventually be acquired by the National Gallery of Art in Washington, D.C. In Palma, Miró's studio is preserved just as he had left it on his last day. There is a Joan Miró Foundation in Barcelona dedicated to preserving his artistic legacy, and on the centenary of his birth in 1993 its curators mounted a retrospective there and then sent it on to the Museum of Modern Art. The critic Gardner reviewed the exhibition for the *National Review*, and recalled the assertions Miró had once made as a young man about wishing to destroy art. "How gloriously and consistently Miró missed that mark," remarked Gardner, "how nobly he nourished that which he would slay, is now on view at the Museum of Modern Art."

■ Works Cited

Bernier, Rosamond, "The Painter Miró, This Month 87, Is As Lively As Ever," *Smithsonian*, April, 1980, pp. 102-111.

Gardner, James, "The Assassin Who Failed," *National Review*, December 27, 1993, pp. 67-68.

Gibson, Michael, "Miró: 'When I See a Tree . . . I Can Feel That Tree Talking to Me,'" *ArtNews*, January, 1980, pp. 53-56.

Hughes, Robert, "The Last of the Forefathers," *Time*, January 9, 1984, p. 64.

Hughes, Robert, "The Purest Dreamer in Paris," *Time*, October 25, 1993, pp. 74-76.

Meisler, Stanley, "For Joan Miró, Poetry and Painting Were the Same," *Smithsonian*, November, 1993, pp. 62-71.

■ For More Information See

BOOKS

Apollonio, Umbro, *Miró*, translated by Victor Corti, Grosset, 1969.

Breton, Andre, *Surrealism and Painting*, translated by Simon Watson Taylor, Harper, 1972.

Breton, Andre, *What Is Surrealism?: Selected Writings*, edited by Franklin Rosemont, Monad Press, 1978.

Gasser, Manuel, *Joan Miró*, translated by Haydn Barnes, Barnes & Noble, 1965.

International Dictionary of Art and Artists, Volume 2, St. James Press, 1990.

Penrose, Roland, *Miró*, Abrams, 1970.

Read, Herbert, *A Concise History of Modern Painting*, Praeger, 1974.

Sweeney, James Johnson, *Joan Miró*, Tudor, 1971.

PERIODICALS

Art in America, September, 1994, pp. 86-94.

ArtNews, April, 1948.

Arts, November, 1968.

Horizon, July, 1977.

Look, June 10, 1958.

New Republic, December 13, 1993, pp. 46, 48-49.

New York, November 1, 1993, pp. 96-98.

Newsweek, March 23, 1959; May 25, 1987, pp. 70-71; January 2, 1984, p. 69; October 25, 1993, p. 72.

New York Review of Books, December 16, 1993, pp. 45-46, 48-51.

New York Times Book Review, December 4, 1977.

New York Times Magazine, March 15, 1959.

Time, November 3, 1958; July 26, 1968; November 26, 1973; July 1, 1974; April 28, 1980, pp. 68-69; January 2, 1984, p. 82.

USA Today, November, 1993, pp. 40-47.

Vogue, December, 1972; October, 1993, pp. 406, 409, 471-72.

—*Sketch by Carol Brennan*

Perry Nodelman

professor, currently full professor of English. *Member:* Children's Literature Association (editor, *Children's Literature Association Quarterly*, 1982-1987; president, 1988-1989).

■ Personal

Born August 18, 1942, in Toronto, Ontario, Canada; married Billie de Wolf (a writer), February 19, 1971; children: Joshua, Asa, Alice. *Education:* United College (now the University of Winnipeg), B.A. (Honors English), 1964; Yale University, M.A. (English literature), 1965, Ph.D. (English literature), 1969. *Hobbies and other interests:* Reading, writing, cooking, gardening, listening to classical music and classic Broadway music.

■ Addresses

E-mail—perry.nodelman@uwinnipeg.ca. *Agent*—c/o Sterling Lord Literistic, 65 Bleecker St., New York, NY 10012.

■ Career

Writer and educator. University of Winnipeg, Winnipeg, Manitoba, 1968—, started as assistant

■ Awards, Honors

Best Books citation, *School Library Journal*, and Books in the Middle: Outstanding Titles citation, *Voice of Youth Advocates*, both 1995, both for *Of Two Minds*.

■ Writings

FICTION FOR YOUNG ADULTS

The Same Place but Different, Groundwood/Douglas & McIntyre, 1993, Simon & Schuster, 1995.
(With Carol Matas) *Of Two Minds*, Bain & Cox/Blizzard, 1994, Simon & Schuster, 1995.
(With Carol Matas) *More Minds*, Simon & Schuster, 1996.
A Completely Different Place, Groundwood/Douglas & McIntyre, 1996, Simon & Schuster, 1997.
Behaving Bradley, Simon & Schuster, 1998.
(With Carol Matas) *Out of Their Minds*, Simon & Schuster, 1998.

PICTURE BOOKS

Alice Falls Apart, illustrated by Stuart Duncan, Bain & Cox/Blizzard, 1996.

NONFICTION

Words About Pictures: The Narrative Art of Children's Picture Books, University of Georgia Press, 1988.
The Pleasures of Children's Literature, Longman, 1992, revised edition, 1996.

OTHER

Contributor of more than one hundred articles to scholarly journals on various aspects of children's literature. A Winnipeg theater company has performed several plays written by Nodelman.

■ Work in Progress

A Meeting of Minds, a fourth in the "Minds" series, with Carol Matas, for Simon & Schuster; a third Johnny Nesbit book, for Groundwood/Douglas & McIntyre.

■ Sidelights

With almost thirty years experience as an English professor at the University of Winnipeg, Perry Nodelman is widely recognized as one of Canada's leading authorities on children's literature. Aptly described as an "academic children's literature specialist" by Toronto *Globe and Mail* book reviewer Elizabeth MacCallum, Nodelman is a successful educator, researcher, writer, editor, and conference speaker. Not content to rest on these laurels, however, Nodelman continues to expand his horizons. Most recently, he has joined the ranks of Canadian authors writing for young people.

The idea for Nodelman's first book for young people came to him while he was reading Katharine Briggs's *Dictionary of Fairies, Brownies, Bogies, and Other Supernatural Creatures*, and thought about how different the fairies in it were from the sentimental fairies of greeting cards and many children's books. "As I read it," Nodelman told Groundwood Books in a publicity release, "I was astonished at how thoroughly nasty all these evil little creatures that people once used to believe in used to be. It made me happy to learn how non-icky they were. And I began to wonder—if these nasty creatures still existed and somehow made their way back to our world again, how would we cope with them?"

Nodelman's whimsical speculation resulted in *The Same Place but Different*, a tale about a crossover between contemporary society and the world of fairy. Set largely in Winnipeg's Churchill Drive Park, which lies across the road from Nodelman's home, the story centers around Johnny Nesbit's realization that "Strangers" have invaded his neighborhood, kidnapped his baby sister, and left a changeling in her place. The plot thickens in traditional fairy tale style as Johnny, intent on rescuing his sister, travels to the Strangers' world and agrees to a task set by their queen.

Johnny Nesbit, up to the shape-shifting challenges and derring-do required of him, is a thoroughly contemporary hero. Nodelman admits to living somewhat vicariously through him. In correspondence to Groundwood Books, he wrote, "I suspect that Johnny Nesbit comes out of all the nasty adolescent cynicism I try to keep stored up inside me in my real life as a theoretically mature adult. He says all the stuff I don't usually have the guts to say." The unusual combination of traditional plot and Nesbit's "now" style attracted reviewers' attention. Roger Sutton of the *Bulletin of the Center for Children's Books* asserted: "Where many contemporary fantasies get lost in portentous mists, this one confidently juggles, tosses, and flips old material with a fresh hand, balancing the levity with some seriously scary moments and a solid quest-adventure core." Sarah Guille, writing for *Horn Book*, concluded, "The tone is smart and flip but reverberates in a plot that is well-grounded in British myth and folklore."

The abundance of material that inspired *The Same Place but Different* prompted *A Completely Different Place*, Nodelman's sequel to his first Johnny Nesbit book. "After I finished *The Same Place but Different*, I still had good stories about fairies and such left that I hadn't managed to use," he commented to Groundwood Books. He was further motivated by a book-signing encounter with a young reader who had enjoyed his first book so much she suggested her teacher read it to the class—but the teacher read just a few pages, was horrified, and adamantly refused. "As I worked on the new book," Nodelman continued, "I kept thinking, I hope it's the kind of book that children love and that a lot of narrow-minded adults won't much like them loving."

Indeed, some adults did have problems with *A Completely Different Place*. A *Kirkus Reviews* commentator considered the novel about a boy who has been shrunk, placed in a bottle, and transported to a diabolical man's estate a "weak outing . . . better in its parts than its sum." In *School Library Journal*, however, contributor Steven Engelfried maintained that "Johnny narrates the tale with a lively, mildly amusing sarcastic tone," concluding that the "combination of traditional magic with unconventional heroes will appeal to many readers."

Dynamic Duo

In between bouts with Johnny Nesbit, Nodelman continued to busy himself with literary criticism. Author Carol Matas, discussing how she writes her award-winning children's books, told the Canadian Children's Book Centre, "The first draft is the most fun. Then I give it to my friend and critic, Perry Nodelman, who critiques it for me and I do a major rewrite."

During the early 1990s, in response to Nodelman's critiques of her first and second drafts of a fantasy for young adults, Matas ended up challenging Nodelman to flesh out the character of the male protagonist. Nodelman seized the opportunity and, in so doing, began a collaboration that has resulted in a series of very well-received books.

Of Two Minds and its sequel, *More Minds*, co-written by Matas and Nodelman, began with the story proposal Matas originally presented to Nodelman. Nodelman liked the concept but felt that some of the ideas weren't fully developed. In a *School Library Journal* dialogue Nodelman told Matas, "I loved the idea—people with the ability to make whatever they imagined real—but I was disappointed that you hadn't taken any of all those wonderful opportunities to have fun with it."

The eventual collaboration, featuring the adventures of a stubborn young princess and a shy clumsy prince, began with Matas writing portions of the book from Princess Lenora's viewpoint and sending them to Nodelman. In turn, Nodelman wrote segments from Prince Coren's perspective and mailed them to Matas. After many such exchanges, the two authors only sat down in the same room and worked together on the manuscript as a whole at the final copy-editing stage. In the end, they claim they can't remember who

The award-winning *Of Two Minds* was the first of several fantasy novels Nodelman would write with Carol Matas.

wrote what parts of the book. They do agree, however, that the process for the second book was, comparatively, "so easy."

Of Two Minds was recognized by *School Library Journal* as one of the "Best Books" offered in its year of publication. Joanne Findon, writing for *Quill & Quire*, commented, "The alternating perspectives of the two characters dovetail nicely, as do the writing styles of Matas and Nodelman, whose unusual dual authorship of this book is surprisingly successful."

Nodelman and Matas have completed *Out of Their Minds*, further adventures of Princess Lenora and

Prince Coren, and are working on a fourth book in the series, *A Meeting of Minds.* He also has a third Johnny Nesbit book underway that will pit Johnny against horrors worthy of Dante's Inferno. While all the books have fantastical themes, Nodelman notes differences between those he writes with Matas and those he writes on his own. "My work with Carol is lighter in tone and comedic. It approaches comic fantasy," he once stated. "My own writing tends to be about the world falling apart. Although it's fast paced and light in tone, it's about situations spilling over into horror. What interests me is what happens when something that shouldn't be there breaks through into your ordinary world and a perfectly ordinary place becomes a different place. I like the idea that

In this sequel to *The Same Place but Different,* Nodelman writes about a boy who has been shrunk, placed in a bottle, and transported to a diabolical man's estate.

you don't have to go away to have an adventure."

Realism or Satire?

Nodelman's 1998 novel *Behaving Bradley,* however, avoids a darker tone in telling the story of life in a contemporary high school. "But while there are no fantasy elements in it," the author once commented, "it might strike some readers as not being all that realistic: it's a satiric farce, with a certain amount of exaggeration and stretching of the truth for the sake of comedy. Or is it? Some people I know who are familiar with life in high schools tell me there's no exaggeration at all—that the people in the schools they know often behave at least as badly and even as humorously as the characters in the book do. And my daughter Alice, upon some events in whose life the book is very loosely based, tells me that the school in the book is a much nicer place than the actual high school she herself attended—and that what really happened to her was much more nightmarish than what happens to Bradley."

The novel follows the efforts of junior Bradley Gold as he becomes involved in his high school's attempts to create a Code of Conduct. Usually a "non-joiner" who stays in the background observing things, Brad somehow end up being put in charge of the student committee working on the Code. His position gives Brad ample opportunity to comment on the hypocrisy he encounters from teachers, parents, and students, which he does in his daily journal. "Nodelman has written a high-concept screwball comedy that has many moments of wacky humor," Ilene Cooper noted in *Booklist,* although she added that at times "the fun seems forced." "In spite of its tongue-in-cheek attitude," *School Library Journal* contributor Janet Hilbun observed, the novel contains "situations and characters [which] are realistically drawn," as well as "a serious tone" that counters the school's madcap atmosphere. Patricia S. McCormack, offering an assessment of *Behaving Bradley* in the *New York Times Book Review,* asserted: "Nodelman has a good ear for the rhythms of the classroom and a good eye for the absurdities of high school life."

Nodelman said that since the novel's first-person account shows Brad's "keen eye for all the ways in which the people around him (especially the adults) fail to live up to the standards they claim

If you enjoy the works of Perry Nodelman, you may also want to check out the following books:

Meredith Ann Pierce, *The Pearl of the Sul of the World*, 1990.
Pat O'Shea, *The Hounds of the Morrigan*, 1987.
Josepha Sherman, *Windleaf*, 1993.

to live by, . . . the book might seem to some readers to be just a tad cynical and negative. But I don't think it is. Perceptive readers will realize how often Brad's perceptions of things are distorted by his own feelings of inadequacy, that they are never quite the whole story. And he often realizes just how implicated he himself is in the human condition, how he too is often less noble than he might like to think he is, how the inevitable failure of all of us human beings to live up to our own ideals does not mean that they are wrong ideals or that we should not always keep on trying to live up to them. That I see as true and positive, and not cynical at all."

■ Works Cited

Canadian Children's Book Centre, *Writing Stories, Making Pictures: Biographies of 150 Canadian Children's Authors and Illustrators*, Canadian Children's Book Centre, 1994, pp. 218-20.
Review of *A Completely Different Place*, *Kirkus Reviews*, May 15, 1997, p. 804.
Cooper, Ilene, review of *Behaving Bradley*, *Booklist*, June 1, 1998.
Engelfried, Steven, review of *A Completely Different Place*, *School Library Journal*, June, 1994, pp. 124-25.
Findon, Joanne, review of *Of Two Minds*, *Quill & Quire*, December, 1994, p. 33.
Guille, Sarah, review of *The Same Place but Different*, *Horn Book*, September-October, 1995, pp. 601-2.
Hilbun, Janet, review of *Behaving Bradley*, *School Library Journal*, June, 1998.
MacCallum, Elizabeth, article in Toronto *Globe and Mail*, July 10, 1993, p. C15.
Matas, Carol, and Perry Nodelman, "A Meeting of the Minds," *School Library Journal*, July, 1996, pp. 28-29.
McCormack, Patricia S., review of *Behaving Bradley*, *New York Times Book Review*, July 19, 1998.
Nodelman, Perry, correspondence to Groundwood Books, March 26, 1996.
"Perry Nodelman" (information sheet), Groundwood/Douglas & McIntyre, undated.
Sutton, Roger, review of *The Same Place but Different*, *Bulletin of the Center for Children's Books*, July-August, 1995, p. 393.

■ For More Information See

ON-LINE

Perry Nodelman's Web site, located at http://www.uwinnipeg.ca/~nodelman.

PERIODICALS

Canadian Book Review Annual, 1993, p. 6174.
Canadian Children's Literature, number 72, 1993, pp. 86-87.
Canadian Materials, September, 1993, pp. 153-54.
Kirkus Reviews, June 1, 1998, p. 815.
Publishers Weekly, July 3, 1995, p. 61; July 20, 1998, p. 222.
Riverbank Review, Spring, 1999, pp. 15-16.
School Library Journal, May, 1995, p. 109; October, 1995, p. 136.

Janette Oke

D.H.L., Bethel College, Mishawaka, IN, 1987; President's Award, Evangelical Christian Publishers Association, 1992, in recognition of contribution to Christian fiction.

■ Writings

Love Comes Softly, Bethany House (Minneapolis), 1979.
Love's Enduring Promise, Bethany House, 1980.
Once Upon a Summer, Bethany House, 1981.
Hey, Teacher, Bethel Publishing (Elkhart, IN), 1981.
Love's Long Journey, Bethany House, 1982.
Spunky's Diary, Bethel Publishing, 1982.
When Calls the Heart, Bethany House, 1983.
Love's Abiding Joy, Bethany House, 1983.
Quiet Places, Warm Thoughts, Bethel Publishing, 1983.
New Kid in Town, Bethel Publishing, 1983.
Love's Undying Legacy, Bethany House, 1984.
The Prodigal Cat, Bethel Publishing, 1984.
When Comes the Spring, Bethany House, 1985.
The Impatient Turtle, Bethel Publishing, 1986.
When Breaks the Dawn, Bethany House, 1986.
When Hope Springs New, Bethany House, 1986.
The Winds of Autumn, Bethany House, 1987.
Janette Oke: My Favorite Verse, Accent Books (Denver), 1987.
Love's Unfolding Dream, Bethany House, 1987.
Winter Is Not Forever, Bethany House, 1988.
Love Takes Wing, Bethany House, 1988.
The Father Who Calls, Bethany House, 1988.
Spring's Gentle Promise, Bethany House, 1989.

■ Personal

Surname pronounced "oak"; born February 18, 1935, in Champion, Alberta, Canada; United States citizen born abroad; daughter of Fred G. (a farmer) and Amy M. (Ruggles) Steeves; married Edward L. Oke (a professor), May 13, 1957; children: Terry L., Lavon C., Lorne D., Laurel J. *Education:* Mountain View Bible College, diploma, 1957. *Religion:* Missionary Church.

■ Career

Writer. Canadian Bank of Commerce, Champion, Alberta, teller and ledger keeper, 1952-54; National Bank & Trust Co., South Bend, IN, proofreader and bookkeeper, 1957-58; Adlake, Elkhart, IN, mail clerk, 1958-59. Also worked at Mountain View Bible College, Reimer Industries, and Royal Bank of Canada, all in Didsbury, Alberta. *Member:* Women's Missionary Society.

■ Awards, Honors

Gold Medallion Award, Evangelical Christian Publication Association, 1983, for *Love's Long Journey;*

The Father of Love, Bethany House, 1989.
Love Finds a Home, Bethany House, 1989.
Maury Had a Little Lamb, Bethel Publishing, 1989.
The Calling of Emily Evans, Bethany House, 1990.
Julia's Last Hope, Bethany House, 1990.
Father of My Heart, Bethany House, 1990.
Trouble in a Fur Coat, Bethel Publishing, 1990.
Roses for Mama, Bethany House, 1991.
A Woman Named Damaris, Bethany House, 1991.
This Little Pig, Bethel Publishing, 1991.
They Called Her Mrs. Doc, Bethany House, 1992.
The Measure of a Heart, Bethany House, 1992.
A Bride for Donnigan, Bethany House, 1993.
Heart of the Wilderness, Bethany House, 1993.
The Faithful Father, Bethany House, 1993.
Pordy's Prickly Problem, Bethel Publishing, 1993.
Too Long a Stranger, Bethany House, 1994.
Who's New at the Zoo, Bethel Publishing, 1994.
Janette Oke's Reflections on the Christmas Story, Bethany House, 1994.
The Bluebird and the Sparrow, Bethany House, 1994.
A Gown of Spanish Lace, Bethany House, 1995.
The Red Geranium, Bethany House, 1995.
The Canadian West Saga, Inspirational Press (New York City), 1995.
Drums of Change: The Story of Running Fawn, Bethany House, 1996.
(With T. Davis Bunn) *Return to Harmony*, Bethany House, 1996.
Nana's Gift, Bethany House, 1996.
(With Bunn) *Another Homecoming*, Bethany House, 1997.
The Tender Years, Bethany House, 1997.
The Matchmakers, Bethany House, 1997.
Spunky's First Christmas, Bethany House, 1997.

A video of *Spunky's First Christmas* has been made available by Tyndale Family Video, 1997; *When Calls the Heart* was produced as a musical with text by David Landrum and music by Orpha Galloway.

■ Sidelights

Author Janette Oke has been hailed as "the Laura Ingalls Wilder of the Bible set." The description seems apt, for Oke, like Wilder, is known for her homespun romance and historical novels with swift-moving plots and wholesome, old-fashioned family values. However, any comparison of Oke and the creator of the *Little House on the Prairie* saga must end there. Unlike Wilder, whose writing were secular in nature, the Canadian-born Oke

This 1981 work details the relationship between an orphaned boy and the aunt who raised him.

unabashedly places strong conservative Christian values front and center in her books, which she has described to *Calgary Herald* religion editor Gordon Legge as her "paper missionaries."

Oke's 1979 debut novel *Love Comes Softly* came out of nowhere to set the publishing world on its ear; that book sold more than a million copies and blazed the trail in what freelance journalist Carol Toller, writing in the Toronto-based *Financial Post*, has described as the $3-billion-per-year Christian publishing industry. Despite such success, Oke's novels are ignored by mainstream literary critics and bestseller lists, and the author's name remains largely unknown outside the Christian publishing world. However, sales of Oke's novels often outpace those of many "big name" writers, and she is one the world's most successful and prolific authors. An added twist to Oke's amazing story is that she did not write her first book until she was forty-two years old; "I had a lot of catching up to do," she quipped in a 1998 interview with Dennis E. Hensley of *Writer's Digest*. Oke has done just that, penning more than fifty books over the past two decades; in addition to her signature fiction, she has written poetry, children's stories, and a book of her own reflections on the Christmas story. Oke's legions of fans adore her, for according to Hensley each new Janette Oke novel "sell[s] from 250,000 to 400,000 copies within six months of release." Total sales of her books now exceed fifteen million copies, and her work has been translated into a dozen languages.

Janette Oke was born February 18, 1935, on a farm near Champion, Alberta, a remote farming community an hour's drive southeast of Calgary. The sixth of nine children born to Fred and Amy Steeves, Janette grew up during the lean, hungry years of the Great Depression. Fred Steeves farmed for a living, while his wife Amy was a stay-at-home farm wife who cared for the children. A deeply religious woman, Amy Steeves "found God" following the death in infancy of one of her two sons; as a result, the Steeves children were raised according to the conservative teachings of the Missionary Church, an evangelical sect.

In the fall of 1938, the Steeves family moved north to Hoadley, Alberta, in the foothills of the Canadian Rockies, about sixty miles southwest of Edmonton. Farm produce prices were low at the time, and life was difficult. The Steeves' wooden homestead had no electricity, indoor plumbing, or central heating; the children slept in a common second floor loft, where they snuggled together for warmth on the frigid winter nights. Despite all of the hardships, the Steeves were a loving and closely-knit family. Together, they not only survived, but eventually prospered; indeed, the story of their life together has a kind of down-home *Little House on the Prairie* flavor to it.

When time and weather conditions permitted, Janette and her siblings attended a local one-room country school. Since the school was two-and-a-half miles from their door, the children walked back and forth each day; they were heavily bundled in coats and boots in winter, and they ran barefoot when spring came. Although young Janette was a shy, quiet girl, she burned with a keen intelligence and was an excellent student.

Apart from playing with her siblings, her chief recreation was reading, especially western novels. According to Oke's daughter Laurel, who has recounted her mother's early life in a 1996 biography entitled *Janette Oke: A Heart for the Prairies*, "Janette . . . [read] all the books she could get her hands on. Since the school had little in the way of a library, books were precious indeed. The students brought their own books from home, exchanging them with one another and faithfully returning them to their owners."

Oke recalled in her interview with Hensley of *Writer's Digest* how the teacher in her rural school would rest Norman Rockwell covers from the *Saturday Evening Post* magazine against the black-

Continuing to follow the characters who appear in *Love Comes Softly* and *Love's Enduring Promise*, in this 1982 novel Oke sends Missie and Willie LaHaye on a difficult journey across the American West.

board ledge and then ask the students to write a story about what was happening in the pictures. "I loved that," Oke told Hensley. "I would let my imagination run wild. My teacher praised my writing efforts." For her own amusement, Oke began keeping a journal and writing short stories and verse—"very poor verse," she confided to reporter Chris Dafoe of the Toronto *Globe and Mail* in a 1996 interview. Oke and a girlfriend spent many happy hours together talking about the girlfriend's plans to one day become a writer. Oke harbored no such dreams of her own; anything of the sort seemed impossibly far-fetched to her.

By age seventeen, Oke has missed so many classes due to bad weather, her own illnesses, and fam-

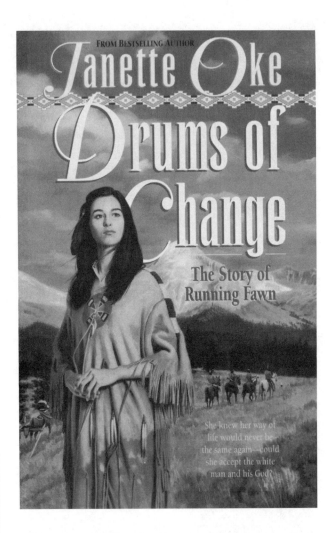

Running Fawn's days as a Blackfoot Indian living in her idyllic home are abruptly changed when white men destroy all she loves and send her and her tribe to a reserve.

ily circumstances beyond her control that she still had not finished high school. However, she was keen to start paying her own way in the world, and so she left school to accept a $25-per-week job at the local bank. After two years of working there, she had saved enough money to enroll at Mountain View Bible College in the town of Didsbury, just north of Calgary, Alberta. There, Janette met and fell in love with Edward Oke, the son of a tractor dealer. After they were married on May 13, 1957, Janette resumed her banking career, while her husband continued his studies in preparation for a career in the ministry of the Missionary Church. The Okes lived in Indiana from the fall of 1957 through to mid-1959 (and again in 1981) so that Edward could attend Bethel College in Mishawaka, a suburb of South Bend; afterward, the couple returned home to Alberta. There, Oke worked at a variety of pink collar jobs, one of which included a brief stint at a weekly newspaper called the *Elkhart Truth.*

Throughout this period, Oke continued to write poems and short stories as a hobby. By now, she was musing about becoming a writer, but she still did not feel that she was ready to put pen to paper. "Janette had taken a couple of writer's aptitude tests, one for a commercial writing course and the other for Christian Writer's Institute," Laurel Oke noted. On both occasions, although her mother achieved high marks, she did not pursue the training. In fact, a representative of the secular firm once called upon Janette Oke. However, when she informed him that she did not have enough time to read as she "would like," he took that as an excuse and left. Later, when Oke began tracking her reading habits to satisfy her own curiosity, she realized that "she usually read more than one hundred books a year." In her own mind, she wished it could be many more.

In 1960, Edward Oke was appointed president of his alma mater, Mountain View Bible College, and he and his wife settled into a comfortable life in Didsbury. Their first child was born on November 19, 1960—after Janette had lost a newborn son, who died shortly after being born in Indiana (which gave her the right to claim American citizenship, if she desired it.) Three other babies would follow over the next five years. When the children were old enough, Oke began teaching Sunday school classes and went back to work. It was not until 1977, when she was working in the office of a concrete company, that an offhand re-

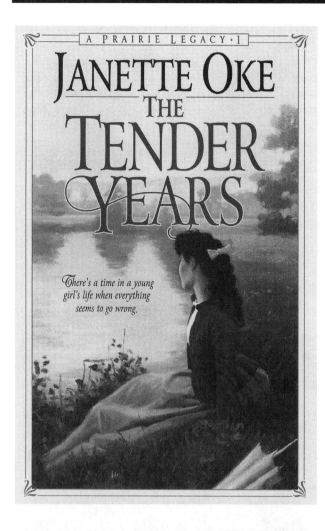

A PRAIRIE LEGACY • 1

JANETTE OKE
THE TENDER YEARS

There's a time in a young girl's life when everything seems to go wrong.

Picking up the story of Marty and Clark Davis's five grandchildren, Oke launched a new series called the "Prairie Legacy" that once again ties together prairie life and wholesome values.

mark someone made set Oke thinking anew about becoming a writer; she realized she was now forty-two, and that time was slipping away. "[Janette Oke's] mind went to the short stories she had stuffed away here and there, and she considered gathering them up under the title 'Twice Twenty-One' and sending them to a publisher," Laurel Oke wrote. "She felt that by the time a person had reached her age, she surely must have learned *something* about life."

Writing As a Mission

While Oke loved contemporary novels, she was growing increasingly uneasy with many of the novels she read, which she felt were "tainted" by too much sex and violence. Oke felt strongly that there should be an alternative for Christians like herself. "In the beginning, her idea was simply to provide a clean, entertaining piece of fiction to fill a void in the market," Laurel Oke explained. As she thought about writing, Janette Oke realized that it might be an ideal way to share her religious faith with others.

After much soul searching and praying for guidance on how to proceed, Oke came to the realization that her God was happy to let her use her literary talents to write whatever stories she wanted to write. This filled her with an enormous sense of contentment and self-confidence. "To write Christian fiction was never a choice for me," Oke told Jerry Horton of the Canadian literary publication *Quill & Quire* in a 1994 interview. "I am a Christian, so anything I write will reflect my faith."

In the summer of 1977, she began working on some new stories to fill up the book that she was now planning. However, when one of these tales seemed to take on a life of its own in her mind, she decided it should be a novel instead of a short story. Thus inspired, Oke began writing in old school scribblers in longhand whenever she could find a spare moment. Three weeks later, she had completed the first draft of an historical romance novel called *Love Comes Softly*. The comments from family and friends who read the manuscript were encouraging, so Oke sent it to Bantam Books, a well-known publisher of paperback novels. "I got it back with this nice little note saying, 'We do not accept unsolicited manuscripts,'" Oke told Dafoe. "And since I knew they wouldn't be soliciting it, I thought I better find out what to do with it."

Initially, that was nothing because Oke was unsure of her next step. Then, about six months later, her husband bought home a book from the library that offered some tips on how a would-be author might find a publisher. Acting on the book's advice, Oke wrote query letters to several publishers who specialized in inspirational and religious literature. She got two replies, both of which asked for sample chapters. Oke complied. One publisher rejected what she had sent; the other, Bethany House, decided to give Oke a chance. "Janette sent us three chapters and a synopsis of *Love Comes Softly*, and I immediately connected from the heart with what she was sharing on paper," recalled Carol Johnson, the editorial director of Bethany House.

Love Comes Softly, a pioneer-era farm tale about the adventures of Marty and Clark Davis and their young family, was published in July of 1979. At the time, there was very little Christian fiction available commercially, and the novel was virtually ignored by literary critics and book reviewers from the mainstream media. "No one knew if [the novel] would sell. But we found we had a larger audience than we anticipated," Oke told interviewer W. Terry Whalin, the author of an online literary newsletter that bears his name. Sales of *Love Comes Softly* took off, and by December that book had become a runaway bestseller. In the process, it opened the publishing industry's eyes to a vast new, untapped literary market—aging Baby Boomers who are seeking spiritual guidance as well as "a good read." In a 1995 article on the growing market for Christian fiction, Martha Duffy of *Time* reported that figures compiled by the Christian Booksellers Association show that "ninety per cent of buyers are women, and the average age of readers is forty-two"—the same age as Oke when she wrote her first novel!

While Oke, herself, was delighted that people were buying her novel, she was not surprised; in her heart, Oke was convinced that any success her writing enjoyed was part of God's divine plan. And besides, she knew that she was filing a glaring void in the literary marketplace. "I wasn't finding material that corresponded with my own wants and needs," Oke told Chris Dafoe. "I felt that as a Christian community we really had a responsibility to our own to give them a choice of reading materials and it wasn't being done."

Book Becomes Series

Oke originally intended that her next book would be about an orphan boy named Joshua Jones. "But reader requests began to come in the form of letters, wanting to know 'what happened next' to the Davis family," Laurel Oke explained in the biography she wrote about her mother. As a result, Oke's editor at Bethany House asked her to write a sequel to *Love Comes Softly.* Oke responded by gathering some scribblers, a supply of sharp pencils, and retreating to a quiet place where she

could be alone. Four-and-a-half days later, Oke emerged with the first draft of another novel, which she called *Love's Enduring Promise.* After some rewriting and polishing, that book was published in September of 1980. Sales again were strong, proving that the success of *Love Comes Softly* had been no fluke. Encouraged by all of this, Oke now wrote her story about the orphan boy Joshua Jones, which she called *Once Upon a Summer.* It, too, sold strongly, and Bethany House was eager to publish a lot more novels by Oke. "Janette's original pace of one book per year soon doubled," Laurel Oke noted.

Oke wrote an animal story for children in 1982, and the following year another novel called *Love's Long Journey,* which relates the further adventures

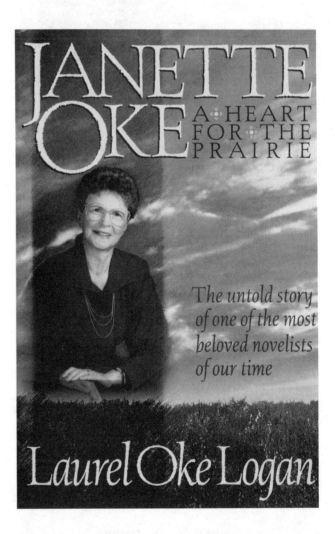

Oke's daughter wrote this 1993 biography to reveal the life of her famous author mother to her reading public.

of some of the same characters who had appeared in *Love Comes Softly* and *Love's Enduring Promise.* Reviewing *Love's Long Journey,* Virginia Sankey of the *Voice of Youth Advocates* wrote that while "Church and Christian day school libraries will want this as well as the other [books] in the series," it seemed likely that the book's religious content and allusions "would probably keep it out of most junior highs." Such comments did nothing to slow sales of the book or prevent it from becoming another bestseller. At the same time, Oke realized that she had unexpectedly, and quite inadvertently, launched a series. In fact, Oke eventually wrote six more novels about the Davis family—for a total of eight. The public appetite for the books was so strong that this would become a pattern for Oke. And in 1997, she revisited the Davis family in a novel called *The Tender Years.* In picking up the story of Marty and Clark Davis's five grandchildren, Oke launched a whole new series called the "Prairie Legacy"—intentionally this time.

The Tender Years focuses on the coming-of-age struggles of a fourteen-year-old girl named Virginia. Despite what she felt was some "forced" dialogue and a "contrived" ending, reviewer Judy Sasges of *Voice of Youth Advocates* wrote that "Oke's fans will be pleased with Virginia's story." The book's "basic plot, strong family values, prairie setting, personal growth, and the natural integration of religion and God into the storyline" make for a "wholesome" story. Melissa Hudak of *Library Journal* agreed. "Fans of the 'Love Comes Softly' series will certainly demand this compelling and well-written follow-up."

Several others books that Oke wrote about new characters she created also evolved into serials. Oke's Joshua Jones tale became a multi-book saga, dubbed the "Seasons of the Heart" series, while another series chronicled the pioneer-era adventures of a Russian immigrant family, and another told of a young Indian woman named Running Fawn. Reaction to these books from Oke's growing audience continued to be highly positive, even if some of the critics who had by now started paying attention to her books were less impressed with what they were reading. For example, reviewing *Winter is Not Forever,* the 1998 novel that was the third installment of Joshua Jones's adventures, Mary Hedge of *Voice of Youth Advocates* hailed the protagonist as "a well-developed character," whose trials and tribulations would give

If you enjoy the works of Janette Oke, you may also want to check out the following books:

Patricia MacLachlan, *Sarah, Plain and Tall,* 1985.
Joan Lowery Nixon, "The Orphan Train Quartet," 1987-89.
Glendon Swarthout, *The Homesman,* 1988.

readers insights into their own lives. However, Hedge cautioned that Oke's fiction may not appeal to everyone. "The slower pace of life is reflected in the rather slow pace of the plot. Because of this, readers used to modern novels may not be able to endure more than the first few chapters," she wrote.

The millions of readers who bought Oke's books obviously disagreed, and as a result other writers and publishers began venturing into the Christian fiction genre. Oke, herself has continued to write at a dizzying pace. While she is best known for her own novels and children's stories, Oke has shown she is willing and able to move in new directions. In 1996, she teamed with fellow Christian writer T. Davis Bunn to write a novel called *Return to Harmony.* In an interview with Sanchez, Oke noted that she and Bunn "were surprised and pleased with the way the story began coming together." They collaborated again on *Another Homecoming* in 1997.

For all her literary successes and despite the awards she has won—including the 1992 President's Award of the Evangelical Christian Publishers Association, Oke is still largely ignored by reviewers in the mainstream media and many bookstores do not even sell her books. None of this troubles her in the least; she is content with the path she has chosen, for as she told Chris Dafoe of the Toronto *Globe and Mail,* "I think I could write a good wholesome book without religion in it. I could choose writing as an occupation. But I choose to see writing as a ministry." In fact, Oke devotes much of the money she has earned from her books to fund the fieldwork of the Missionary Church, of which she and her family are members. Nonetheless, Oke has said in terms of relative importance in her life writing will always take a back seat to that of her family. "I don't see myself as a professional writer. I see myself as a wife and mother and grandmother who writes," she told Dafoe. "It's a busy corner of my life, but it's just a corner."

■ Works Cited

Dafoe, Chris, "A writer's sturdy faith," *Globe and Mail* (Toronto), May 2, 1996, pp. C1, 2.

Duffy, Martha, "The Almighty to the Rescue," *Time*, November 13, 1995, pp. 105-7.

Hedge, Mary, review of *Winter Is Not Forever, Voice of Youth Advocates*, October, 1998, p. 183.

Hensley, Dennis E., "Janette Oke: 15 million sold—and counting," *Writer's Digest*, September, 1998, pp. 32-36.

Horton, Jerry, "Mighty Oke," *Quill & Quire*, December, 1994, p. 18.

Hudak, Melissa, review of *The Tender Years: A Prairie Legacy*," *Library Journal*, September 1, 1997, p. 168.

Legge, Gordon, "Paper Missionary," *Calgary Herald*, November 18, 1995, p. H10.

Logan, Laurel Oke, *Janette Oke: A Heart for the Prairie*, Bethany House, 1993.

Sankey, Virginia, review of *Love's Long Journey, Voice of Youth Advocates*, April, 1983, p. 40.

Sasges, Judy, review of *The Tender Years, Voice of Youth Advocates*, February, 1998, pp. 388-89.

Toller, Carol, "Onward Christian Authors," *Financial Post*, January 27-29, 1996, pp. 22-23.

Whalin, Terry W., "Romance in the Life of Janette Oke—a Prairie Romance Novelist," *W. Terry Whalin Newsletter*, http://www.terrywhalin.com (January 14, 1999).

■ For More Information See

PERIODICALS

Booklist, August, 1995, p. 1911; March 15, 1996, p. 1220; September 1, 1996, p. 65.

BookPage, August, 1996; December, 1996.

Library Journal, September 1, 1996, p. 164.

School Library Journal, August, 1995, p. 157.

Voice of Youth Advocates, April, 1983, p. 40; October, 1988, p. 183; October, 1995, p. 222; October, 1996, p. 212.*

—Sketch by Ken Cuthbertson

Sara Paretsky

85. *Member:* Private Eye Writers of America, Authors Guild, Authors League of America, Sisters in Crime (founder and president, 1987-88), Crime Writers Association, National Abortion Rights Action League (director of Illinois chapter, 1987—), Chicago Network.

■ Awards, Honors

Award from Friends of America Writers, 1985, for *Deadlock*; named one of *Ms* magazine's Women of the Year, 1987; Silver Dagger award, Crime Writer's Association, 1988, for *Blood Shot.*

■ Writings

V. I. WARSHAWSKI MYSTERIES

Indemnity Only, Dial, 1982.
Deadlock, Dial, 1984.
Killing Orders, Morrow, 1985.
Bitter Medicine, Morrow, 1987.
Blood Shot, Delacorte, 1988, published in England as *Toxic Shock*, Gollancz, 1988.
Burn Marks, Delacorte, 1990.
Guardian Angel, Delacorte, 1991.
Tunnel Vision, Delacorte, 1994.
Windy City Blues (short stories), Delacorte, 1995, published in England as *V. I. for Short*, Hamish Hamilton, 1995.
Three Complete Novels (contains *Indemnity Only, Blood Shot,* and *Burn Marks*), Wings (New York City), 1995.

■ Personal

Born June 8, 1947, in Ames, IA; daughter of David Paretsky (a scientist) and Mary Edwards (a librarian); married Courtnay Wright (a physicist and professor), June 19, 1976; stepchildren: Kimball, Timothy, Philip. *Education:* University of Kansas, B.A., 1967; University of Chicago, M.B.A. and Ph.D. (history), 1977. *Avocational interests:* Singing, baseball (especially watching the Chicago Cubs).

■ Addresses

Home—1507 East 53rd St., #223, Chicago, IL 60615. *Agent*—Dominick Abel, 498 West End Ave., New York, NY 10024.

■ Career

Freelance writer. Urban Research Corp., Chicago, IL, publications manager, 1971-74; freelance business writer, 1974-77; Continental National America (insurance company), Chicago, manager of advertising and direct mail marketing programs, 1977-

OTHER

(Editor) *Beastly Tales: The Mystery Writers of America Anthology*, Wynwood Press (New York City), 1989.
(Editor) *A Woman's Eye* (mystery short stories), Delacorte, 1991.
(Editor) *Women on the Case: 26 Original Stories by the Best Women Crime Writers of Our Times*, Delacorte, 1996.
Ghost Country (novel), Delacorte, 1998.

Also author of *Case Studies in Alternative Education*, 1975. Contributor to anthologies, including *The Eyes Have It*, Mysterious Press, 1985, and *The Eyes Have It, Volume II*, Mysterious Press, 1986. Contributor to periodicals, including *American Girl*, *Black Mask Quarterly*, and *Women: A Journal of Liberation*.

■ **Adaptations**

Indemnity Only was adapted as the 1991 film *V. I. Warshawski*, starring Kathleen Turner.

■ **Sidelights**

There was a time when the female detectives of mystery novels were prim and proper ladies who either solved crimes from the parlor rooms of their country homes (á la Agatha Christie's Ms. Marple) or else they would have to call on their gentlemen friends for help when their cases turned really dangerous (as did P. D. James's Cordelia Gray). The role of hardboiled private eye was reserved for the Sam Spades and Philip Marlowes of the genre. All that changed in the early 1980s with the debut of the self-reliant female detectives who gave the tried-and-true formulas a kick in the pants by giving mysteries a real feminist edge. And the woman who led this literary revolution is Sara Paretsky, creator of the V. I. Warshawski series.

Warshawski, a former public defender from a working-class, southside Chicago family, is a private detective with an intimate knowledge of the city's seedy side. She takes no guff from anyone, including the men in her life, and this has resulted in one divorce and several other short relationships. She has a taste for Black Label whisky, loves to watch Cubs baseball, is a terrible house-keeper, and doesn't like to cook. As a karate expert, she can hold her own in almost any fistfight. Paretsky does not try to make V. I. (which stands for Victoria Iphigenia, though she prefers initials) a gorgeous heartthrob, either, describing her character as having dark hair and gray eyes and weighing in at 140 pounds on a five-foot-eight frame. V. I. is athletic, too, enjoying long swims and runs along the Chicago waterfront. In short, she's one tough cookie, and not at all like any of the fictional female private eyes who preceded her, although others have followed in her footsteps. Paretsky's creation, as Neal J. Ney wrote in *Arm-*

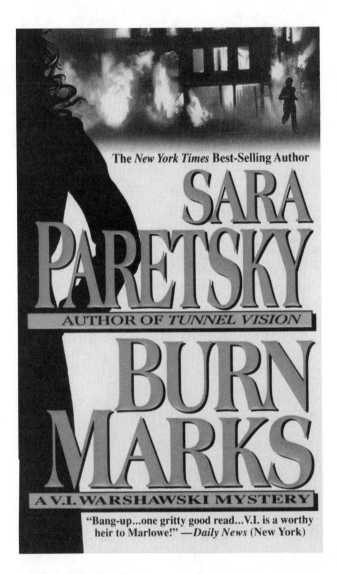

When V. I. Warshawski tries to help her drunken Aunt Eena after she is burned out of her apartment building, the private detective soon finds herself tangled in a web of corruption and intrigue.

chair Detective, "is not the only nor the first example of a female hardboiled detective, but she is one of the best."

Paretsky's Early Life

The story of how V. I. came to make her debut in 1982's *Indemnity Only* is an involved one. While her creator comes from a background quite different from the detective's, there are some parallels. Paretsky, born in Ames, Iowa, is one of five children born to a scientist and a librarian. She enjoyed a comfortable lifestyle as a child. The family moved to Lawrence, Kansas, when Paretsky was still a girl, and it was there that she spent most of her early years. Growing up in the 1950s and 1960s, the young Paretsky was not expected to go to college. Instead, her parents figured she would marry, have children, and spend her days as a mother and wife. But Paretsky had other ideas. She was a bright student and paid her own way through the University of Kansas, working as a dishwasher and a secretary while her parents paid for her brothers' education.

Like others of the generation that came of age on American campuses in the 1960s, Paretsky became politicized and socially aware. Her first trip to Chicago, where she worked as an intern at an inner city summer camp, was a life-changing experience. Until then, Paretsky had been relatively sheltered from the harsh realities of urban life—the poverty, crime, drug abuse, and misery. It was during her student days that Paretsky's ideas of social justice and gender equity really took shape, including her advocacy of abortion rights, which later led to her membership in the National Abortion Rights Action League. These concerns are often apparent in her Warshawski novels.

Moving to Chicago after her 1967 graduation, Paretsky eventually found a job working for the Urban Research Corporation as a publications manager. She then decided to go back to school, studying at the University of Chicago, where she graduated with an M.B.A. and a doctorate in history. One of the main reasons she attended graduate school, she remarked to *Lear's* Helen Dudar, was "to prove to my family that I was as smart as my brothers." And while she certainly managed to do that, Paretsky was not really certain what her goal should be. She didn't want to become a university professor like her father or her

husband, whom she married in 1976. Instead, she got a job at the insurance company Continental National America as a manager of advertising and direct mail marketing programs. She worked there from 1977 to 1985.

Becoming a successful executive, wife, and mother of three stepsons, Paretsky still did not feel fulfilled. She decided there was still something missing in her life, and that something was a love of writing that she had been denying herself since childhood. It was an interest that began when she was only five years old. She had tried to write her first play then, but because her parents gave her no encouragement, she grew up believing it was never a practical pursuit. By the late 1970s, however, Paretsky decided she was ready to try her hand at writing again. She had always loved mystery novels—she read two dozen mysteries at the same time she was supposed to be studying for her Ph.D. oral exams—and Paretsky decided she could write one, too. She wanted to make the lead character female, while still being as strong a character as one of Raymond Chandler's heroes. However, her first efforts weren't working out because she tended to lapse into parody.

Paretsky Resolves to Be an Author

Feeling frustrated, Paretsky promised herself that she would complete a solid novel by the end of 1979 or give up trying. Following a friend's advice, she took a class at Northwestern University taught by Stuart Kaminsky, the creator of the Toby Peters mysteries. "Kaminsky's thoughtful critiques proved decisive in the development of both Paretsky's writing style and her character, V. I. Warshawski," wrote Nancy Shepherdson in a *Writer's Digest* article. "In particular, he helped her banish 1930s slang from her detective's vocabulary: She no longer calls electricity *juice* or cash *scratch*." With the support of a skilled mentor, Paretsky completed her first novel in 1980. In some ways, that was the easy part. Selling the book proved difficult. Publishers saw the potential in Paretsky's writing, but they were resistant to the liberties that she took with traditional literary formulas. "Paretsky had a hard time selling her first manuscript," reported *Newsweek* contributor Laura Shapiro, "in part because publishers wanted to equip V. I. with a male partner. (The Chicago setting was a problem, too; New York publishers feared a Midwestern city would seem 'alien' to readers.)" Paretsky prevailed, however, and after thirteen rejection letters from publishers, *Indemnity Only* was published in 1982 to strong reviews. *New Republic* critic Robin W. Winks termed the book a "thoroughly convincing" and "gritty" mystery.

In writing *Indemnity Only*, Paretsky did no research, instead borrowing heavily from her own experiences as a student and insurance company employee. The story involves a University of Chicago student who has gone missing and unscrupulous doings in the insurance industry that lead to a murder. Adding spice to the plot, Paretsky also throws in gangsters, scheming union leaders and bank officials, and secret identities. While the storyline of deceit and treachery is a traditional one, it is the character of V. I. that adds uniqueness to Paretsky's writing. From the start, the reader finds an independent woman who, though she enjoys a relationship with another man, has no desperate need for one in her life. As Robert Sandels related in an *Armchair Detective* article, "After many encounters with thugs and gangsters in *Indemnity Only*, [V. I.] visits her lover in the hospital, where he is recovering from a bullet wound he never would have received had he listened to her. 'I've been falling in love with you,' he says, 'but you don't need me.' V. I. and the reader agree with him, and so ends the relationship."

But Warshawski does have strong ties to her family. She comes from a mixed background of Italian, Polish, and Jewish ancestors; her father is a retired police officer, her mother an opera singer who abandoned her career when she fled Fascist Italy. Readers become more acquainted with V. I.'s family in the 1984 novel *Deadlock*. In that book, Warshawski delves into the murder of her favorite cousin. She has a strong bond with "Boom Boom" Warshawski, an ex-hockey player turned shipping company employee. When Boom Boom dies from an "accidental drowning" at a shipyard, V. I. investigates to uncover a corporate war between shipping magnates that has led to more than one murder. As with one *Publishers Weekly* reviewer who called *Deadlock* an "absorbing, well-written tale," other critics had praise for Paretsky's second novel. *New York Times Book Review* critic Newgate Callendar especially lauded the author's further development of V. I., whom he calls a "much more believable character than she was in" *Indemnity Only*.

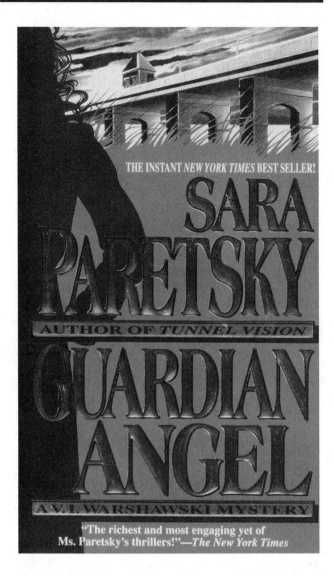

Warshawski runs to the aid of her favorite neighbor, Mr. Contreras, when she accepts an assignment to search for a missing former union member who turns up dead in a canal in this 1991 installment of the popular series.

In *Killing Orders* the reader learns even more about V. I.'s family. Her aunt calls upon the detective to solve the theft of millions of dollars in share certificates from a monastery. It's in this novel that the audience learns about how V. I.'s mother escaped from Italy during World War II. V. I. also goes up against the usual thugs, but manages to uncover an underground Catholic organization whose illegal doings lead the detective all the way to the archbishop. While a *Publishers Weekly* writer felt the novel helped to solidify Warshawski as a "welcome addition to the growing canon of hardboiled, female private eyes," T. J. Binyon, writing in the *Times Literary Supplement*, considered *Killing Orders* "not overly convincing as a story," although he enjoyed the fast pace and local color.

The V. I. Difference

One characteristic of the V. I. Warshawski mysteries that several commentators have noted is how Paretsky's heroine is developed from installment to installment. The reader learns more about her family and her past with each book. In an interview for *Contemporary Authors*, Jean W. Ross asked the author about this. "I realized [as I wrote the sixth book in the series] that I'm the equivalent of V. I.'s analyst," Paretsky said, "that what's interesting for me in telling these stories is to learn about her life and her past, and that if I find a way of tying a mystery into that, then I will be better able to come up with a story line." The author later added, "When I started with *Indemnity Only* [V.I.] wasn't such an independent character from me personally. But as I've learned more about her life, it's turned out to be quite different from my own; she's taken on a much more separate identity. So in some ways I've become more separate from her. But, at the same time, when I get very involved in actually writing about her, by the time I'm a third of the way through or so, I find myself dreaming about episodes in the book, and it's very unsettling."

Besides the strong characterization in the V. I. mysteries, another common thread is the heroine's championing of the "little guy" against big corporations, big institutions, or other powerful figures. V. I.'s investigations typically start off as murder investigations but soon reveal a bloody trail that can be traced to nefarious corporations and secret organizations. In 1987's *Bitter Medicine*, the villains are immoral hospital administrators who allow a pregnant teenager and her infant to die. The teenager happens to be one of Warshawski's friends. At first, it appears that her death is just an unfortunate tragedy possibly aggravated by the girl's diabetes. But as V. I. digs deeper into the case, she learns that more unsavory factors are at work. In a side story, V. I.'s friend Lotty, who operates a clinic that performs abortions, comes under attack by right-to-lifers, thus allowing Paretsky to comment on one of her personal causes, the right for women to have

abortions. T. J. Binyon, writing in another *Times Literary Supplement* article, had considerable praise for *Bitter Medicine*, which he called "more thoughtful, more credible and better organized" than the author's earlier efforts. And *New York Times Book Review* critic Newgate Callendar praised Paretsky's "sympathy and understanding for the downtrodden."

The *Armchair Detective* article by Sandels penetrated even more deeply in its criticism of the V. I. Warshawski novels. Calling Paretsky's creation "a Frankenstein's monster put together from the bodies of male detectives long dead and a few female shoppers," Sandels found nothing extraordinary or innovative about the fictional detective. The critic also dismissed notions that Paretsky offers valuable social commentaries in her books, writing that "no matter how much Warshawski peels back the layers of greed or corruption in the various institutions she approaches, she never quite confronts those institutions." Sandels went on to argue that the Warshawski books aren't even really all that feministic, attacking not so much the male-dominated institutions of the world but more often the family, which he felt Paretsky portrays as "depressing caricatures." Sandels concluded that "Paretsky's novels seem less social than familial, less subversive than confessional. Her detective seems more concerned with emotional perfection and material satisfaction than with raising questions about the structures of society which her villains inhabit."

Despite such critical analyses, other reviewers have repeatedly noted that Paretsky's writing improves with each novel. Such is the case with 1988's *Blood Shot*, in which V. I.'s search for her childhood friend's father unexpectedly leads her into an investigation involving criminal pollution of the environment and corruption among big-time industrialists and government officials. *Newsweek* contributor Katrine Ames, who declared *Blood Shot* to be Paretsky's "best book yet," lauded the author's characterizations, from her villains to her heroine. Ames noted how Paretsky keeps V. I. in balance with both good and bad traits, thus making her much more believable as a person who is "full of moral indignation, but she is not a saint." There is also more material in *Blood Shot* covering V. I.'s personal history, continuing the author's character study. In addition to the continuing development of the main character, an ongoing attribute of any V. I. Warshawski story is the violence, much of it committed against V. I. herself. Paretsky's detective has been pounded, slashed with a knife, tied up in blankets and left in a polluted swamp to drown, and has even had acid thrown at her. The question as to whether there is too much violence in Paretsky's mysteries was posed to the author by Jean Ross. Paretsky confessed that "it's a thing I struggle with, the concept of violence and what it means and how violent V. I. can be without crossing a line where she's no longer a credible human being, let alone a credible woman. I'm interested in what role violence plays in Chicago, what role it plays in American life, in the way we look at women and the way we look at men. These are the issues that I struggle with as a writer, and that a lot of readers find I've resolved unsatisfactorily for their taste. A lot of readers feel V. I. is far too violent for a woman. So I keep trying to think about those problems without coming up with a satisfactory answer."

Sisters in Crime

Still, Paretsky would be reticent to tone down her character and make her more "feminine." She is intent on helping to create a strong image of women in literature—both as characters and with regard to the female authors who create them. To this end, in 1987 she founded Sisters in Crime, an organization of women mystery authors who strive to get women writers the critical attention they deserve. Sisters in Crime started by surveying various newspapers and periodicals, beginning with the *New York Times*. Paretsky told Ross, "We found that, while women are writing about thirty to forty percent of the mysteries that are published within a given year, only about six to thirteen percent of the books the *Times* was reviewing were by women." After writing to the *Times*, Sisters in Crime did manage to see more women authors getting reviews. "[T]hey did a full-page review independent of Newgate Callendar of Sue Grafton's . . . book, *E Is for Evidence*. I think that review is a tribute to the work that Sisters in Crime has done in focusing attention on the *Times*'s overlooking mysteries in the past."

After founding Sisters in Crime, Paretsky released her next novel, *Burn Marks*, a couple years later. In this book, V. I. is drawn into the mystery when she tries to help her poor Aunt Eena, who has been burned out of the seedy hotel room where

If you enjoy the works of Sara Paretsky, you may also want to check out the following books:

The suspense thrillers of Patricia D. Cornwell, including *Postmortem*, 1990.
The works of Sue Grafton, including *A Is for Alibi*, 1982.
Laurie R. King, *A Grave Talent*, 1993.

she lived. However, the case quickly turns into an investigation of arson, political corruption, and murder, as well as giving Paretsky the chance to comment on the plight of the homeless. Reviewer Jo-Anne Goodwin of the British publication *New Statesman* praised *Burn Marks* as being "hugely enjoyable."

By the time the novel was published, Paretsky was finally beginning to realize financial success as an author. Up until that point, she had been working full time and taking care of her family while trying to work on her writing. After five novels, she was starting to earn enough money to quit work and focus on her books. It was also at this time that her first novel, *Indemnity Only*, was being made into a film. *V. I. Warshawski*, released in 1991, starred Kathleen Turner. Although it was not a success, the exposure it gave Paretsky's work helped make her an even bigger name in mystery fiction.

Some critics have noted that with Paretsky's 1991 novel, *Guardian Angel*, the author was starting to push the edges of the traditional mystery story. V. I. has always been a bit different from the usual hardboiled detective, and not just because of her gender. The Philip Marlowes and Sam Spades of the genre were always loners, always separate and distant from the flawed world that spun around them. But although V. I. is a divorcee and lives alone, she has a circle of close friends that includes Dr. Lotty Herschel, who runs a rundown medical clinic in a bad part of Chicago; old Mr. Contreras, who is V. I.'s neighbor and who is always looking out for her; and her dog, Peppy. The novel *Guardian Angel*, in which the detective is again pitted against crooked politicians and lawyers, delves deeply into V. I.'s friendship with Lotty and examines the main character even more than in previous novels.

New Statesman critic Nick Kimberly also noted that, stylistically, Paretsky is trying "to write crime novels with none of the stigmas associated with merely popular fiction." There's more of an attempt at "literary" writing, as well as digressions such as "pages of wholly superfluous musical appreciation" and V. I.'s recollections of hearing "Martin Luther King speak in 1966." Charles Champlin, writing in the *Los Angeles Times Book Review,* praised *Guardian Angel* as Paretsky's best to date. "The author has few peers as a plotter," declared Champlin, who later concluded that "Paretsky gets better and better, the stories at once more imaginative and more personal, giving not a sign that laurels are being rested upon."

Turning again to her concern for the homeless—first expressed in *Burn Marks*—Paretsky's 1994 novel *Tunnel Vision* is about a money-laundering scheme disguised by an organization called Home Free, which builds houses for the homeless. As usual, V. I. discovers corruption at high levels from the Senate on down, and her contempt for those who walk all over the poor and disadvantaged is once again shown to be justified. Many critics declared that *Tunnel Vision,* the eighth book in the V. I. Warshawski series, proved that "Paretsky is still the best if not the best-selling writer about female detectives," as Pat Dowell put it in the *Washington Post Book World.* Charles Champlin echoed that praise when he wrote in the *Los Angeles Times Book Review* that in "a series of such uniformly high quality it's hard to make comparisons, but I think the new book is one of Paretsky's very best."

After *Tunnel Vision,* Paretsky began stretching her writing skills even more. The first test was her 1995 short story collection *Windy City Blues,* which contains stories written since 1982. Although these stories all feature V. I., the detective sometimes takes a back seat to other characters. Also, as Josh Rubins pointed out in a *New York Times Book Review* article, after the opening story in the collection, "A Walk on the Wild Side," "few of the stories . . . try to sketch in the menacing, earthy textures of V. I.'s Chicago or to suggest her flinty commitment to the city's underdogs." Rubins felt that the result was "quite a letdown." Paul Skenazy, writing in the *Washington Post Book World,* also observed that most of the stories lack "the rich complexity that have made Paretsky's Warshawski novels into one of the finest detective series going."

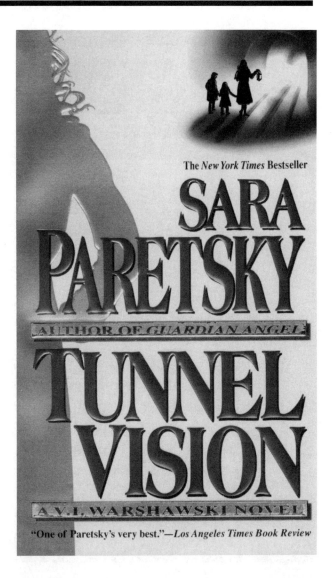

Paretsky mixes a murder mystery with social concerns in this story of domestic abuse and homeless families.

Paretsky Temporarily Abandons Warshawski

Although *Windy City Blues* was a literary experiment, Paretsky took an even bigger step in 1998 when she set aside her now-famous detective altogether to write a novel called *Ghost Country.* In an online interview with Murray Ryerson, the author explained her rationale: "V. I. and I have been close for a long time. I needed time away from her so I could keep writing about her with a fresh voice," she said. Paretsky went on to explain that the story "was inspired by something a minister working to help the homeless once told her. "[He] said he often imagines Jesus on the

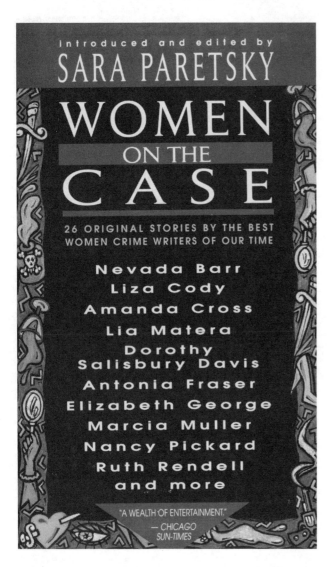

introduced and edited by
SARA PARETSKY
WOMEN
ON THE
CASE

26 ORIGINAL STORIES BY THE BEST
WOMEN CRIME WRITERS OF OUR TIME

Nevada Barr
Liza Cody
Amanda Cross
Lia Matera
Dorothy
Salisbury Davis
Antonia Fraser
Elizabeth George
Marcia Muller
Nancy Pickard
Ruth Rendell
and more

"A WEALTH OF ENTERTAINMENT."
— CHICAGO
SUN-TIMES

Paretsky, an ardent supporter of women writers, edited this collection of mysteries in order to showcase their talents.

steps of a Chicago hospital, turned away because he doesn't have a green card," she said. That notion led the author to think more about people's faith, as well as her ongoing concern for the plight of the poor. She consequently worked on *Ghost Country* for the next three years.

Ghost Country is about many different characters who all find themselves drawn to a remarkable, mysterious woman called Starr, who some come to think has divine abilities. The cast of characters include the homeless Madeleine Carter, who thinks she sees the Virgin Mary's blood on the wall of a hotel; Dr. Hector Tammuz, a resident

psychiatrist; Luisa Montcrief, a former opera singer who has become destitute alcoholic; and Harriet and Mara Stonds, two sisters at odds over the attention of their famous grandfather, neurosurgeon Abraham Stonds. All these characters are profoundly affected in one way or another by the appearance of Starr. "Whether Starr has divine powers, or is just a woman of such empathy that people project all their desires on her is something you have to decide for yourself," the author tells Ryerson.

Ghost Country received mixed reactions from critics. A *Kirkus Reviews* contributor felt that while Paretsky wasn't "quite up to the task of breathing life into this psychotic saint," the book deserves a "honorable place in the gallery of straight fiction by mystery writers." On the other hand, *Booklist* critic Emily Melton called *Ghost Country* perhaps "[Paretsky's] best book yet; it shows amazing depth and emotion, offers richly complex characters and a stunningly original plot."

Despite the author's excursions into mainstream fiction, fans of the V. I. Warshawski novels need not fear that they have seen the last of Paretsky's gutsy femme detective. Now that she has taken a few years off, she is ready to return to the dangerous streets of Chicago. Paretsky told Murray Ryerson in her on-line interview that she's "at the start of a new adventure, [but] one too young for me to tell you much, except that it's politics as usual in the greater Chicago area."

■ Works Cited

Ames, Katrine, review of *Blood Shot, Newsweek,* September 26, 1988, pp. 73-74.

Binyon, T. J., review of *Killing Orders, Times Literary Supplement,* June 20, 1986, p. 683.

Binyon, T. J., review of *Bitter Medicine, Times Literary Supplement,* November 13, 1987, p. 1262.

Callendar, Newgate, review of *Deadlock, New York Times Book Review,* March 18, 1984, p. 27.

Callendar, Newgate, review of *Bitter Medicine, New York Times Book Review,* August 2, 1987.

Champlin, Charles, "Criminal Pursuits," *Los Angeles Times Book Review,* February 16, 1992, p. 8.

Champlin, Charles, review of *Tunnel Vision, Los Angeles Times Book Review,* June 12, 1994, p. 8.

Review of *Deadlock, Publishers Weekly,* December 23, 1983, p. 54.

Dowell, Pat, review of *Tunnel Vision, Washington Post Book World,* June 19, 1994, p. 6.

Dudar, Helen, interview with Sara Paretsky, *Lear's,* August, 1991.

Review of *Ghost Country, Kirkus Reviews,* April 1, 1998, p. 432.

Goodwin, Jo-Ann, "The Big Idea," *New Statesman,* June, 1990, pp. 38-39.

Review of *Killing Orders, Publishers Weekly,* March 22, 1985, p. 55.

Kimberly, Nick, "Clever Dicks," *New Statesman,* June 5, 1992, p. 37.

Melton, Emily, review of *Ghost Country, Booklist,* March 1, 1998, p. 1045.

Ney, Neal J., "Windy City Detectives," *Armchair Detective,* fall, 1990, pp. 449-50.

Ross, Jean W., interview with Sara Paretsky, *Contemporary Authors,* Volume 129, Gale, 1990, pp. 334-38.

Rubins, Josh, review of *Windy City Blues, New York Times Book Review,* October 8, 1995, p. 24.

Ryerson, Murray, interview with Sara Paretsky, http://www.saraparetsky.com.

Sandels, Robert, "It Was a Man's World," *Armchair Detective,* fall, 1989, pp. 388-96.

Shapiro, Laura, "The Lady Is a Gumshoe," *Newsweek,* July 13, 1987, p. 64.

Shepherdson, Nancy, "The Writer behind Warshawski," *Writer's Digest,* September, 1992, pp. 38-41.

Skenazy, Paul, review of *Windy City Blues, Washington Post Book World,* November 19, 1995, p. 6.

Winks, Robin W., review of *Indemnity Only, New Republic,* March 3, 1982.

■ For More Information See

PERIODICALS

Armchair Detective, spring, 1988, p. 148.

Entertainment Weekly, October 20, 1995, p. 58.

Los Angeles Times Book Review, April 1, 1984, p. 4.

New York Times Book Review, January 24, 1993, p. 24.

School Library Journal, January, 1989, p. 39.

Voice of Youth Advocates, June, 1990, pp. 108-9.

Washington Post Book World, September 18, 1988, p. 6.

Wilson Library Bulletin, December, 1991, pp. 104-5.*

—Sketch by Kevin S. Hile

Lisa Scottoline

Everywhere That Mary Went; Edgar Allen Poe Award, 1994, for *Final Appeal.*

■ Personal

Born c. 1956, in Philadelphia, PA; divorced; one daughter. *Education:* University of Pennsylvania, B.A. (English, with honors); University of Pennsylvania Law School, graduated cum laude, 1981.

■ Addresses

Home—Philadelphia, PA.

■ Career

Writer, 1993—. Worked as a clerk for state appellate judge in Pennsylvania; Dechert, Price & Rhoads, Philadelphia, PA, lawyer; also worked as a part-time clerk for a federal appellate judge.

■ Awards, Honors

Edgar Allen Poe Award nomination for best original paperback, Mystery Writers of America, 1993,

■ Writings

Everywhere That Mary Went, Harper, 1993.
Final Appeal, Harper, 1994.
Running from the Law, Harper, 1996.
Legal Tender, HarperCollins, 1996.
Rough Justice, HarperCollins, 1997.
Mistaken Identity, HarperCollins, 1999.

Also author of an unpublished novel, "Fairy Tale"; works have been translated and published in over twenty languages.

■ Sidelights

Lisa Scottoline has joined the ranks of former lawyers who have turned to writing fictional thrillers about it instead. Her particular milieu is the upper crust and underbelly of the legal scene in her hometown, Philadelphia, where her books are set and where they have enjoyed excellent sales since their debut. On a larger scale, Scottoline has won praise for her clever yet sympathetic attorney-heroines. *People* magazine's Cynthia Sanz called her "the female John Grisham" for her ability to put these protagonists in inadvertent peril, but also first providing them with the wherewithal to extricate themselves and bring events to a satisfying, good-over-evil conclusion.

Scottoline, born in the mid-1950s, grew up in the Philadelphia suburb of Bala Cynwyd. She won entry to the prestigious University of Pennsylvania, where literary giant Philip Roth was one of her professors in the upper-level courses she took toward her English degree with a concentration on the contemporary American novel. But Scottoline then decided to pursue a law degree, and graduated from her alma mater's equally well-regarded law school in 1981. She clerked for one of the judges on Pennsylvania's Supreme Court bench, a coveted assignment, and became an attorney in private practice at a Philadelphia firm, where she specialized in employment discrimination cases. She also married, had a daughter in the mid-1980s, and then went through a divorce.

For a time, Scottoline was a single parent, clerking for a judge part-time, and making ends meet by using her credit cards for life's necessities, so she decided to try her hand at another line of work. She began writing a women's novel called "Fairy Tale," and sent it to seven agents whose names she gleaned from the annual *Writer's Market*. Several editors bid for it, but in the end, Scottoline realized that she could write a successful work of fiction, and decided not to publish her novel because she didn't want to be restricted to writing women's novels. Instead she turned to her legal career for inspiration: lawyer-centered thrillers had become a popular fiction genre with the rise of Scott Turow and John Grisham in the late 1980s. After signing with an agent, Scottoline began writing her own attorney-in-danger cliffhanger.

Finds Success With Legal Thriller

Her next manuscript sold in a week, and Scottoline signed with the paperback division of HarperCollins. That manuscript became *Everywhere That Mary Went*, published in the fall of 1993. Its title, based on the nursery rhyme "Mary Had a Little Lamb," hints at the misfortune that seems to follow protagonist Mary DiNunzio. As it opens, this Philadelphia corporate attorney is defending a hardware store in a discrimination suit filed by its employees. DiNunzio is still somewhat grief stricken over the unsolved death of her husband, who was struck by a car while on his bicycle. Like Turow, Scottoline writes in the present tense, letting the action unfold as DiNunzio's life becomes even more distressing.

Not surprisingly, DiNunzio's blue-chip workplace is a hotbed of intrigue occupying seven floors of pricey Philadelphia high-rise real estate; DiNunzio compares each of the floors to the Seven Deadly Sins—with Sloth at the entry level and Pride at the penthouse. She believes she resides in Envy, partly because she and a good friend, her California-transplant colleague, Judy Carrier, are each slated to be promoted to partner soon. However, another attorney at her firm, Ned Waters, a man DiNunzio once dated in college, is also up for one of the two slots. Against her better judgment, the

LISA SCOTTOLINE

EVERYWHERE THAT MARY WENT

EDGAR AWARD NOMINEE

"What Fun! Lisa Scottoline Brings Something New To The Lawyer-Mystery —A Brilliant Sense Of Humor." —SUSAN ISAACS

Lawyer Mary DiNunzio, who has lost her husband in a suspicious auto accident, finds herself the victim of a stalker who might be from her own office in Scottoline's debut novel.

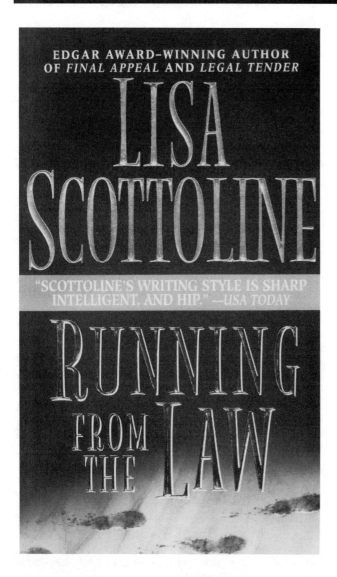

EDGAR AWARD–WINNING AUTHOR
OF *FINAL APPEAL* AND *LEGAL TENDER*

LISA SCOTTOLINE

"SCOTTOLINE'S WRITING STYLE IS SHARP INTELLIGENT, AND HIP." —USA TODAY

RUNNING FROM THE LAW

Rita Marrone should have thought twice about defending her lover's father—a judge accused of sexual harassment—before the case turned to murder and a threat on her own life.

two begin dating again. Ned is supportive when she starts receiving silent prank phone calls, both at home and work, that coincide with her hectic schedule. DiNunzio also realizes that someone has been snooping around her desk and altering her computer files.

Scottoline created a tough, smart character in *Everywhere That Mary Went,* but also one with working-class Italian-American parents, a twin sister who has become a nun, and a treasured male secretary. When he's fatally struck by the same car that DiNunzio has spotted following her, she

enlists the help of a police detective to look into the similarities between this death and that of her husband's. Soon she begins to believe someone wants her dead, and most clues point to Ned. She also discovers that her new paramour—whose abusive father heads a rival Philly firm—has been prescribed mood-controlling drugs.

A satisfying, though suspenseful, ending was hinted at by most reviewers. "An engaging, quick read, sprinkled with corny humor and melodrama in just the right proportions," opined a critic in *Publishers Weekly.* "Scottoline knows her milieu and re-creates it flawlessly," declared Alice Joyce in *Booklist.* A *Philadelphia Inquirer* reviewer praised the author for creating a likable, smart character with a penchant for very astute one-liners. "Scottoline loves Mary DiNunzio," the review asserted. "Because she does, an alchemy takes place that makes Mary come alive. Once that happens, we all love her and tremble for her when she's put in harm's way."

Everywhere That Mary Went was nominated for an Edgar Award, the top prize in suspense fiction from the Mystery Writers of America, and an outstanding coup for a debut novelist. Scottoline's next book, *Final Appeal,* would win the award in 1994. For it, she created another Italian-American legal eagle, Grace Rossi, but like the author herself, Rossi is a Philadelphia single mother who clerks part-time for a judge in the federal appeals court. Like many other women she knows, Rossi harbors a secret crush on Judge Armen Gregorian, but he is apparently happily married. After he requests Rossi's specific assistance on a high-profile case, their first night working together leads to romance.

The next morning Judge Gregorian is dead. On the surface it appears a suicide, but Rossi begins her own investigation. Some of her better leads come from her friendship with a mysterious homeless man who, in the end, is revealed to be a federal agent. The author, opined a reviewer in *Publishers Weekly,* "has again pulled together an intriguing cast of characters and a smart mystery to make an exciting, action-packed read." *Final Appeal* would also be the final of Scottoline's titles to be published in paperback only, as many mass-market mysteries are. As a result of her Edgar Award and strong local sales, HarperCollins issued her next work in hardcover, a prestigious bump upstairs for such a relatively new author. Though

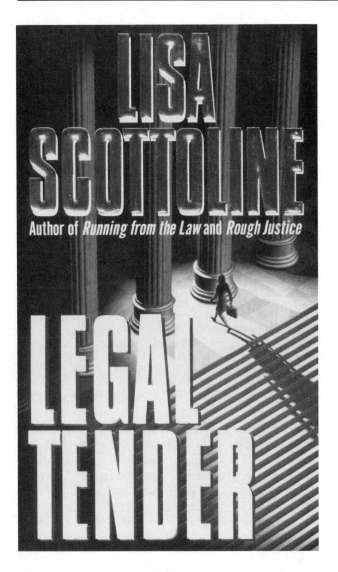

An attorney who makes it her business to prosecute crooked police finds herself the object of a murder investigation in Scottoline's 1996 novel.

Scottoline's first two novels had not set any nationwide sales records, the hardcover strategy signaled that HarperCollins editors and executives felt she had great promise as an author.

In *Running from the Law*, Scottoline again merged a winning combination of sex, unscrupulous legal conduct, and a smart, attractive protagonist who suddenly finds her life in grave danger. Rita Morrone, however, is a more complex character than Scottoline's previous two heroines, exhibiting a decidedly more devious streak than the warmhearted Mary DiNunzio or virtuous Grace Rossi. Morrone is a lawyer who hates to lose a case,

known for her tenacity and ability to manipulate a jury and even a judge on occasion. She is close to her butcher father, who voices his disapproval of the sometimes even bloodier legal world, and has a fiancé, Paul Hamilton, scion of an old-money Philadelphia family.

As *Running from the Law* begins, Morrone is embroiled in a scandalous local case that involves Paul's father, Fiske Hamilton, a distinguished federal judge accused by his young, attractive secretary of sexual harassment. Soon Morrone, defending the senior Hamilton, finds that there is more to the case than meets the eye, and learns that her fiance has been cheating on her with the plaintiff. Then the secretary is found dead, and Hamilton becomes a suspect in her murder. Morrone begins to delve into the case on the sly, and her relationship with Paul disintegrates. The shooting of her father in a robbery at his store seems connected, but Morrone's good standing at the weekly poker games with her father's friends provide her with the leads that bring her to the true culprit. "The strengths of this book lie in character and dialogue," wrote Eva C. Schegulla of *Armchair Detective*, who found only Rita's romance with Paul Hamilton implausible. "The witty repartee and down and dirty fighting are sharp and memorable."

Hits the Jackpot

In 1996, after the critical success of her first three books, Scottoline won a contract with HarperCollins to publish her next two novels in hardcover as well, and was signed to a seven-figure-deal with the house. *Legal Tender* was published that same year, her fourth thriller and her fourth Italian-American attorney-heroine. Benedetta "Bennie" Rosato, a partner in a small Philadelphia firm, is blond, tall, and an expert rower who goes out on the Schuykill River in the middle of the night for physical exercise and case-related contemplation. Then her partner—also her ex-boyfriend—tells her he is dissolving the partnership, which effectively puts her out of work. When he is found murdered, Rosato becomes the number-one suspect. Matters worsen when the murder weapon turns up at her home, the newspapers track her as a suspect in the salacious case, her clients abandon her, and then she is accused of killing the executive of a pharmaceutical company.

To extricate herself, Rosato dons a series of disguises to uncover the real culprits. Scottoline also creates for her heroine some everyday troubles, such as a recently acquired boyfriend and a mother with psychological problems. A *Publishers Weekly* reviewer called Bennie "a delightful heroine . . . and, again, Scottoline merits a big round of applause." A critic in *Kirkus Reviews* found the fourth novel rife with "nonstop action, smart narration, and dozens of helpful tips on going underground in your own hometown." Only an *Entertainment Weekly* assessment by Gene Lyons was critical, finding "flashes of sardonic wit" but a "cliched situation, shallow characterization, and formulaic plot."

In her fifth book, 1997's *Rough Justice,* Scottoline cleverly brings together several characters from her previous books to form a Philly legal powerhouse. Mary DiNunzio and Judy Carrier, from *Everywhere That Mary Went,* are lawyers at Bennie Rosato's new firm. Rosato & Associates has been hired on the sly by another Philadelphia lawyer, Marta Richter, a top criminal defender who has been tricked by her client into believing that he was innocent of the murder of a homeless man. After Richter delivers her stunning closing argument and the jury goes into deliberation, slumlord Elliott Steere confesses his guilt to Richter with a certain amount of relish. She's infuriated, but the tenets of attorney-client privilege doesn't automatically mean she can change the outcome of the trial. Instead Richter enlists the legal aid of Rosato & Associates to help overturn the case.

But after Steere is back in jail, temporarily, Carrier and DiNunzio mysteriously disappear and Richter's life is in danger. A massive snowstorm that paralyzes the city is the setting for the book's dramatic conclusion. A *New York Times Book Review* assessment of *Rough Justice* found the "run-for-your-life plot," a hallmark of Scottoline's work and common to the legal-thriller genre, a bit overworked—here "recycled for a blizzard that has two lawyers *skiing* for their lives," Marilyn Stasio noted somewhat disdainfully. Other reviewers were more positive. Scottoline, wrote a *Publishers Weekly* contributor, "skillfully depicts personal quirks that give her characters dimension . . . and her skill as a novelist makes her plot sizzle with cliffhanger intensity." The author planned *Rough Justice* as the first in a series set at Rosato & Associates, and Sanz, reviewing it for *People,* found great promise in the idea. She termed the book

"a wonderfully engrossing, sometimes hilarious thriller that will delight courtroom junkies and cement her standing."

Scottoline has her own site on the World Wide Web, for which she spent several thousand dollars of her own money promoting via advertisements in the *New York Times Book Review.* In early 1999 she offered an intriguing proposition to her cyber-fans: on her Web site she published a draft of the first chapter of her forthcoming book, *Mistaken Identity,* and invited fans to edit it them-

Scottoline brings together several of her characters from previous novels in this thriller in which attorney Marta Richter is tricked into believing her client is innocent of a murder charge, and has to work fast to turn the tables of justice and save her own life.

If you enjoy the works of Lisa Scottoline, you may also want to check out the following books and films:

John Grisham, *The Firm*, 1991.
Laurie R. King, *A Grave Talent*, 1993.
Presumed Innocent, a film starring Harrison Ford, 1990.

selves and send it back. She told Scott Kirsner of *The Standard*, an on-line news source, that the several hundred e-mails she receives from fans each week often provide her with very good suggestions. "It's the best kind of editor . . . they have great ideas, but no power."

■ Works Cited

Review of *Everywhere That Mary Went*, *Philadelphia Inquirer*, January 9, 1994.

Review of *Everywhere That Mary Went*, *Publishers Weekly*, September 27, 1993, p. 59.

Review of *Final Appeal*, *Publishers Weekly*, October 3, 1994, p. 65.

Joyce, Alice, review of *Everywhere That Mary Went*, *Booklist*, September 1, 1993.

Kirsner, Scott, "Publishing: Edit This Book," *The Standard*, http://wwwthestandard.com, November 23, 1998.

Review of *Legal Tender*, *Kirkus Reviews*, September 1, 1996, pp. 1278-79.

Review of *Legal Tender*, *Publishers Weekly*, September 9, 1996, p. 62.

Lyons, Gene, Review of *Legal Tender*, *Entertainment Weekly*, November 8, 1996, p. 62.

Sanz, Cynthia, review of *Rough Justice*, *People*, September 8, 1997, p. 41.

Review of *Rough Justice*, *Publishers Weekly*, July 7, 1997, p. 48.

Schegulla, Eva C., review of *Running from the Law*, *Armchair Detective*, winter, 1996, pp. 105-6.

Stasio, Marilyn, review of *Rough Justice*, *New York Times Book Review*, September 7, 1997, p. 34.

■ For More Information See

ON-LINE

Lisa Scottoline's homepage is located at http://www.scottoline.com/newhome.cfm.

PERIODICALS

Armchair Detective, winter, 1994, p. 87.

Entertainment Weekly, July 18, 1997, p. 75.

Library Journal, October 1, 1995, p. 121; August, 1997, p. 135.

New York Times Book Review, November 5, 1995, p. 27.

Philadelphia Inquirer, March 13, 1994, p. MC3.

Publishers Weekly, August 28, 1995, p. 101; June 10, 1996, p. 46; February 22, 1999.

San Francisco Examiner, October 17, 1995.*

—*Sketch by Carol Brennan*

J. Michael Straczynski

■ Personal

Full name, Joseph Michael Straczynski; born July 17, 1954, in Paterson, NJ; son of Charles (a manual laborer) and Evelyn (Pate) Straczynski; married Kathryn May Drennan (a writer), 1983. *Education:* Attended Kankakee Community College, 1972-73, and Richland College, 1973; Southwestern College, A.A., 1975; San Diego State University, B.A., 1978.

■ Addresses

Home—Glendale, CA. *Agent*—Ilse Lahn, Paul Kohner Agency, Inc., 9169 Sunset Blvd., Los Angeles, CA 90069; and Valerie Smith, Virginia Kidd Agency, 538 East Harford St., Milford, PA 18337.

■ Career

San Diego State University, San Diego, CA, personal and academic counselor, 1975-77; *Racquetball News,* El Cajon, CA, editor in chief, 1978; *Daily Californian,* El Cajon, special correspondent and reviewer, 1978-79; KSDO-AM Radio, San Diego, entertainment editor and theater and film reviewer, 1979-80; Airstage Radiodrama Productions, San Diego, artistic director and resident writer, producer, director, workshop instructor, and facilitator, 1980-81; *Writer's Digest,* Cincinnati, OH, contributing editor and author of column, "Scripts," 1982-91; executive story consultant, story editor, and writer, *Captain Power and the Soldiers of the Future,* 1986-87; story editor and writer, *The Real Ghostbusters* (animated), 1986-89; KPFK-FM radio, Los Angeles, host of weekly program "Hour 25," 1987-92; story editor, *The New Twilight Zone,* 1987-88; executive story consultant, *Jake and the Fat Man,* 1989-90; producer, *Murder, She Wrote,* 1991-92; producer, *Walker, Texas Ranger,* 1993; creator, executive producer, and writer, *Babylon 5,* beginning 1993. Instructor at Grossmont Junior College, 1978, and San Diego State University, 1979. *Member:* Writers Guild of America West, Psi Chi (life member).

■ Awards, Honors

Writers Guild Award nomination and ACE Award nomination, c. 1989, both for screenplay *The Strange Case of Dr. Jekyll and Mr. Hyde;* named one of *Newsweek*'s fifty "most influential thinkers-innovators," 1995; Hugo Awards for dramatic presentation, World Science Fiction Convention, 1996, for *Babylon 5:* "The Coming of Shadows," and 1997, for *Babylon 5:* "Severed Dreams"; Space Frontier

Foundation Award for Best Vision of the Future, and American Cinema Foundation Award, both for series *Babylon 5.*

■ Writings

SCREENPLAYS AND TELEPLAYS

Marty Sprinkle (teleplay), broadcast by KPBS-TV, 1977.

Love or Money (film), CrossOver Productions, 1978.

Disasterpiece Theater (television variety), broadcast by XETV-TV, 1980.

He-Man and the Masters of the Universe (animated series), 9 episodes, syndicated, 1984.

She-Ra, Princess of Power (animated series), 9 episodes, syndicated, 1985.

Jayce and the Wheeled Warriors (animated series), 14 episodes, syndicated, 1986.

Captain Power and the Soldiers of the Future (series), 11 episodes, syndicated, 1986-87.

The Real Ghostbusters (animated series), 23 episodes, ABC-TV, 1986-89.

The New Twilight Zone (series), 12 episodes, CBS-TV, 1986-88.

The Strange Case of Dr. Jekyll and Mr. Hyde (TV movie), Showtime, 1989.

Nightmare Classics (series), 2 episodes, Showtime, 1989.

Jake and the Fatman (series), 5 episodes, CBS-TV, 1989-90.

Murder, She Wrote (series), 7 episodes, CBS-TV, 1991-92.

Walker, Texas Ranger (series), 1 episode, CBS-TV, 1993.

Babylon 5: The Gathering (series pilot), syndicated, 1993.

Babylon 5 (series), 93 episodes, syndicated, 1993-97, Turner Network Television (TNT), 1998.

Babylon 5: In the Beginning (TV movie), TNT, 1998.

Babylon 5: Thirdspace (TV movie), TNT, 1998.

Babylon 5: The River of Souls (TV movie), TNT, 1998.

Babylon 5: A Call to Arms (TV movie), TNT, 1999.

PLAYS

Death in Stasis (one-act), first produced in Chula Vista, CA, 1977.

Parting Gesture (one-act), first produced in San Diego, CA, 1977.

Memos From the Other Side (one-act), first produced in Chula Vista, 1977.

Snow White (two-act; first produced in Chula Vista, 1977), Performance Publishing, 1978.

The Last Pirate Show (one-act), first produced in San Diego, 1978.

Last Will and Estimate (one-act), first produced in San Diego, 1979.

Movies, Movies (two-act), first produced in San Diego, 1979.

The Apprenticeship (three-act), first produced in San Diego, 1980.

FICTION

Demon Night, Dutton, 1988.

Tales from the New Twilight Zone (stories; adapted from his teleplays), Bantam, 1989.

OtherSyde, Dutton, 1990.

OTHER

(And producer and director) *The Other Side of the Coin* (radio play), first broadcast by KCR-AM/FM Radio, 1978.

(And producer and director) *Where No Shadows Fall* (radio play), first broadcast by KPFK-FM Radio, 1982.

The Complete Book of Scriptwriting: Television, Radio, Motion Pictures, the Stage, Writer's Digest, 1982, revised version (includes a complete *Babylon 5* script), 1996.

Also author of radio play *Encounter at Twilight,* 1980. Work represented in anthologies, including *Shadows Six,* edited by Charles Grant, Doubleday, 1983. Scriptwriter for radio series "Alien Worlds," 1979-80. Contributor of nearly two hundred articles to magazines, including *San Diego, Talent Spotlight,* and *City,* and to newspapers. Editor of *Post Scripps,* 1979, and *Tuned In,* 1980.

■ Work in Progress

Producing and writing for *Crusade: The Babylon Project,* a television series.

■ Sidelights

"I'm a writer. I never really wanted the pointy hat that says PRODUCER," J. Michael Straczynski admitted in a 1996 Compuserve Forum Conference. "If I were offered staff writer, for crappy money, no power, but they wouldn't change the words, I'd take it in a hot second." Nevertheless, in bringing his science fiction saga *Babylon 5* to the small screen, Straczynski has become one of the most visible television producers in the business. Not only does he oversee the development and production of the series and its spinoffs, he wrote more than ninety of the show's 111 hour-long episodes and has maintained an ongoing dialogue with the show's fans over the internet. The result, according to *Newsweek* contributor Adam Rogers, "has been some of the most intelligent science fiction on television," earning the ardent devotion of millions of viewers as well as two Hugos from the science fiction community.

Straczynski was born in New Jersey in 1954, and he grew up "hearing tales of the old country," as he recalled in a 1983 interview with *Contemporary Authors*. Stories of all kinds appealed to him, from science fiction to legends to plays. "I grew up reading the classics," he told a 1998 Compuserve Forum Conference. "I was into Greek mythology when I was barely eleven or twelve. I was dragged off as a kid by the school to see *Oedipus Rex* in theater in the round when I was maybe about twelve, and having never seen anything like that before, it just blew my brains out the back of my head." Straczynski read widely and enjoyed classic authors—such as William Shakespeare, Charles Dickens, and Christopher Marlowe—and contemporary writers. Science fiction, fantasy, and horror writers such as Ray Bradbury, Harlan Ellison, H. P. Lovecraft, Eric Frank Russel, and J. R. R. Tolkien were particular favorites, while Rod Serling's *Twilight Zone* series showed him that television could also provide a good medium for storytelling.

Not content with just reading or hearing stories, Straczynski wanted to create some of his own. "I always knew I'd be a writer," he commented in his *Contemporary Authors* interview. "While I was young, I collected and was fascinated by paper clips, blank sheets of paper, pens, pencils, staplers—the basic paraphernalia of writing." In high school, the young student wrote poetry, short stories, and scripts, and by his senior year he had directed and appeared in his own assembly-length play. Straczynski entered college, hoping that what he learned would advance his goal of being a writer. He discovered instead that the best way to learn to write is through practice. While attending classes at Southwestern College and San Diego State University in California, he had several

plays produced and sold his first television sitcom script. By the time he earned his bachelor's degree in 1978, Straczynski had also published nearly eighty articles in various magazines and newspapers.

Following college, Straczynski moved from journalism into scriptwriting, penning several more plays for stage, television, and radio. His experience led to a regular scriptwriting column for *Writer's Digest* and a nonfiction book, *The Complete Book of Scriptwriting*, which dealt with the creation, marketing, and production of all types of scripts. By the late 1980s, Straczynski had worked as a scriptwriter and story editor for several children's programs, including *Captain Power and the Soldiers of the Future* and *The Real Ghostbusters*. The high point of this period, however, was most likely his work for *The New Twilight Zone*. He wrote twelve episodes of this series between 1987 and 1988, and "[b]etter than any of the other writers who worked on various revivals of *The Twilight Zone*, Straczynski perfectly entered into and maintained the ambience of Rod Serling's original vision," Gary Westfahl noted in the *St. James Guide to Horror, Ghost and Gothic Writers*. Straczynski later adapted these teleplays into short stories and collected them in the 1989 book *Tales from the New Twilight Zone*.

From Television to Terror

Straczynski remained a fan of science fiction, fantasy, and horror of all types, and in 1987 he began hosting a weekly two-hour radio show that examined those genres. Refusing to be pigeon-holed as a scriptwriter, he also continued writing nonfiction articles and contributing short stories to magazines such as *Amazing Stories* and *Twilight Zone*. He also began his first novel. *Demon Night* was published in 1988, and some reviewers compared it to Stephen King's horror classic *'Salem's Lot*. The novel follows Eric Matthews as he returns to his boyhood home in Maine after suffering from recurring nightmares and strange telekinetic events. He finds that mysterious happenings in the town are somehow linked to the discovery of strange Native American artifacts in a nearby cave. After a demonic force called "the Night" is loosed, Eric discovers that his heritage gives him both the power and the responsibility to combat its evil. Many reviewers found *Demon Night* to be formulaic, but they praised the author's

Straczynski's popular sci-fi television series *Babylon 5*, which he wrote and produced himself, is about a space station with a mission to foster peace between humans and alien races.

storytelling ability. A *Publishers Weekly* critic called the novel "atmospheric and fast moving"; a *Science Fiction Chronicle* reviewer found it "a frequently scary story with an extremely good series of closing scenes."

Straczynski continued working in television—earning both Writers Guild and Cable ACE Award nominations for his 1989 script *The Strange Case of Dr. Jekyll and Mr. Hyde*—even as he penned a second horror novel. *OtherSyde* was published in 1990, and "must be regarded as his crowning achievement in prose," according to Westfahl. In this novel, sixteen-year-old Chris Martino moves from New Jersey to Los Angeles and befriends another outsider, nerdy Roger Obst. As the two write invisible-ink notes to each other, strange communications from the "OtherSyde" are inserted into their messages. Roger learns how to respond to the creatures from the OtherSyde, and they are soon helping him revenge himself against the

teens who have made him an outcast. As a rash of teen "suicides" strikes his school, Chris begins to resist the OtherSyde and finds himself facing off against his former friend. Calling the book a "non-stop read," a *Publishers Weekly* reviewer noted that "when sticking to the demonic events and the increasing bewilderment of his recognizable characters, Straczynski holds us transfixed." While observing that the Faustian idea of the vengeful outsider is "highly familiar," *Locus* contributor Edward Bryant called the author's treatment "highly professional" and added that *OtherSyde* "doesn't really push the envelope of horror fiction, but it's still ample evidence that the author has the ability to do exactly that when he wishes." Meanwhile, Gary Westfahl, writing in the *St. James Guide to Horror, Ghost, and Gothic Writers*, concluded: "The novel is authentic and evocative throughout because its horrors . . . are effectively linked to real-world horrors of modern life like bullying, child abuse and urban crime. Furthermore, its final scenes of a Los Angeles engulfed in darkness, flames, and looters . . . constitute a genuinely frightening vision of a modern apocalypse."

Even as his first novels were attracting attention, Straczynski was climbing the career ladder in the television industry. After a stint as an executive story consultant for the series *Jake and the Fatman,* he worked as a producer for two more successful series: *Murder, She Wrote* and *Walker, Texas Ranger.* A producer has more control over the execution of a story idea than a screenwriter does. Straczynski explained in an April, 1993 posting on Compuserve that "when I was a freelancer, I wanted to be story editor; when I was story editor, I wanted to be producer; when I was producer, I wanted to be executive producer/show runner with a series of my own." When it comes to television, he added, "the highest you can go is to create your own series, run it, and tell your stories."

Straczynski had a very specific story he wanted to tell, one that had fascinated him for almost a decade. "I'd had two notions in my head back around 1986," he related in a 1998 Compuserve Forum Conference: "a small, contained story set on a space station that could be done inexpensively, and on the other hand, I wanted to do a huge, star-hopping space saga. I was in the shower one morning, and suddenly these two ideas collided and I realized that they were the same thing." For a year the author worked on fleshing out the concept, and came up with a five-year story arc following the events on a space station that serves as a center of commerce and diplomacy for several space-faring races of beings. "I knew that the best series set up places where the stories come to you, in a police station or a hospital or a law office," Straczynski said in a 1995 Compuserve Forum Conference, "and decided in a science fiction environment a space station would work well for that. . . . [I] added the backdrop of myth and archetype, constructed a Hero's Journey, and took it from there."

But bringing a series to television is not as simple as just developing an idea, and so Straczynski and fellow producers John Copeland and Douglas Netter spent several years searching for a company to finance and find broadcast outlets for the series, which the author titled *Babylon 5.* "I knew that this was something I wanted to do, and that

one way or another, by sheer force of will if necessary, it *would* be made," Straczynski said in an April, 1993 Compuserve posting. "In the long run, I think we can do something really amazing with this show, and done right, it could be a perfect cap to my career. Mainly, it's just a story that I want to tell. And I'm amazingly stubborn about story telling, when I want to be." The producer's stubbornness paid off, and in 1993 *Babylon 5* debuted in syndication throughout the United States.

The Dawn of the Third Age

The pilot episode of *Babylon 5* introduced viewers to the galaxy's "last, best hope for peace." It is the year 2258, ten years after a war between Earth and the alien Minbari, and the Babylon 5 space station has been established to promote understanding and cooperation among various races. Besides humans and Minbari, there are the Centauri, an imperialistic race lamenting their loss of influence in the galaxy; the Narn, a reptilian-looking race overcoming one hundred years of subjugation to the Centauri; and the Vorlon, a silicon-based race whose science and motives are mysterious. Not only do Commander Jeffrey Sinclair (played by Michael O'Hare) and his staff have to mediate between the ambassadors of various races, they must deal with critics back home on Earth. As the first season progressed, viewers were gradually given clues as to the reasons behind the surprising resolution of the Earth-Minbari War; the role of Earth's telepathic Psi Corps in interstellar politics; and the intentions of the secretive Vorlon. While the intrigue led to the examination of such significant issues as self-determination and political responsibility, the series also had a sense of humor. In a review of the series pilot, *Entertainment Weekly* contributor Ken Tucker noted that it "features an inviting combination of crackerjack computer-generated special effects and a funky goofiness." *New York Times* critic John J. O'Connor similarly praised the costumes, makeup, and special effects of the pilot—"not least the visiting ships that enter and leave like dazzling insects"—and added that "*Babylon 5* could prove fun to have around."

The series quickly found an audience, earning very good ratings for a syndicated show and even beating network programming in some markets. By the time the second season began, there were enough fans that *TV Guide* devoted an article to

Straczynski shares his knowledge of how to be a successful screen and stage writer in this 1996 book.

reassuring them that the replacement of Commander Sinclair with Captain John Sheridan (played by Bruce Boxleitner) did not mean a deviation from Straczynski's "story arc." Because Sinclair was the only captain to win a battle during the Minbari war, his presence on the station leads to further political complications. As the series progresses through seasons two and three, however, it becomes clear that there are greater problems facing the station than mere political squabbles—mainly the threatening "Shadow" race which seems bent on destroying the fragile peace. Sinclair, Minbari Ambassador Delenn (played by Mira Furlan), and their allies must prepare for the coming conflict while attempting to deflect forces in Earth's government which would turn the station into a partisan, dictatorial state. The eventual defeat of the Shadows in season four does not

resolve all problems, for Sheridan and Delenn have enemies in their home governments that seek to destroy them. *TV Guide* contributor Bruce Newman noted that what makes "*Babylon 5* . . . not only always something, but something truly unique, is the obsessive attention to detail of series creator J. Michael Straczynski." Part of this attention to detail led Straczynski to pen every episode in the third and fourth season of the show—making him the first person to ever write a full season of an hour-long drama series. The effort is one he is not keen to duplicate. "It's kind of like trying to tap dance while they're throwing a chain saw at you," Straczynski told Newman.

As the series progressed, its fan base grew ever larger and more vocal. Hundreds of websites devoted to *Babylon 5* and its stars sprang up on the Internet, and discussions of the show's merits appeared in various television and science fiction forums. Straczynski made appearances at fan conventions, and the *Babylon 5* universe branched out into novels, comics, and merchandise. After the fourth season, the series was picked up by cable network Turner Network Television, ensuring that fans would see the completion of the five-year saga. Several two-hour movies also appeared, one of which, *A Call to Arms,* set up the story for a spinoff series, *Crusade.* When asked what it was about *Babylon 5* that inspired such devotion, the author replied in the 1996 Compuserve Forum Conference: "What I think it comes down to is passion. I feel strongly about the stories I'm telling, the actors feel strongly about their characters, and in the episodes the tales are rendered with emotion, and passion, and weight, and that's all too rare on most American TV. I try desperately to make the audience *feel* something, to construct something that echoes myth and the sagas we grew up on in SF . . . to reinterpret myths for contemporary times, and point to our past and our future simultaneously," he further explained. "B[abylon]5 is *history*, a history of the future, and it speaks with the voice of our ancestors and our inheritors simultaneously, and that's a very powerful voice."

Babylon 5 proved there was a place on television for complex, intelligent science fiction and that viewers would accept a series set outside of the *Star Trek* universe. It pioneered the use of computer-generated images—it was the first to rely completely on them for its special effects—and

If you enjoy the works of J. Michael Straczynski, you may also want to check out the following films:

Star Trek: First Contact, starring Patrick Stewart, 1996.
Star Trek 2: The Wrath of Khan, starring William Shatner and Ricardo Montalban, 1982.
Star Wars, directed by George Lucas, 1977.

earned Emmys for both visual effects and makeup. With its relatively low budget and long-range story arcs, the show provided a new template for science fiction series television to follow. As for Straczynski, although the original series has now ended, he fully intends to remain involved in the creation of spinoff books, comics, and television series related to the *Babylon 5* universe. There have even been discussions about the possibility of a feature film. Straczynski has also spoken of returning to novel-length fiction in the future, for he still has more stories he would like to tell. It is for his stories he would like to be remembered, as he told a 1996 Compuserve Forum Conference: "He told a good story. He entertained us and made us think. He tried never to hurt anybody. And he never started a fight . . . but he always finished it."

■ Works Cited

Bryant, Edward, review of *OtherSyde, Locus,* July, 1990, pp. 17, 19, 21, 57.
Review of *Demon Night, Publishers Weekly,* June 3, 1988, p. 67.
Review of *Demon Night, Science Fiction Chronicle,* April, 1989, pp. 39-40.
Newman, Bruce, "Babylon Believers," *TV Guide,* July 27, 1996, pp. 36-39.
O'Connor, John J., "Beaming Up New Science-Fiction," *New York Times,* February 22, 1993, p. 16.
Review of *OtherSyde, Publishers Weekly,* June 15, 1990, p. 55.
Rogers, Adam, "Master and Slave of 'Babylon 5,'" *Newsweek,* June 9, 1997, p. 63.
Straczynski, J. Michael, interview in *Contemporary Authors,* Volume 109, Gale, 1983, pp. 457-58.
Straczynski, J. Michael, comments posted to Compuserve Forum, April 9, 1993.
Straczynski, J. Michael, comments in Compuserve Convention Center formal conference, December 2, 1995.
Straczynski, J. Michael, comments in Compuserve Convention Center formal conference, April 6, 1996.
Straczynski, J. Michael, comments in Compuserve Babylon 5 Forum formal conference, January 31, 1998.
Tucker, Ken, review of *Babylon 5* (pilot), *Entertainment Weekly,* February 19, 1993, p. 52.
Westfahl, Gary, "J. Michael Straczynski," *St. James Guide to Horror, Ghost and Gothic Writers,* St. James Press, 1998, pp. 575-76.

■ For More Information See

BOOKS

Bassom, David, *The A-Z Guide to Babylon 5,* Dell, 1997.
Bassom, David, and J. Michael Straczynski, *Creating Babylon 5: Behind the Scenes of Warner Bros. Revolutionary Deep Space Drama,* Del Rey, 1997.
Lane, Andy, *The Babylon File: The Definitive Unauthorized Guide to J. Michael Straczynski's TV Series Babylon 5,* London Bridge, 1997, Volume 2, Virgin Publications, 1999.
Parliament of Dreams: Conferring on Babylon 5, edited by Edward James and Farah Mendelsohn, The Science Fiction Foundation, 1998.

ON-LINE

The official *Babylon 5* website is located at http://www.babylon5.com.
Of the scores of unofficial websites, one of the most thorough is "The Lurker's Guide to *Babylon 5,*" at http://www.midwinter.com/lurk.
Compuserve users can access a *Babylon 5* forum with transcripts of Straczynski's Compuserve postings and conferences by typing GO BABYLON5.

PERIODICALS

Booklist, July, 1990, p. 2074.
Entertainment Weekly, January 28, 1994, p. 40.
New York, January 5, 1998, p. 56.
TV Guide, November 5, 1994, p. 32.
Variety, January 24, 1994, p. 69.

—Sketch by Diane Telgen

Erika Tamar

tor for *Search for Tomorrow* television serial. Play Troupe of Port Washington, Long Island (community theater), actress and director. *Member:* Authors Guild, PEN, Society of Children's Book Writers and Illustrators.

■ Personal

Accent is on last syllable of surname; born June 10, in Vienna, Austria; came to the United States as a child; daughter of Julius (a physician) and Pauline (a homemaker; maiden name, Huterer) Tamar; divorced; children: Ray, Monica, Michael. *Education:* New York University—Washington Square College, B.A.; Stanford University, TV/Film Institute graduate. *Politics:* "Sometimes Democrat, mostly independent." *Religion:* Jewish. *Hobbies and other interests:* Visual and performing arts, especially jazz and photography; taking painting classes; volunteering at the Metropolitan Museum of Art.

■ Addresses

Home—399 East 72nd St., New York, NY 10021.

■ Career

Freelance writer, 1982—. Leo Burnett Co., Inc., New York, NY, production assistant/casting direc-

■ Awards, Honors

Books for the Teen Age list, New York Public Library, 1983, for *Blues for Silk Garcia*, 1984, for *Goodbye, Glamour Girl*, and c. 1994, for *The Things I Did Last Summer;* Young Adult Books for Reluctant Readers list, American Library Association (ALA), and IRA Young Adult's Choice, both 1990, for *It Happened at Cecilia's;* IRA Young Adult's Choice, 1991, for *High Cheekbones;* Best Book for Young Adults, ALA, Books for the Teen Age list, New York Public Library, both 1993, Nevada Young Readers' Award nominee, 1997, and Garden State Master list, all for *Fair Game;* California Young Readers' Medal winner, Intermediate List, 1998, and South Carolina Children's Book Award nominee, 1997-98, third place, Sequoyah Children's Book Award, Oklahoma Library Association, 1998, Rebecca Caudill Young Readers' Award master list, and Bank Street College Children's Books of the Year citiation, all for *The Junkyard Dog;* Child Study's Children's Books of the Year citation, and commended title, Consortium of Latin American Studies Programs (CLASP), both for *Alphabet City Ballet;* Golden Kite Award nomination, Society of Children's Book Writers and Illustrators, Notable

Trade Book in the Field of Social Studies citation, National Council of Social Studies-Children's Book Center, and CLASP commended title citation, all for *The Garden of Happiness*.

■ Writings

YOUNG ADULT NOVELS

Blues for Silk Garcia, Crown, 1983.
Good-bye, Glamour Girl, Lippincott, 1984.
It Happened at Cecilia's, Atheneum, 1989.
High Cheekbones, Viking, 1990.
Out of Control, Atheneum, 1991.
The Truth about Kim O'Hara, Atheneum, 1992.
Fair Game, Harcourt Brace, 1993.
The Things I Did Last Summer, Harcourt Brace, 1994.

MIDDLE GRADE NOVELS

Soccer Mania!, Random House, 1993.
The Junkyard Dog, Knopf, 1995.
Alphabet City Ballet, HarperCollins, 1996.

PICTURE BOOKS

The Garden of Happiness, illustrated by Barbara Lambase, Harcourt Brace, 1996.
Donnatalee, illustrated by Lambase, Harcourt Brace, 1998.

Tamar has also contributed articles and fiction to *DC Health* and *Cosmopolitan*, and had a fashion/beauty column for *Elite*, 1988-89.

■ Work in Progress

The Long Way Home, a mid-grade novel for Knopf; an adult suspense novel.

■ Sidelights

A teenage girl seeks the truth about her long-absent father; local athletes gang-rape a mentally handicapped girl and the town is eager to cover up the crime; a Jewish refugee from Nazi Europe wants to leave her heritage behind in her new land; a young girl learns there are hidden costs to becoming a model; a summer romance with an older woman teaches a teenage boy hard lessons about the difference between physical and emotional love. These are just some of the incidents that inform the young adult novels of Erika Tamar, whose books for young adults explore, as she once noted, "the unexpected truth that lies under the perceived image of a person, as well as the many contradictory perceptions people have of the same event."

In titles such as *Blues for Silk Garcia*, *Good-bye, Glamour Girl*, *High Cheekbones*, *Out of Control*, *Fair Game*, and *The Things I Did Last Summer*, Tamar delves into the world of young adults with a "fine eye for urban adolescent *angst*," as *Kirkus Reviews* noted in its review of *It Happened at Cecilia's*. Tamar has created a memorable male protagonist, Andy Szabo, whom she follows through three linked novels, *It Happened at Cecilia's*, *The Truth about Kim O'Hara*, and *The Things I Did Last Summer*. Additionally, Tamar has also written novels for younger readers, including *Soccer Mania!* and the award-winning *The Junkyard Dog*, as well as the picture books *The Garden of Happiness* and *Donnatalee*.

"I loved reading as long as I can remember," Tamar once commented, "and I've always liked telling a story. I think I always wanted to be a writer." Born in Vienna, Austria, Tamar came to the United States at the age of four as a refugee from the Nazis. She and her older brother lived with a foster family in Houston, Texas, for several months until her parents were able to join them. Thereafter the family settled in New York City where her father was a physician. "I was young enough to pick up English very easily," Tamar recalled, "yet old enough to be conscious of learning another language; perhaps that contributed to my awareness of words and their nuances of meaning."

Tamar attended New York University where she majored in English with an emphasis on creative writing. However, a class in screenwriting led her to other classes in film production, and by the time of her graduation she wanted to direct television or film, "another way of telling a story." Out of college, Tamar discovered that this new dream of directing "was probably . . . rather unrealistic . . . in that pre-feminist era." Instead, she became for five years a production assistant and casting director for a live television serial, *Search for Tomorrow*. Marriage and children soon followed; with the birth of her first child, the family moved to Port Washington on Long Island. "I was a full-time mom," she once related, "and satisfied my creative urge by getting involved with community theater. I didn't concentrate seriously on writing for many years; the necessary solitude of writing clashed with my rather gregarious and extroverted personality and it took some maturity to muster the self-discipline. It was the young adult novels that my children brought home that spurred me—the 'I can do that' syndrome." A writing workshop at the New School with Margaret Gabel was very helpful. Her work with television and film gave her a keen visual sense. "I still find that my ideas for books start with visual images," she once stated. And her work with community theater instilled the idea of character creation in her. "I see a strong correlation between acting and writing—the ability to slip into character is what I rely on when I'm working on a book." Soon Tamar had completed a novel in class, and submitting it to Crown, she was amazed when this first publisher took the book. "I was hooked!" Tamar recalled.

Semi-autobiographical Debut

That first novel, *Blues for Silk Garcia*, not surprisingly, included large doses of personal experience. Set in a facsimile of Port Washington, the book also dealt with jazz, a favorite musical form of Tamar's. Her daughter's virtuosity with classical guitar was also built into the story, and even a parakeet the family had at the time makes appearances in the novel. As Tamar once commented, "My experiences and feelings, people I've known, things that move me or make me laugh, go into my novels in big fictionalized chunks—and that's what makes writing so much fun."

The novel's protagonist, Linda Ann Garcia, fifteen, resembles her long-absent father, down to her talent for music. Now she hears that Silk Garcia, the noted guitarist, is dead at thirty-eight. Her mother refuses to talk of the man who abandoned them, and Linda's search for truth takes her into the world of nightclub musicians, where she slowly pieces together new levels of truth about her dad. Tamar's first novel was well received. *Booklist's* Ilene Cooper observed that Tamar skillfully combines Linda's quest for her father with her first romance and thereby provides readers a "full-blown, memorable heroine capable of growth and change," concluding that "in every respect [the

Tamar's 1993 young adult novel about gang rape is based on a true story.

book is] a well-crafted first novel." Christy Tyson, writing in *Voice of Youth Advocates*, noted that "this is a carefully-developed coming-of-age story enriched by a credible rock/jazz background," while *School Library Journal* contributor Linda Wicher felt that *Blues for Silk Garcia* "will be popular with young adults and is an admirable book for a first novel." Chosen as one of the New York Public Library's "Books for the Teen Age," Tamar's first novel was on all accounts successful and encouraged her on to further writing.

With her second novel, Tamar mined her own life more closely, going back to her first years in America when she herself became assimilated via

If you enjoy the works of Erika Tamar, you may also want to check out the following books and films:

Norma Fox Mazer, *Out of Control*, 1993.
Anna Quindlen, *Object Lessons*, 1991.
The Accused, a film starring Jodie Foster, 1988.

the movies. Liesl is a Jewish refugee from Nazi-occupied Vienna in *Good-bye, Glamour Girl*. She is determined to leave her Central European heritage behind and transform herself into an all-American glamour queen just like her movie idol, Rita Hayworth. When not busy reading movie magazines, Liesl joins her new boyfriend, the reckless Billy Laramie, in adventures. When Billy finally asks her to run away with him, Liesl is confronted with the final decision of choosing between her dreams and reality. *Kirkus Reviews* noted that "Tamar provides wry, touch-true details of Austrian refugee life" and "also gives a full-blown portrait of the movie-star cult." Sandra Dayton, writing in *Voice of Youth Advocates*, observed that "The reader . . . should be inspired by Liesl's consistently positive outlook and hope for a brighter tomorrow," while *Bulletin of the Center for Children's Books* wrote that in Tamar's description of friendship changing to love and the bitter-sad parting from Billy, "Liesl gives up the self-dramatization which has been a major theme throughout her adolescence." *Publishers Weekly* summed up its positive review of the book by stating that Tamar "seems to write out of total recall for an era she brings to life in a vibrant novel."

The Tales of Andy Szabo

For her third YA novel, Tamar employed stories her own children had regaled her with when working in restaurants to help put themselves through college, and also introduced Andy Szabo, the male protagonist whom she employed in two further titles. "The story concerns the ups and downs of a Cajun-Hungarian restaurant," Tamar recalled. The book was also set in New York's Greenwich Village, a locale dear to Tamar since her own college days at NYU. In *It Happened at Cecilia's*, Andy is fourteen, sensitive, a secret writer, and the son of the Hungarian half of the Cecilia's,

a Greenwich Village restaurant. His mother is dead and soon a customer, the dancer Lorraine, becomes interested in his father. Marriage plans are announced and Andy fears displacement. Meanwhile, the restaurant has become ultra-popular after a review, so much so that the Mafia begins to show interest in it. Andy and Lorraine are forced to team up to protect the man they both love, creating the "beginnings of a warm family relationship," according to Cindy Darling Codell in *School Library Journal*. Codell also noted "the well-constructed dialogue, the absolutely hilarious restaurant antics, and the believ-

Seventeen-year-old Andy thinks he has found true love one summer when he meets an au pair who introduces him to his first sexual experience, until Andy later finds out that she is married.

able portrayal of a family restructuring itself" which all contribute to making this "an entertaining book." Shirley Carmony, writing in *Voice of Youth Advocates*, felt that this was a book with a male protagonist that "will appeal to a great many junior high age students," while Zena Sutherland observed in *Bulletin of the Center for Children's Books* that the "characters are distinctive . . . and the fairly happy ending is not made pat and incredible by having everything sugar-iced." *Kirkus Reviews* concluded its review by noting that the "promised sequel will be welcome."

In fact, two sequels followed: *The Truth about Kim O'Hara* and *The Things I Did Last Summer*. Andy is fifteen in *The Truth about Kim O'Hara*, and in love with the girl of the title, a Vietnamese-born beauty. The only problem is that Kim keeps him at arm's length sexually, and soon Andy begins to suspect there is more to her reticence than shyness; that perhaps there are secrets she has brought with her from Vietnam that have her in their grip. *Booklist*'s Susan DeRonne noted that through the many incidents of the book Andy learns that "the essence of a deep relationship is not just sex, but friendship." DeRonne concluded that the story "is compelling reading with a multicultural twist." *The Things I Did Last Summer* is "a poignant story of a boy's first love," according to Larry Condit in *Voice of Youth Advocates*. Andy is seventeen now and spending the summer with his pregnant stepmother on Bay Island. The first day on the beach he meets a beautiful *au pair* who works for the wealthy Carlyles and is smitten. If he's not with the woman, Susan, he is working part-time as a journalist for the local paper. The older Susan initiates Andy to sex and soon he has dreams of the two of them sharing a life together. Such dreams are smashed, however, when Andy learns the truth about Susan—that she is actually Mrs. Carlyle.

Marilyn Makowski observed in *School Library Journal* that "in the end [Andy] is wiser and headed for a better future," while Deborah Stevenson concluded in *Bulletin of the Center for Children's Books* that the novel is "a well-written, absorbing story about first love and disillusionment." *Kirkus Reviews* summed up much critical opinion by stating that "Tamar (who has never written better) probes deeply into the emotions that make first love so wonderful and so terrible. A book that should win a wide readership among mature YAs."

Tamar also took a look at the perils of modeling in the award-winning *High Cheekbones*, and at the lives of members of a teen rock band in *Out of Control*, a book *Publishers Weekly* dubbed "Rashomon-like" for its narrative diversity. One of Tamar's hardest-hitting YA novels, however, is *Fair Game*, the story of the gang-rape of a mentally handicapped girl by the athletes from a small-town baseball team. Patterned after true events, *Fair Game* is set on Long Island and is told from several points of view: Cara, the retarded girl; Laura Jean, the girlfriend of one of the athletes involved in the rape and who initially is out to protect her man; and Julio "Joe" Lopez, an athlete who refuses to take part in the rape, but does nothing to stop it, either. Cara is a five-year-old in an attractive teen body who wants only to fit in. She will do anything to please, and one day a group of all-American boys have her do it all, even assaulting her with a bottle and broom handle. At first the incident is covered-up, but soon the media get hold of the story, and it will not go away. Laura Jean thinks Cara is a "slut" and that it was all her fault that the boys did what they did, until she interviews Cara, trying to trick her into clearing the boys. Instead, she comes face to face with the truth and finally understands the brutality of what was done to Cara.

Publishers Weekly thought the book was "Meticulously rendered and narrated in speedy, staccato language," and that it was a "must-read for any teen who has considered the implications of foul play." *Kirkus Reviews* decided the book was "well wrought and compelling" and Stevenson, in *Bulletin of the Center for Children's Books*, concluded that "this is a challenging book dealing with the interconnection of many complicated issues (racism, sexism, violence)—a book that could provoke some heated discussions."

It is no coincidence that recent Tamar titles deal with the inner city, for she moved from Long Island and now makes her home in the city. "I live in Manhattan again and I enjoy the restaurants, theater, art galleries, films, walking everywhere and observing the street life," Tamar once noted. "I often meet with other writers for critique, shop talk, or just delicious gossip. I work out and swim regularly, a necessary antidote to being crunched over my computer. Sometimes it's really hard to spend long hours at my desk, yet my greatest interest, still and always, is writing."

■ Works Cited

Review of *Alphabet City Ballet, Publishers Weekly,* November 11, 1996, p. 76.

Carmony, Shirley, review of *It Happened at Cecilia's, Voice of Youth Advocates,* June, 1989, p. 108.

Codell, Cindy Darling, review of *It Happened at Cecilia's, School Library Journal,* March, 1989, p. 202.

Condit, Larry, review of *The Things I Did Last Summer, Voice of Youth Advocates,* June, 1994, p. 94.

Cooper, Ilene, review of *Blues for Silk Garcia, Booklist,* August, 1983, pp. 1468-69.

Dayton, Sandra, review of *Good-bye, Glamour Girl, Voice of Youth Advocates,* April, 1985, p. 52.

DeRonne, Susan, review of *The Truth about Kim O'Hara, Booklist,* December 1, 1992, pp. 659, 662.

Review of *Fair Game, Kirkus Reviews,* September 15, 1993.

Review of *Fair Game, Publishers Weekly,* October 25, 1993, p. 65.

Review of *The Garden of Happiness, Kirkus Reviews,* April 1, 1996, pp. 537-38.

Golodetz, Virginia, review of *The Junkyard Dog, School Library Journal,* June, 1995, pp. 114-15.

Review of *Good-bye, Glamour Girl, Bulletin of the Center for Children's Books,* December, 1984, p. 75.

Review of *Good-bye, Glamour Girl, Kirkus Reviews,* November 1, 1984, p. J-108.

Review of *Good-bye, Glamour Girl, Publishers Weekly,* October 12, 1984, p. 51.

Review of *It Happened at Cecilia's, Kirkus Reviews,* April 15, 1989, p. 631.

Review of *The Junkyard Dog, Kirkus Reviews,* June 15, 1995, p. 864.

Makowski, Marilyn, review of *The Things I Did Last Summer, School Library Journal,* April, 1994, p. 155.

Review of *Out of Control, Publishers Weekly,* October 4, 1991, p. 89.

Stevenson, Deborah, review of *Fair Game, Bulletin of the Center for Children's Books,* November, 1993, p. 103.

Stevenson, Deborah, review of *The Things I Did Last Summer, Bulletin of the Center for Children's Books,* April, 1994, p. 271.

Sutherland, Zena, review of *It Happened at Cecilia's, Bulletin of the Center for Children's Books,* March, 1989, p. 183.

Review of *The Things I Did Last Summer, Kirkus Reviews,* June 15, 1994, p. 852.

Tyson, Christy, review of *Blues for Silk Garcia, Voice of Youth Advocates,* October, 1983, p. 209.

Wicher, Linda, review of *Blues for Silk Garcia, School Library Journal,* May, 1983, p. 86.

■ For More Information See

PERIODICALS

Booklist, February 1, 1990, pp. 1079-80; September 15, 1991, pp. 142-43; November 15, 1993, p. 614; May 1, 1995, pp. 1575-76.

Bulletin of the Center for Children's Books, September, 1995, p. 31; January, 1997, p. 187.

Horn Book, May, 1994, pp. 358-61.

Kirkus Reviews, September 1, 1996, p. 1329.

Publishers Weekly, May 6, 1996, p. 80.

School Library Journal, August, 1990, p. 165; July, 1998, p. 84.

Voice of Youth Advocates, February, 1993, pp. 342-43; December, 1993, pp. 302-3.*

—Sketch by J. Sydney Jones

Cynthia Voigt

English teacher, 1968-69, department chair, 1971-79, part-time teacher and department chair, 1981-88; author of books for young readers, 1981—.

■ Awards, Honors

Notable Children's Trade Book in the field of social studies, National Council for Social Studies/Children's Book Council, and American Book Award nominee, both 1981, for *Homecoming;* American Library Association (ALA) Best Young Adult Books citation, 1982, for *Tell Me If the Lovers Are Losers;* ALA Best Children's Books citation, 1982, and Newbery Medal, ALA, 1983, both for *Dicey's Song;* ALA Best Young Adult Books citation, 1983, and Newbery Honor book, ALA, 1984, both for *A Solitary Blue;* Edgar Allan Poe Award for best juvenile mystery, Mystery Writers of America, 1984, for *The Callender Papers;* Silver Pencil Award (Dutch), 1988, and Deutscher Jugend Literatur Preis, 1989, both for *The Runner;* Alan Award for achievement in young adult literature, 1989; California Young Reader's Award, 1990, for *Izzy, Willy-Nilly.*

■ Writings

"TILLERMAN FAMILY" BOOKS

Homecoming, Atheneum, 1981.
Dicey's Song, Atheneum, 1982.
A Solitary Blue, Atheneum, 1983.

■ Personal

Born February 25, 1942, in Boston, MA; daughter of Frederick C. (a corporate executive) and Elise (Keeney) Irving; married first husband September, 1964 (divorced, 1972); married Walter Voigt (a teacher), August 30, 1974; children: Jessica, Peter. *Education:* Smith College, B.A., 1963. *Politics:* Independent. *Hobbies and other interests:* "Reading, eating well (especially with friends), tennis, movies, hanging around with our children, and considering the weather."

■ Addresses

Home—Deer Isle, ME. *Agent*—Merrilee Heifetz, Writers House, Inc., 21 West 26th St., New York, NY 10010.

■ Career

J. Walter Thompson Advertising Agency, secretary, 1964; high school English teacher in Glen Burnie, MD, 1965-67; The Key School, Annapolis, MD,

The Runner, Atheneum, 1985.
Come a Stranger, Atheneum, 1986.
Sons from Afar, Macmillan, 1987.
Seventeen against the Dealer, Macmillan, 1989.

JUVENILE FICTION

Tell Me If the Lovers Are Losers, Atheneum, 1982.
The Callender Papers, Atheneum, 1983.
Building Blocks, Atheneum, 1984.
Jackaroo, Atheneum, 1985.
Izzy, Willy-Nilly, Atheneum, 1986.
Tree by Leaf, Macmillan, 1988.
On Fortune's Wheel, Macmillan, 1990.
The Vandemark Mummy, Atheneum, 1991.
David and Jonathan, Scholastic, 1992.
Orfe, Macmillan, 1993.
The Wings of a Falcon, Scholastic, 1993.
When She Hollers, Scholastic, 1994.
The Bad Girls, Scholastic, 1996.
Bad, Badder, Baddest, Scholastic, 1997.

OTHER

Stories about Rosie (picture book), Macmillan, 1986.
Glass Mountain (adult fiction), Harcourt, 1991.

Also compiler of stories and poems, with David Bergman, for *Shore Writers' Sampler II,* Friendly Harbor Press, 1988.

■ Sidelights

Cynthia Voigt is an accomplished storyteller noted for her well-developed characters, interesting plots, and authentic atmosphere. In her novels for children and young adults, she examines such serious topics as child abandonment, verbal abuse, racism, and coping with amputation. Reviewers have praised Voigt's fluent and skillfully executed writing style, compelling topics, and vividly detailed descriptions. Critics also have described Voigt's themes as universal and meaningful to young adults, particularly noting her expertise in fashioning convincing characters and rich relationships in which both adults and children grow in understanding. In a *Twentieth-Century Children's Writers* essay, Sylvia Patterson Iskander described the qualities that have made Voigt's writings appealing to readers: "Voigt's understanding of narrative techniques, power to create memorable

characters, admirable but not goody-goody, knowledge of the problems of youth, and desire to teach by transporting readers into the characters' inner lives result in reversing unpromising, perhaps tragic, situations to positive, optimistic ones."

Voigt was born in Boston, Massachusetts, the second of her parents' five children. Most of her childhood was spent in small-town southern Connecticut. "I actually remember very little of my childhood," Voigt once stated. "I am not certain what to make of that," she also commented. "We were not neglected children." It was in this atmosphere that Voigt began to develop an interest in books. She recalled: "My grandmother lived in northern Connecticut, in a house three stories high; its corridors lined with bookcases."

Voigt noted that she had already become an avid reader, with books such as *"Nancy Drew, Cherry Ames, The Black Stallion,* and the Terhune book[s]," when one day at her grandmother's house she "pulled *The Secret Garden* off one of her shelves and read it. This was the first book I found entirely for myself, and I cherished it. There weren't any so-called 'young adult' books when I was growing up. If you were a good reader, once you hit fourth grade, things got a little thin. I started to read adult books, with my mother making sure what I had chosen was not 'too adult.' I read Tolstoy, Shakespeare, Camus, and many classics, except for *Moby Dick,* which I finally read in college. It knocked me out. I came to Dickens and Trollope later in life."

By the time Voigt began high school, she had set her sights on a career as a writer. She began writing short stories and poetry, and upon entering Smith College, a women's college in Massachusetts, she enrolled in creative writing courses. Her work, however, received little encouragement from her teachers. "Clearly what I was submitting didn't catch anyone's eye," she once remarked. "I never had a bad teacher like my character, Mr. Chappelle in *A Solitary Blue.*" On the other hand, she did find that some of her teachers at Smith "resented teaching women, feeling themselves too good for the position. We had very little patience with that attitude."

Following graduation from Smith College, Voigt moved to New York City where she worked for the J. Walter Thompson Advertising Agency. "I married in 1964 and moved with my first husband to Santa Fe, New Mexico," she recalled. "I was to work as a secretary to help support us while he was in school. But even with my New York experience it was difficult to find a job. I drifted into the Department of Education one day and asked what I would have to do to qualify myself to teach school. They learned that I'd attended Smith College and signed me up for accrediting courses at a Christian Brothers college. Within six months I met the terms of certification. I vowed I would never teach when I left Smith, and yet, the minute I walked into a classroom, I loved it."

In this award-winning continuation of *Homecoming,* from the "Tillerman Cycle" of novels, thirteen-year-old Dicey Tillerman tries to raise her siblings in her grandmother's house.

By the time of her divorce from her first husband, Voigt had settled in Annapolis, Maryland. "I had been writing throughout college, but during most of my first marriage, I didn't write much at all," Voigt once commented. Voigt had worked at the high school in Glen Burnie, Maryland. She then was hired by The Key School in Annapolis: "I was assigned to teach English in second, fifth and seventh grades. The second graders were a kick and a half. I assigned book reports to my fifth graders. I would go to the library and starting with the letter 'A' peruse books at the fifth, sixth, and seventh-grade age level. If a book looked interesting, I checked it out. I once went home with thirty books! It was then that I realized one could tell stories which had the shape of real books— novels—for kids the age of my students. I began to get ideas for young adult novels and juvenile books. That first year of teaching and *reading* really paid off in spades! I felt I had suddenly discovered and was exploring a new country."

Tillerman Family Stories Earn Honors

In 1974, the author married Walter Voigt, a teacher of Latin and Greek at The Key School. "I was teaching full time, but was able to continue the writing I'd begun while I was living alone by sticking to my regime of one hour a day," the author recalled. When Voigt became pregnant, she switched to teaching part-time and dedicated more of her time to writing. "The summer I was pregnant I wrote the first draft of *The Callender Papers.* When my son, Peter, was an infant, I took him to school and taught with him in a 'Snuggli.' When he was a year old, I wrote *Tell Me If the Lovers Are Losers,* and the next year (he was in a playpen in the faculty lounge next to my classroom), I began *Homecoming.*

"One day while I was writing *Tell Me If the Lovers Are Losers,* I went to the market and saw a car full of kids left to wait alone in the parking lot. As the electric supermarket doors whooshed open, I asked myself 'What would happen if nobody ever came back for those kids?' I made some jottings in my notebook, and let them 'stew' for a year, the way most of my ideas do. When I sat down to write the story that grew from my question (and this is typical of my process) I made a list of character names. Then I tried them on to see if they fit. I knew Dicey was the main character, but was not sure precisely *who* she was.

If you enjoy the works of Cynthia Voigt, you may also want to check out the following books:

Sue Ellen Bridgers, *Notes for Another Life,* 1981.
Patricia Calvert, *When Morning Comes,* 1989.
Cynthia D. Grant, *Uncle Vampire,* 1993.
Colby Rodowsky, *Julie's Daughter,* 1985.

The more I wrote about her, the more real she became to me. I'd planned a book about half the size of *Homecoming.* But a few chapters into the novel, the grandmother became central and I began to see that there was a lot more going on than would fit in one book." *Homecoming* became Voigt's first published novel, appearing 1981.

With *Homecoming,* the author begins the saga of the Tillermans, four fatherless children aged six through thirteen who are abandoned in a shopping mall parking lot by their mentally ill mother. Dicey, the eldest, takes it upon herself to care for all four, and they eventually move to their grandmother's home in distant Maryland. "The plot is well developed, fast paced, with some suspense. The book deals with the pain of losses—death, separation, poverty—but also with responsibility, friends, wisdom, happiness, survival," wrote *Christian Science Monitor* critic Joanna Shaw-Eagle. Although many critics questioned whether the length of the work and its often-negative portrayal of adults made it inappropriate for young adult readers, Kathleen Leverich of the *New York Times Book Review* took these elements into consideration when she concluded that "the accomplishments of this feisty band of complex and . . . sympathetically conceived kids makes for an enthralling journey to a gratifying end."

Dicey's Song continues the Tillermans' story, concentrating on young Dicey's emerging understanding of her new life in her grandmother's house in Maryland and her relationships with her siblings and grandmother. Even better received than *Homecoming, Dicey's Song* was praised for its cohesive plot and the depth of its characterizations, particularly of Dicey and her eccentric grandmother. In her review in *Bulletin of the Center for Children's Books,* Zena Sutherland called *Dicey's Song* "a rich and perceptive book." In 1983, Voigt

was awarded with the prestigious Newbery Medal for *Dicey's Song.* In *A Solitary Blue,* Voigt centers on Jeff, a friend of Dicey's introduced in the earlier Tillerman novels, whose mother abandons him to the care of his remote father while she goes off to help needy children. The story depicts the evolution of Jeff's understanding of his parents and of himself. According to Gloria P. Rohmann in her review in *School Library Journal,* the book "ultimately disappoints"; but other critics, while noting flaws, praised the depiction of the relationship between Jeff and his father. Jane Langton in her critique in the *New York Times Book Review* called *A Solitary Blue* "beautifully written," comparing it to Charles Dickens's *Bleak House. A Solitary Blue* was named a Newbery Honor book in 1984.

The Runner is another spin-off from the Tillerman novels, this time set a generation before the others and centered on Samuel "Bullet" Tillerman, whose obsession is long-distance running and whose torment is his autocratic father. The plot turns on Bullet's prejudice against black people, which is eventually softened by his association with Tamer Shipp, a black runner. Although some critics found the plot contrived and the writing overdone, Alice Digilio of *Washington Post Book World* concluded, "Voigt sails *The Runner* through some heavy seas, but always with a steady hand." In *Come a Stranger,* Voigt supplements the Tillerman series with another novel that takes racism as its focus. The plot centers on Mina Smiths, a character first introduced in *Dicey's Song,* whose experience of being the only black girl at ballet camp one summer impels her to try to identify with whites. Tamer Shipp appears as Mina's minister, to whom she goes for guidance. Though some critics faulted the author for stereotyping her black characters, others praised Voigt for the depth of her characterizations and smooth writing style.

Voigt completed her Tillerman series with the books *Sons from Afar* and *Seventeen against the Dealer.* She once commented on the writing process for the Tillerman books: "Bullet's story, which is what *The Runner* is, crossed my mind when I was writing *Homecoming* and put him in there. It had been in the back of my mind for that two- or three-year period. In the meantime I was writing two other Tillerman books, which had come naturally one out of the other. The ideas get in my head, and then there's a time when it's the right time to write them, I hope. And that's when I sit down to do them."

Mystery and Fantasy Fill Juvenile Books

Tell Me If the Lovers Are Losers, Voigt's second published novel, focuses on three female college freshmen who become roommates, then teammates on the same volleyball team, and then friends. While some critics faulted the novel for what *New York Times Book Review* critic Kathleen Leverich called "exaggeration of character and the sacrifice of the theme to improbable theatrics," others, like Sally Estes of *Booklist*, dubbed *Tell Me If the Lovers Are Losers* "both provocative and rewarding for older, more perceptive high school age readers." Voigt's next publication was *The Callender Papers*, a Gothic mystery set in late-nineteenth-century New England. Thirteen-year-old Jean Wainwright agrees to sort through the papers of Irene Callender, who died under mysterious circumstances and whose child then disappeared. Jean eventually finds the answer to the mystery, learning some lessons about life in the process. A number of critics observed that *The Callender Papers* was lighter fare than Voigt usually offers her readers, but most also found the mystery satisfying and well written.

Voigt created another novel for slightly younger adolescents in her 1984 work, *Building Blocks*. In what Zena Sutherland of *Bulletin of the Center for Children's Books* described as "an interesting time-travel story," Voigt depicts a strengthening relationship between a father and son through understanding gained when the son is transported from 1974 to the Depression. There he becomes friends with the 10-year-old boy who will become his father. *Building Blocks* was generally well-received, even by critics who did not admire the science-fiction element in the plot. *New Directions for Women* reviewer Elizabeth Sachs wrote: "Though the transition back in time is awkward, the scenes of Brann with his young boy father are beautiful." Voigt also utilizes magical elements in *Jackaroo*, a book Karen P. Smith described in *School Library Journal* as "an intense and elegantly written historical adventure-romance." Set in a mythical place during the Middle Ages, *Jackaroo* features a strong teenage heroine who takes on the persona of the legendary Jackaroo in order to save her family and community. Mary M. Burns remarked in an article in *Horn Book*: "As in all of

By the Newbery Medal-winning author
CYNTHIA VOIGT
THE RUNNER
SCHOLASTIC

A spinoff of the Tillerman novels, this book features Bullet, a long-distance runner who begins to overcome his racial prejudice when he is forced to train with an African American athlete.

Cynthia Voigt's books, the style is fluid. . .; the setting is evoked through skillfully crafted description; the situations speak directly to the human condition."

In *Izzy, Willy-Nilly*, Voigt depicts the trauma faced by an active teenager whose leg is amputated after a car accident. Through this incident, and with the help of Roseamunde, an awkward girl who embodies all that Izzy did not before her accident, Voigt's protagonist finds resources and wisdom within herself that she might otherwise never have known. Though some critics complained about the book's length and some unrealistic elements in the plot, Patty Campbell of *Wilson Library Bulletin* dubbed *Izzy, Willy-Nilly* the "best young adult novel of the season, and perhaps of the year." Voigt's next book, *Stories about Rosie,* is a departure from the author's earlier works. This picture book features humorous stories about the Voigt family dog from the dog's perspective. While some critics felt that the stories were too long and complex for the picture-book audience, a *Publishers Weekly* reviewer concluded: "*Rosie* is a lightweight, just-right book for dog fans everywhere."

In 1993, Voigt published *Orfe,* a novel which explores the underworld of the music business by following the title character's rock-and-roll career, her friendship with Enny, her manager, and her troubled relationship with Yuri, a recovering drug addict. Critics generally found the novel too dark, and Beverly Youree concluded her review in *Voice of Youth Advocates:* "Readers expecting a story similar to those of the Tillerman novels or her fantasy novels will be disappointed." Voigt's *The Vandemark Mummy* was more warmly received. A mystery for younger adolescents, the plot centers on a brother and sister who go with their father when he is hired as the curator for an Egyptian collection at Vandemark College. When the collection's mummy is stolen and then found in a damaged condition, the sister disappears trying to uncover the thief. A reviewer for *Junior Bookshelf* wrote: "Serious issues are under debate, but the story is exciting and highly entertaining." In *David and Jonathan,* Voigt returns to more weighty matters for the older adolescent with a story that deals with the Holocaust, the Vietnam war, and homosexuality. A *Junior Bookshelf* contributor called *David and Jonathan* "highly serious," adding, "It is equally highly readable."

Voigt continued the story begun in *Jackaroo* with *On Fortune's Wheel,* and then resurrected the setting again in *The Wings of a Falcon,* a novel a *Kirkus Reviews* critic called "grand, thought-provoking entertainment." This work centers on Oriel and his friend Griff, who escape from an island of slavery to travel across unknown lands only to be captured by Wolfers, a destructive band of barbarians, before escaping and settling on a farm in the north. Reviewers noted the book's length and mature themes in their generally positive reviews. In her review in *School Library Journal,* Susan L. Rogers compared Voigt's fantasy trilogy to her Tillerman series: "Each volume stands on its own, but together they create a tapestry more complex, meaningful, and compelling than its individual parts."

Voigt's books have earned her acclaim from readers and critics, for both their thoughtful themes and entertaining prose. While the products of her work have achieved success in the publishing world, Voigt once commented that the actual process of writing also has an important place in her life: "Awards are external, they happen after the real work has been done. They are presents, and while they are intensely satisfying they do not give me the same kind of pleasure as being in the middle of a work that is going well. . . . Writing is something I need to do to keep myself on an even keel. It's kept me quiet; it's kept me off the streets." Voigt's advice to aspiring writers reflects this ethic: "Do it, not for awards, but for the pleasure of writing."

■ Works Cited

Burns, Mary M., review of *Jackaroo, Horn Book,* March-April, 1986, p. 210.

Campbell, Patty, review of *Izzy, Willy-Nilly, Wilson Library Bulletin,* November, 1986, p. 49.

Review of *David and Jonathan, Junior Bookshelf,* February, 1992, p. 38.

Digilio, Alice, "What Makes Bullet Run?," *Washington Post Book World,* July 14, 1985, p. 8.

Estes, Sally, review of *Tell Me If the Lovers Are Losers, Booklist,* March 15, 1982, p. 950.

Iskander, Sylvia Patterson, "Cynthia Voigt," *Twentieth-Century Children's Writers,* 3rd edition, St. James Press, 1989, pp. 1004-5.

Langton, Jane, review of *A Solitary Blue, New York Times Book Review,* November 27, 1983, pp. 34-35.

Leverich, Kathleen, review of *Homecoming, New York Times Book Review,* May 10, 1981, p. 38.

Leverich, Kathleen, review of *Tell Me If the Lovers Are Losers, New York Times Book Review,* May 16, 1982, p. 28.

Rogers, Susan L., review of *The Wings of a Falcon, School Library Journal,* October, 1993, p. 156.

Rohmann, Gloria P., review of *A Solitary Blue, School Library Journal,* September, 1983, pp. 139-40.

Sachs, Elizabeth, review of *Building Blocks, New Directions for Women,* spring, 1986, p. 13.

Shaw-Eagle, Joanna, "Cynthia Voigt: Family Comes First," *Christian Science Monitor,* May 13, 1983.

Smith, Karen P., review of *Jackaroo, School Library Journal,* December, 1985, p. 96.

Review of *Stories about Rosie, Publishers Weekly,* September 26, 1986, p. 82.

Sutherland, Zena, review of *Dicey's Song, Bulletin of the Center for Children's Books,* October, 1982, p. 38.

Sutherland, Zena, review of *Building Blocks, Bulletin of the Center for Children's Books,* April, 1984, p. 158.

Review of *The Vandemark Mummy, Junior Bookshelf,* April, 1993, pp. 79-80.

Review of *The Wings of a Falcon, Kirkus Reviews,* August 1, 1993, p. 1009.

Youree, Beverly, review of *Orfe, Voice of Youth Advocates,* December, 1992, p. 288.

■ For More Information See

BOOKS

Children's Literature Review, Volume 13, Gale, 1987.

PERIODICALS

ALAN Review, spring, 1994, pp. 56-59.

Bulletin of the Center for Children's Books, September, 1993, p. 25.

Horn Book, August, 1993, pp. 410-13.

Kliatt, January, 1993, p. 13.

Publishers Weekly, July 18, 1994, pp. 225-26.

School Library Journal, December, 1992, pp. 133-34.

—*Sketch by Mary Gillis*

Will Weaver

■ Personal

Born January 19, 1950, in Park Rapids, MN; son of Harold Howard (a farmer) and Arlys A. (Swenson) Weaver; married Rosalie Mary Nonnemacher (a teacher), March 2, 1975; children: Caitlin Rose, Owen Harte. *Education:* Attended Saint Cloud State University, 1968-69; University of Minnesota, B.A., 1972; Stanford University, M.A., 1979. *Politics:* Progressive. *Hobbies and other interests:* Mountain hiking, hunting and fishing.

■ Addresses

Home—Bemidji, MN. *Office*—Bemidji State University, 1500 Birchmont Dr., Bemidji, MN 56601. *Agent*—Lazear Agency, 326 South Broadway, Suite 214, Wayzata, MN 55391. *E-mail*—weaverww @vax1.bemidji.msus.edu.

■ Career

Writer and educator. Farmer, Park Rapids, MN, 1977-81; Bemidji State University, Bemidji, MN, part-time writing instructor, 1979-81, associate professor, 1981-90, professor of English, 1990—.

■ Awards, Honors

Minnesota State Arts Board Fellowship for Fiction, 1979, 1983; "Grandfather, Heart of the Fields" was named one of the "Top Ten Stories of 1984," PEN and the Library of Congress; "Dispersal" was named one of the "Top Ten Stories of 1985," PEN and the Library of Congress; Bush Foundation fiction fellow, 1987-88; Friends of American Writers Award, 1989; Minnesota Book Award for Fiction, 1989; Best Books list, American Library Association, and Distinguished Book Award, International Reading Association, both 1996, Best Books for Teens lists in Texas and Iowa, all for *Farm Team.*

■ Writings

Red Earth, White Earth (adult novel), Simon & Schuster, 1986.
A Gravestone Made of Wheat (short stories), Simon & Schuster, 1989.
Striking Out (young adult novel), HarperCollins, 1993.
Farm Team (young adult novel), HarperCollins, 1995.
Hard Ball (young adult novel), HarperCollins, 1998.

Contributor to periodicals, including *Loonfeather, Prairie Schooner, Hartford Courant, San Francisco Chronicle, Kansas City Star, Chicago Tribune, Minneapolis Tribune, Newsday, Northern Literary Quarterly, Milkweed Chronicles, Library Journal, Chapel Hill*

Advocate, and *Minnesota Monthly.* Weaver's short stories for young adults have been collected in several anthologies: "Stealing for Girls," in *Ultimate Sports,* edited by Don Gallo, Delacorte, 1995; "The Photograph," in *No Easy Answers,* edited by Gallo, Delacorte, 1997; and "Bootleg Summer," in *Time Capsule,* edited by Gallo, Delacorte, 1999.

■ Adaptations

Red Earth, White Earth was adapted as a television film, airing on the Columbia Broadcasting System (CBS-TV) in 1989.

■ Work in Progress

Memory Boy, a natural disaster novel for young readers, set in the future; a young adult short story collection.

■ Sidelights

Will Weaver's country is the upper Midwest, the heartland. It's his home and his material; he occupies the terrain in his fiction as naturally as he does in life. Here is Weaver on a prairie thunderstorm witnessed by the protagonist of his adult novel, *Red Earth, White Earth:* "Outside [Guy] stood among the flax and watched the oncoming weather. Now waist-high and blooming blue on the higher swells of the field, the flax's uncertain colors matched the sky. Southwest were the high, shining cumulus cloud towers. . . . From the Northwest came the lower, darker, faster-moving clouds of the cold front. Guy for a half-hour watched the two fronts collide. Their clouds in slow motion churned and tumbled and rolled upward dark and bulbous. Supported now by yellow spider legs of lightning, the two fronts were no longer clouds but great spiders struggling for control of the reservation sky."

It is this sort of textured writing that has earned Weaver praise as "a writer of uncommon natural talent," according to Frank Levering in *Los Angeles Times Book Review,* and as a writer who views "America's heartland with a charitable but candid eye," in the words of Andy Solomon in the *New York Times Book Review.* Weaver turned his ample talents to young adult fiction after a highly successful adult novel and story collection, and the

result is a trio of books built around the central character of Billy Baggs; books containing the same nuance of detail and depth of characterization as his adult fiction. Billy is a farm boy for whom baseball becomes a release, a passion, a metaphor for life's potentials. But Weaver's are not simply baseball books. "They are not play-by-play sports novels," Weaver told *Authors and Artists for Young Adults (AAYA)* in an interview. "The score of the game is not what is important. It is the *human* game that is important."

Red Barn, White House

Raised on a dairy farm near Park Rapids, Minnesota, Weaver knows intimately whereof he writes. "I grew up in the upper Midwest," Weaver told *AAYA,* "on a traditional dairy farm—a red barn with a white house on one-hundred and sixty acres." One of three children, Weaver attended the local country school. "It was the old-fashioned sort with two classes per room, and the teacher would divide her time between the classes. The younger kids started out school in the basement, and then you would work your way up the floors of the building through the various grades." At home, life was simple, but close. "We had what you might call a very plain style of living. A Scandinavian household that focussed on the scriptures and where silence was not a bad thing. My parents did not believe that everything modern was necessarily good. We grew up without a television, and I still credit the growth of my imagination to that."

Farm life could be hard, but it had its advantages. "There was so much independence on the farm. Sure there was work every day of the year, but there was also the kind of freedom for a young kid there that you could not find in town. You could drive at a young age and go fishing and hunting." Without the interruption of television, there was plenty of time for the imagination and for getting outside and doing things. Books came in the form of condensed novels initially. "I remember with real clarity the *Readers Digest* condensed books we used to get. They got me started with reading; they introduced me to the feel of story and march of words."

Part of the legacy of his farm youth, however, was also the feeling of being an outsider. "When I went to school in Park Rapids, I felt as though I was miles behind these other kids in ways. I felt that the town kids were more sophisticated, and they were. Also, the absence of television made me feel even more out of it. But this feeling of being outside is not a bad thing for a writer to have. Of course I had no intention of being a writer back then." A steady 'B' student, Weaver enjoyed being out in nature more than stuck at a desk earning higher grades. In high school one English teacher took an interest in Weaver, encouraging his writing and appreciation of literature. "This altered my direction," Weaver told *AAYA*. "Here was a teacher showing interest in my abilities and it gave me great confidence."

Weaver attended college at both Saint Cloud State University and at the University of Minnesota to earn his bachelor's degree. His was the first generation in his family to attend college, and for Weaver it was a time to process changes, to take a long look at the world and see where he fit.

Growth of a Writer

It was not until after college that Weaver began writing. "I didn't even take a creative writing course in Minnesota," Weaver recalled. "It was just not in my mind. I studied literature, not writing." Upon graduation, Weaver left for California. Like his grandfather before him, Weaver had applied for and been granted a conscientious objector status. Separated by generations, and reacting to different wars, the two Weavers nonetheless responded to the same sort of inner voice. In California Weaver believed he would find more possibilities for alternate service to fulfill his CO status, but in fact there were few to be found. Soon the draft ended as the Vietnam War wound down and Weaver was spared alternate service.

Staying on in California, in and around the Bay Area, Weaver began writing. "I was lonely for the Midwest and started to write about it. The early sketches led to short stories." Soon he was joined in California by his girlfriend from college days and the two were married. On the strength of a couple of short stories, Weaver was admitted to Stanford's prestigious writing program, where once again he felt the consummate outsider. "Here I was, this rube from the Midwest, with a few tattered pages of short stories in my notebooks while other students had stories published in major magazines or were sons or daughters of famous

He needs a hit for the home team

This first novel to feature Billy **Baggs** chronicles his guilt over his brother's death, his internal struggles with a stern father who insists he stay on the farm, and the discovery of his baseball pitching talents.

writers. It was a somewhat traumatic experience at first, but then later I discovered the value of the experience." Weaver and his wife also began careers in California's Silicon Valley. Starting as a technical writer, Weaver soon became manager of a high-tech company. "We were on our way, but neither I nor my wife really wanted that life. We both missed the Midwest and finally decided to move back to Minnesota."

At first settling in Minneapolis-St. Paul, the couple soon migrated farther north. In 1976, Weaver took over the running of his father's dairy farm, but quickly learned that such a routine could be more draining than expected. "There's an old joke about two farmers," Weaver told *AAYA*. "One says to the other, 'What would you do if you had a million dollars?', and the other one answers, 'Farm until it's all gone.' That was sort of our experience on the farm, plus there was very little time or energy to continue with my writing." The Weavers spent two years on the farm, and during this time Weaver also began teaching at a nearby college, Bemidji State University. Eventually the teaching and writing won out over farming, and Weaver began fashioning his short stories into a much larger work, the novel *Red Earth, White Earth.*

Recording a Disappearing Lifestyle

Weaver spent two years on his first novel, a tale of the return of a prodigal son to the Minnesota of his youth. Like Weaver, this fictional protagonist also returns from Silicon Valley, and once back in the Midwest must confront unrest between Native Americans and local farmers. *Red Earth, White Earth* earned critical praise and became a television movie three years after its publication. Suddenly Weaver was a literary figure, a Midwestern voice. His collection of short stories, *A Gravestone Made of Wheat,* confirmed the promise of his first novel. "I began to see that I wanted to capture with my writing some of the small-farm texture that is so rapidly disappearing," Weaver told *AAYA*. "I want to record that in a texture of aesthetic realism."

Weaver set to work on another long realistic novel about the Midwest but part way through suddenly made a discovery. "My children were in middle school at the time," he told *AAYA*. "They were full of stories from school and about their friends, and there I was hiding out in my study, struggling with my novel. I was trying to balance a tenure faculty position, writing, and being a good father. Listening to my kids talking about middle school, I was reminded of my own youth. I suddenly thought that I would write books my kids might enjoy reading. I'd go with the grain of my family life. Besides, there are certainly affinities for YA in my adult work, large parts of them that younger readers could enjoy as well."

Such a decision coincided with his son starting out in Little League. "This was like a bridge be-

Billy faces the painful decision of giving up baseball when his father goes to jail and he has to run the family farm in Weaver's 1995 novel.

tween me and my son," Weaver explained. "As a kid I loved playing baseball, and watching my son learn the game, I felt a connection across the generations. The irony was that he was one of those town kids; that made me flashback to those days when I felt an outsider around the kids from town."

Weaver took this assorted inspiration, melding it together in a tale of a thirteen-year-old farm boy who uses baseball to transcend his feelings of being an outsider. In Billy Baggs, Weaver found a character at once enigmatic and sympathetic. "His last name is evocative for me," Weaver told *AAYA*. "Billy has a lot of baggage to carry through life." The first title in the series, *Striking Out*, finds Billy trying to deal with the gruesome death of his older brother in 1965, five years earlier. Billy still feels responsible for the accidental death, and the austere life of do's and don't's imposed by his stern father, Abner, make Billy's life that much more difficult. Abner, a victim of childhood polio, expects the worst from life and often gets it. Billy's mother, on the other hand, is still hopeful about life: with saved egg money, she buys a typewriter and teaches herself enough typing skills to get a job in town at the medical clinic. But Abner proposes no such escape for his son—he will work on the farm.

Visiting town one day, Billy sees some kids playing baseball and feels an outsider to them in their sport. Retrieving a ball hit over the fence, he throws it back to the players with the force of an arm built strong through heavy farm work. The coach sees the potential to make a pitcher of the young boy, and eventually talks Abner into letting Billy play baseball. Billy, however, must overcome his own self-consciousness as well as hostility from some of the teammates to find his place on the team and lead them to victory in the final game of the season. "If this plot suggests a throwback to the . . . sports-oriented series from the 1940s and '50s," noted a reviewer for *Publishers Weekly*, "the subplots, involving teenage sex and the mother's decision to take an office job in town, are clearly the stuff of contemporary YA fiction." This same reviewer concluded that a "wealth of lovingly recounted details evokes the difficult daily life on a small dairy farm, while flashes of humor serve as relief." Dolores J. Sarafinski commented in *Voice of Youth Advocates* that "Weaver prevents the plot from becoming too cloying by the realistic representation of life on the farm and Billy's sexual interest in a young neighbor. . . . Weaver writes well and students ten years old and up will enjoy Billy's struggle, the baseball experience, and the vivid description of life on the farm." Betsy Hearne, writing in *Bulletin of the Center for Children's Books*, pointed out the "clearly focussed plot" and the "fine-tuned psychological and physical pacing" that would "hold junior high school and high school readers," while Mary Harris Veeder declared in the *Chicago Tribune Books* that Weaver's name should be added to the list of the "few talented authors for this age group who manage to catch the significance of sports as the language in which much growing up expresses itself." Veeder concluded that "Many boys stop reading for fun in middle school; this book is good enough to change that."

If you enjoy the works of Will Weaver, you may also want to check out the following books and films:

Chris Crutcher, *The Crazy Horse Electric Game*, 1984.
S. E. Hinton, *The Outsiders*, 1967.
Hoosiers, a film starring Gene Hackman, 1986.

Weaver continued the saga of Billy Baggs in *Farm Team* and *Hard Ball*, following Billy's progress at ages fourteen and fifteen respectively. In the former novel, the action picks up where it left off in *Striking Out*, with Billy's father taking revenge on a used car salesman who sold his wife a clunker. Running amok in the car lot with a tractor, Abner is carted off to jail and Billy must spend the summer working the farm with no time for pitching fast balls. Billy's mom comes to the rescue, helping to set up a playing field on their property and initiating Friday night games for some relaxation. Billy leads a makeshift group of country kids on the farm team and they ultimately defeat the pompous town kids in a game ending on a fly ball hit by Billy's rival, King Kenwood, and caught by Billy's dog.

While some reviewers found *Farm Team* less substantive than *Striking Out*, Todd Morning in *School Library Journal* thought that the novel was "a successful sequel," and that the final game was "wonderfully evoked." Morning concluded that "Most readers will come away from this book looking forward to the next installment in the life of Billy Baggs." A reviewer for *Publishers Weekly* commented that "Weaver combines wickedly sharp wit with a love of baseball and intimate knowledge of farm life to yield an emotionally satisfying tale." The same reviewer summed up the optimistic ending: "In a good old-fashioned ending, our hero bests his nemesis, . . . earns Abner's grudging respect and wins the admiration of the girl who makes his heart sing."

The third novel in the series, *Hard Ball*, continues the competition between Billy and King Kenwood, but in this story the two must learn to deal with each other as well as the expectations of their respective fathers. King is from the better side of town, a child of privilege. The boys compete on the baseball field and for the heart of Suzy—a rivalry that adds piquancy to their feud. It does not help that their fathers are as much at odds with one another as the sons are. As a result of a physical fight between Billy and King, the coach suggests that the boys spend a week together, splitting the time between each household. In the process, King discovers a grudging admiration for the harsh farm life Billy leads and also begins to see how difficult Billy's father can be. Billy in turn learns that a softer life does not necessarily mean an easier one.

Claire Rosser, reviewing *Hard Ball* in *Kliatt,* noted that "There's a welcome earthiness here, in the language and in the farm situations, which add humor and realism." Rosser concluded that "Weaver gets this world exactly right, with the haves and have nots living separate lives, even in sparsely populated Minnesota farmland." Mary McCarthy commented in *Voice of Youth Advocates* that "Billy is an engaging, realistic character who leaves the reader rooting for more. . . . An excellent read for a hot summer night, baseball fan or not." *Kirkus Reviews* dubbed the book an "offbeat, exciting narrative," while *Bulletin of the Center for Children's Books* concluded that "Weaver will have readers in the palm of his glove."

Life beyond Baseball

"I don't want to be pigeon-holed as a sports writer," Weaver told *AAYA.* "Partly for that reason I am letting Billy Baggs go his own way for a time. My current projects do not deal with him at all. Also, I feel my characters were getting a little tired of my intrusions—they needed some breathing room. Billy needs to decide whether or not he wants to go ahead and finish high school. But I am sure I'll get back to Billy soon. I know from the letters I get from young readers that they are anxious to know how life turns out for him. That is one of the enjoyable fringe benefits of writing for younger readers—that they take stories seriously and are eager to give feedback. Writing for this audience is a bit like a dialogue."

Weaver brings the same demanding rules of craft to his YA novels that he did to his adult work. "I generally work without an outline; I only like to know a chapter or two ahead—like writing only as far as I can see by headlights. But the trouble is, sometimes you take the wrong turn

In the third book in Weaver's series, Billy and arch-rival King Kenwood compete both on the field and off—until their coach insists they live together for a week.

with this method. You have to be flexible; you need to be able to start all over again, to throw away what does not work." Much of Weaver's writing is confined to the summer months when he is free of his teaching load. "I work about half a day," he told *AAYA.* "I get between three and ten pages a day and I do my writing in a study off the garage."

Weaver is a firm believer in revision. "I always tell aspiring writers that they must be ready to revise. Only Mozart got it right the first time. Some of my short stories have been through twenty revisions; my novels through six to ten rewrites. I am very concerned with quality. If there is anything that will cement a writer's reputation, it's the sense that each book is as good as or better than the last one. That's a real goal of mine."

Weaver's gritty Midwestern realism sets the tone for each of his books, whether adult or YA. He speaks of "stealth literary value," of a "textured readability," and these are the qualities that both reviewers and readers alike have responded to. "If I have a message with all my books, it is that we can do things if we really put our minds to it. But we can't do it alone. We have to trust in humanity, in our family and friends."

■ Works Cited

Review of *Farm Team, Publishers Weekly,* June 26, 1995, p. 108.

Review of *Hard Ball, Bulletin of the Center for Children's Books,* May, 1998, p. 343.

Review of *Hard Ball, Kirkus Reviews,* December 1, 1997, p. 1781.

Hearne, Betsy, review of *Striking Out, Bulletin of the Center for Children's Books,* February, 1994.

Levering, Frank, review of *Red Earth, White Earth, Los Angeles Times Book Review,* October 19, 1986, p. 9.

McCarthy, Mary, review of *Hard Ball, Voice of Youth Advocates,* June, 1998, p. 126.

Morning, Todd, review of *Farm Team, School Library Journal,* July, 1995, p. 96.

Rosser, Claire, review of *Hard Ball, Kliatt,* July, 1998, p. 9.

Sarafinski, Dolores J., review of *Striking Out, Voice of Youth Advocates,* December, 1993, p. 304.

Solomon, Andy, review of *A Gravestone Made of Wheat, New York Times Book Review,* March 12, 1989, p. 22.

Review of *Striking Out, Publishers Weekly,* August 30, 1993, p. 97.

Veeder, Mary Harris, review of *Striking Out, Chicago Tribune Books,* June 19, 1994, p. 6.

Weaver, Will, *Red Earth, White Earth,* Simon and Schuster, 1986.

Weaver, Will, interview with J. Sydney Jones for *Authors and Artists for Young Adults,* conducted January 28, 1999.

■ For More Information See

PERIODICALS

Booklist, November 15, 1993, p. 515; March 15, 1994, p. 1359; September 1, 1995, p. 66; March 15, 1996, p. 1284.

Bulletin of the Center for Children's Books, September, 1995, pp. 32-33.

Kirkus Reviews, November 15, 1993; June 1, 1995.

Kliatt, September, 1996, p. 5.

Los Angeles Times Book Review, March 12, 1989, pp. 1, 13.

Minneapolis Tribune, September 3, 1995.

New York Times Book Review, November 9, 1986, p. 33.

School Library Journal, October, 1993, p. 156

Voice of Youth Advocates, October, 1995, p. 226.

Washington Post Book World, November 2, 1986, p. 8; March 26, 1989, p. 11.

—Sketch by J. Sydney Jones

Barbara Wersba

Personal

Born August 19, 1932, in Chicago, IL; daughter of Robert and Lucy Josephine (Quarles) Wersba. *Education:* Bard College, B.A., 1954; studied acting at Neighborhood Playhouse and at the Paul Mann Actors Workshop; studied dance with Martha Graham.

Addresses

Home—Box 1892, Sag Harbor, NY 11963. *Agent*—McIntosh and Otis, Inc., 310 Madison Ave., New York, NY 10017.

Career

Actress in radio and television, summer stock, off-Broadway, and touring companies, 1944-59; full-time writer, 1959—. Summer lecturer at New York University; writing instructor at Rockland Center for the Arts.

Awards, Honors

Deutscher Jugend Buchpreis, 1973, for *Run Softly, Go Fast*; American Library Association (ALA) Best Book for Young Adults and Notable Children's Book lists, both 1976, and National Book Award nomination, 1977, all for *Tunes for a Small Harmonica*; ALA Best Book for Young Adults, 1982, for *The Carnival in My Mind*; D.H.L. from Bard College, 1977.

Writings

FICTION FOR YOUNG ADULTS

The Dream Watcher, Atheneum, 1968, Longmans Young, 1969.
Run Softly, Go Fast, Atheneum, 1970.
The Country of the Heart, Atheneum, 1975.
Tunes for a Small Harmonica, Harper & Row, 1976, Bodley Head, 1979.
The Carnival in My Mind, Harper & Row, 1982.
Crazy Vanilla, Harper & Row, 1986, Bodley Head, 1986.
FAT: A Love Story, Harper & Row, 1987, Bodley Head, 1987.
Love Is the Crooked Thing, Harper & Row, 1987, Bodley Head, 1987.
Beautiful Losers, Harper & Row, 1988, Bodley Head, 1988.
Just Be Gorgeous, Harper & Row, 1988, Bodley Head, 1989.

Wonderful Me, Harper & Row, 1989.

The Farewell Kid, Harper & Row, 1990, Bodley Head, 1990.

The Best Place To Live Is the Ceiling, Harper & Row, 1990, Bodley Head, 1991.

You'll Never Guess the End, HarperCollins, 1992, Bodley Head, 1992.

Life Is What Happens While You're Making Other Plans, Bodley Head, 1994.

Whistle Me Home, Henry Holt, 1997.

(Reteller) *The Wings of Courage,* by George Sand, George Braziller, 1998.

FICTION FOR CHILDREN

The Boy Who Loved the Sea, illustrated by Margot Tomes, Coward, 1961.

The Brave Balloon of Benjamin Buckley, illustrated by Tomes, Atheneum, 1963.

The Land of Forgotten Beasts, illustrated by Tomes, Atheneum, 1964, Gollancz, 1965.

A Song for Clowns, illustrated by Mario Rivoli, Atheneum, 1965, Gollancz, 1966.

Let Me Fall before I Fly, Atheneum, 1971.

Amanda, Dreaming, illustrated by Mercer Mayer, Atheneum, 1973.

The Crystal Child, illustrated by Donna Diamond, Harper & Row, 1982.

POETRY FOR CHILDREN

Do Tigers Ever Bite Kings?, illustrated by Rivoli, Atheneum, 1966.

Twenty-Six Starlings Will Fly through Your Mind, illustrated by David Palladini, Harper & Row, 1980.

OTHER

Contributor to the *New York Times Book Review.*

■ Adaptations

"The Dream Watcher" (play) starring Eva Le Gallienne, first produced at White Barn Theater, Westport, Conn., August 29, 1975, later produced by the Seattle Repertory Theatre, 1977-78; *The Country of the Heart* was made into a television film, *Matters of the Heart,* that starred Jane Seymour.

■ Sidelights

Over a period spanning the better part of four decades, Barbara Wersba has written more than two dozen books, including several well-received novels for young adults that feature sensitive, artistic teens as protagonists and themes which advocate the individual's right to self-expression. Wersba began her career as a novelist in her mid-twenties after many years in the theater. She spent her teen years at a private school and in theater workshops in New York City, and her familiarity with the glittering, high-rise-canyon milieu of Manhattan and the emotional problems of its affluent, private-school adolescents has become a mainstay of her fiction. Often her novels chronicle the tale of a loner or misfit—usually "suffering from the advantages of a secure childhood," as *School Library Journal* contributor Joanne Aswell remarked—who is at odds with his or her parents, but through an unusual friendship or an unlikely achievement obtains a newfound grasp of and pride in their own singularly special character.

Despite the success of her work, Wersba has always been pestered with the question of why she confines her talents to writing for young people, instead of trying her hand at adult fiction or plays. "Why write for children?" Wersba mused in her autobiographical essay for *Something About the Author.* "Because the form is tantalizingly short, and thus tantalizingly difficult. Because the form implies hope. Because those of us who use this form still experience our childhood in strong and passionate ways. There is no chalk line on the sidewalk with childhood on one side and maturity on the other. It is all the same life, it is all one, and the best children's writers know that they are writing for the child in the adult, and the adult in the child."

Wersba was born in 1932 in Chicago to Kentucky native Lucy Jo Quarles, who had married Robert Wersba, of Russian-Jewish heritage. It was an ill-fated match, and Wersba recalled being affected at a young age by the tense atmosphere in her home. She spent her early years in a suburb of San Francisco, and was a somber child by her own admission, a loner, someone who spent long hours dreaming of escape. "At night, lying in bed, I would hear the sound of trains passing in the valley, and imagine that I was on one of them," Wersba once noted to *Authors and Artists for Young*

Adults (AAYA). "Get away, get away, said the wheels of the trains. Get away, get away, I echoed."

Wersba remembered writing from a very early age, but as a little girl in the 1930s she assumed her path out of the ordinariness of her life would involve show business. Thus at the age of eleven she began working behind the scenes in a community theater in her neighborhood, and was given her first role a few months later. "No matter that I did not like to act, that it frightened me, and almost made me sick," Wersba told *AAYA.* "I had a purpose in life and no longer felt alone." Wersba's parents announced their intention to divorce around this same time, and her mother began planning a move to New York; Wersba's two cats could not come along and would be euthanized, her mother told her. "On the day they were taken away, I crawled into a little space under the house, near the furnace room, and wept," Wersba told *AAYA,* recalling that the loss of her beloved pets was more devastating than the departure of her father.

In New York City, Wersba took advantage of the rich cultural offerings of one of the world's most famous cities. Almost immediately upon her arrival, she spent her money on a theater ticket for a Broadway play, which turned out to be Tennessee Williams's *The Glass Menagerie.* She began frequenting the theaters and saw many great stage luminaries of the era. She still wrote regularly, though she never showed her work to anyone. Wersba was sent to a private school, and was taking afternoon classes at the Neighborhood Playhouse by the age of 15; she also studied dance with Martha Graham for a time. Still, she had never managed to conquer her terrible stage fright, and knew as adulthood approached that she had somehow landed in the wrong direction, the wrong life. "A loner from birth, I felt uneasy in the social atmosphere of the theatre," Wersba noted to *AAYA.* "Every spare moment I had was spent writing stories and poems, but I did not take this seriously. My writing seemed terrible to me, awkward, imitative, trite."

Wersba disobeyed her father by refusing to attend Vassar College, opting instead for the 300-student Bard College. It was a good choice and the beginning of a much happier time in her life, as she was released from the cliquish Manhattan private-school realm. Though she still acted, she also delved into literature courses and even ran a coffee and donut service in the dormitory. "In 1977 I went back to Bard to accept an honorary degree," Wersba told *SATA,* "and the friend who went with me says that I wept the entire day. I do not remember the day clearly, but I suppose I did weep, for everywhere I turned, everywhere I walked, the ghost of my young self was just ahead of me. . . . Thin, blonde, intense, that girl was more real to me than she had been to herself, and as I accepted the degree I felt her by my side."

The Lean Years

After graduation in 1954, Wersba joined a stock company in New Jersey and was given the lead in a Tennessee Williams play, *Camino Real,* for her first role. On opening night, a well-known director came backstage and offered her a Broadway role, but she never called him. "As far as my acting career was concerned, the journey downward had begun," Wersba recalled of this incident in *SATA.* Still, she persisted and moved to New York later that year. She found cheap rents in the East Village, the rougher neighborhood adjacent to Greenwich Village, and lived in a coldwater flat in a building on East Ninth Street that was also home to several other aspiring actresses. There were also rats, roaches, a bathtub in the kitchen, and she and her neighbors would share a single fur coat to make the rounds of theatrical agents. To support herself, Wersba worked at a number of jobs, from waitress to department-store clerk to seed-mosaic artist.

Wersba eventually found solace with her first forays into real writing when she adapted stories into dramatic monologues for the theater company she had formed with some fellow thespians. "The stories were wonderful—by people like Dylan Thomas and Virginia Woolf—and as I shaped and cut them, and turned narrative into dialogue, I knew the first pleasure in working at a typewriter that I had ever known," Wersba told *SATA.* But the cross-country tour exhausted her, and she was diagnosed with hepatitis. She headed to Martha's Vineyard to recuperate, knowing she would never return to acting, and "it was then that my hostess said, 'Barbara, why don't you write something?'" Wersba told *AAYA.* So she sat down and wrote *The Boy Who Loved the Sea,* about a child who dreams so deeply of the sea that he decides to live there. Then her hosts invited an editor from New York to dinner and secretly put Wersba's manuscript in her purse. The woman's boss also loved it, and Wersba was made an offer.

The Boy Who Loved the Sea was published in 1961, and Wersba eagerly began work on her second book, *The Brave Balloon of Benjamin Buckley,* which appeared in 1963. Several more fantasy tales for children followed, as well as a book of poetry, *Do Tigers Ever Bite Kings?* This 1966 volume, asserted Kay E. Vandergrift in *Dictionary of Literary Biography,* "combines love and laughter in a rollicking rhymed tale of a gentle king and a timorous tiger who stage an elaborate drama for a militant and shrewish queen." Vandergrift added: "This whimsical, often absurdly funny story is also a sophisticated message of peace, all the more powerful for its nonsensical delivery."

By the late 1960s Wersba was living in Rockland County, New York and working on an historical novel when "a voice came into my head. This voice, that of a young boy, was so strong and insistent that I put the historical novel away, sat down at the typewriter, and did not get up again for seven months. . . . On the day that I finished this book I burst into tears." The voice belonged to a character she named Albert Scully, the hero of her first book for young adults, *The Dream Watcher.* Published in 1968, the novel is a coming-of-age story about Scully, who at fourteen feels himself an outcast. He is sensitive, likes Shakespeare and gardening, and knows no one like himself, can point to no single group to which he might belong. Then he meets a lovely elderly woman, Orpha Woodfin, who tells him she was once a well-known Broadway actress. Like Scully, she is also a great reader, and their long discussions and her confidence in his intelligence instill a sense of self-worth in him. It is a book "loaded with adult wisdom," opined John Weston in the *New York Times Book Review,* "but Miss Wersba weaves it smoothly into her over-all creation."

New Course in Life

Wersba maintained that *The Dream Watcher* changed her life. The reviews were positive, and sales were strong. She began receiving letters from readers both young and old who had strongly identified with Scully's situation, remembering an older friend who had served as a mentor at one time in their lives. Wersba also began receiving film offers from Hollywood, but then one of her heroines from her Broadway play-going adolescence, Eva Le Gallienne, contacted her via a friend and offered to play the role on stage if Wersba would be willing to adapt it into a play. The author agreed, but it took her several years to teach herself how to write for the stage, despite her fifteen years as an actor. While working on the adaptation, Wersba recalled that she read four plays a day for months.

The stage version of *The Dream Watcher,* starring Le Gallienne as Orpha Woodfin, debuted at a Connecticut venue, the White Barn Theater, in August of 1975. The play was a success, and so out-of-town tryouts, preliminary to a Broadway debut, were planned beginning in Seattle in 1977. Several factors worked against the success of another staging, however, and the play closed shortly afterward. Wersba returned home to the Rockland area, where by this time she was living in a vintage nineteenth-century commercial building. She and a partner ran the downstairs as an old-fashioned country store that was a great hit with New Yorkers out for a country drive. Part of Wersba's recovery from the Seattle debacle was to take up a new project: teaching. She opened a school in her home she called "The Women's Writing Workshop," and later taught writing classes at The Rockland Center for the Arts for several years. Another unusual job that she came to enjoy was caring for an invalid, the famed writer Carson McCullers, before her death in 1967. McCullers, a friend of Tennessee Williams, was a literary celebrity at a young age with her acclaimed novel *The Heart Is a Lonely Hunter,* but she had suffered from a number of personal travails over the years, including numerous strokes. Wersba shopped for her and took dictation for her stories. "She was lonely and wrote about loneliness," Wersba told *Something About the Author.* "Her characters survive through illusion, as she did, and hope to be redeemed by love—and never are."

The success of *The Dream Watcher* inspired Wersba to continue to write for the young-adult market, and from there she began work on a string of novels that met with similar acclaim. Her second such effort, *Run Softly, Go Fast,* tapped perfectly into the zeitgeist of 1970. A child of middle-class affluence, 19-year-old David Marks recounts his story in flashback in a journal after the death of his father. His coming-of-age tale is littered with typical rebellious acts and experiments with drugs. Eventually he strikes out on his own and finds modest success as an artist, but still struggles to come to terms with the loss of his father. *Kirkus Reviews* panned the book, terming both father and son "equally intolerant, unattractive and stereotyped," and found its casual mentions of drug use somewhat offensive. *New York Times Book Review* contributor John Rowe Townsend noted that "technically, *Run Softly, Go Fast* is highly accomplished," but listed among its faults weak characterization and sloppy resolution; in the end, Townsend opined, the work "fails to speak clearly, and only occasionally strikes a responding chord."

Wersba's next novel would later be filmed for television, with Jane Seymour cast in the female lead. *The Country of the Heart* deals with a rather risqué topic: a student has an affair with an older woman, whom he only later learns is dying of cancer. Again, the work is told in flashback form through a personal diary. "Wersba's deft control of tone is remarkably convincing," maintained Georgess McHargue in the *New York Times Book Review*. The novel was adapted for television and released as *Matters of the Heart*, and Wersba later said she was very much pleased with the screen version.

Tunes for a Small Harmonica

Wersba's next work won several American awards after its publication in 1976. *Tunes for a Small Harmonica*, nominated for a National Book Award, sets the tone for what would become a typical Wersba protagonist: the smart but quirky young girl, confidently roaming her way around New York City and trying to find her niche in life. "*Tunes* is the story of J. F. McAllister, a brash young New York woman who falls in love with her rather dim and pale poetry teacher," wrote Audrey Eaglen in an essay on Wersba for *Twentieth-Century Young Adult Writers*. McAllister is misunderstood by her mother, who loves to shop and cannot understand why her daughter will only wear boys' clothes; occasionally the teen must spend an hour in her easily-duped Park Avenue psychiatrist's office. In an attempt to get her to quit smoking, McAllister's best friend gives her a harmonica, but because the object of her desire supposedly needs to return to England to finish his doctorate, McAllister begins busking with it

to raise money for him. When she finds out he has been lying to her about nearly everything in his life, McAllister contemplates suicide.

Wersba was widely praised for *Tunes for a Small Harmonica*. *Publishers Weekly* termed the novel "a honey of a story, laced with humor and tender feelings," and flush with "characters made truly human by the author's expertise." A review by Diane Haas for *School Library Journal* found "occasional stylistic weaknesses," yet a heroine both "winning and believable." Wersba's love of animals provided her with the inspiration for the character of yet another misunderstood young New Yorker and his unlikely comic home life. Wersba never missed an opportunity to pick up a stray dog or cat and take it back to Rockland County, hoping to find a permanent home for it. Once she saw a man on a very hot day in New York City, "disheveled and crazy," Wersba described him in *SATA*, with a crowd gathered around him and a young, skeletal Irish setter in his charge. The dog could no longer stand from the heat and hunger. The man was trying to sell it, but the crowd—"in typical New York fashion," Wersba noted in *SATA*, was uninterested in helping him out, but curious about the spectacle itself. So Wersba took the dog back home and named her Bridie. The setter quickly grew into a large, uncontrollable, undisciplined, but very loving dog that once knocked Wersba down and inadvertently broke her foot in the process. She was devastated when she finally placed Bridie in a good home, though, and so began to write *The Carnival in My Mind*.

Published in 1982, *The Carnival in My Mind* follows the platonic romance between loner Harvey Beaumont, a diminutive 14-year-old and aspiring writer, and Chandler, an actress six years his senior. Harvey's mother provides a home for five Irish setters in their Park Avenue apartment, where he is largely ignored by his parents and composes suicide notes to them on occasion. Chandler lives in a building full of eccentric characters that is not unlike the East Ninth Street place in which Wersba resided during her fur-coat-sharing years. Harvey later discovers that Chandler is not an actress, but a call girl, and has a child being cared for by her rich, Midwest parents, who have disowned her.

"Wersba has created two great characters and a wonderful depiction of adolescent love," declared

After young Noli finds out that her "boyfriend" T.J. is actually gay, she goes on a drinking binge that makes her realize she's an alcoholic.

Voice of Youth Advocates contributor Sari Feldman. The book also won praise for its dry humor and Harvey's wry narrative voice, which one reviewer likened to the tone of a Woody Allen dialogue: "I went into the master bedroom," reads one passage in *The Carnival in My Mind*. "Mother's five dogs were sitting around on old leather sofas watching television. . . . I sat down on one of the couches. Thoren Oakenshield gave me his paw, which he always did when I sat next to him, so I held onto it as we watched the news."

Wersba created another mixed-up scion of affluence in *Crazy Vanilla*, her 1986 novel. Tyler loves nature photography, especially near the family summer home on Long Island, but it is a loner hobby that makes his father suspicious—the fam-

ily is still reeling from the shock of learning that Tyler's accomplished, golden-boy older brother is gay. Their mother drinks, the father is distant, and Tyler feels that "Crazy Vanilla" aptly describes his life: seemingly bland on the surface, but teeming with landmines just below. He finds a friend in Mitzi, who is a year older than Tyler and works as a waitress in the Hamptons. She is streetwise and comes from a decidedly nonconformist family, but shares his love of photography. *Voice of Youth Advocates* contributor Marijo Duncan termed *Crazy Vanilla* "typical Wersba, complete with likable characters who handle tough growing up situations well, and with a sense of humor."

Stories about Rita

Wersba wrote three novels featuring the indomitable Rita Formica, whom readers first encounter as a teen with an eating disorder in 1987's *FAT: A Love Story*. Rita tries to lose weight in order to win the approval of handsome, athletic Robert Swann, who instead pursues her best friend. This trauma lands Rita in a surprise romance with her boss, who owns a cheesecake shop and is nearly twice her age. Rita appears again in *Love Is the Crooked Thing*, which begins with her beloved, Arnold, escaping to Switzerland at the strong suggestion of Mr. and Mrs. Formica. To earn money to join him, Rita decides to become a romance novelist and embarks upon creating a narrative framed by the requisite bodice-ripping scenes. She makes it to Switzerland, but realizes that Arnold is perhaps unfit for a true relationship.

In *Beautiful Losers*, the 1988 conclusion of the trilogy, Arnold has a change of heart, flies home, and the pair move in together in a ramshackle house near the Shelter Island ferry. Rita's parents are so upset that she has chosen not to go to college that they cut her loose, and in order to support Arnold while he writes his masterpiece, Rita takes a job as an assistant to a writer of children's books—"a portrait that unmercifully skewers a whole type of children's author," noted Eleanor K. MacDonald in *School Library Journal*. After weeks of frustration, Rita becomes disillusioned and returns to her parents' home to begin her own book. She soon realizes, however, just how much she misses Arnold. "Rita and Arnold are such delightful, original, authentic characters that their romance never becomes a romantic cliché," declared Cathi Edgerton in *Voice of Youth Advo-*

cates, who also found *Beautiful Losers* "laced with warmth, humor, spirit, and optimism."

Like Rita, Heidi Rosenbloom also finds it difficult to live up to her parents' expectations. In Wersba's 1988 novel *Just Be Gorgeous,* Heidi's situation is made all the worse for the conflicting personalities of her divorced parents. Her mother sees her as a potential debutante, and cannot understand why Heidi shops in secondhand stores; her father, on the other hand, lives in Greenwich Village and considers Heidi a nascent genius. Heidi falls for Jeffrey, a homeless man who dances for money on the street wearing eye shadow and a fur coat. In the end, Jeffrey leaves New York, but not before instilling in Heidi a great dose of self-confidence. Wersba, wrote Aswell in *School Library Journal,* "succeeds in creating in Jeffrey a truly sympathetic and tragically lovable character."

The saga of Heidi as she approaches the age of maturity continues in Wersba's 1989 sequel, *Wonderful Me.* With her abominable grades, Heidi decides against college and launches a career as a Manhattan dog walker. When she begins receiving secret love letters, she discovers they're from one of her teachers. The romance dead-ends, but through it Heidi "learns what is most important in her life and finds the courage to initiate change," wrote Judy Druse in *Voice of Youth Advocates.* Wersba concluded Heidi's story in *The Farewell Kid,* as the heroine opens a dog rescue service, gets her own apartment, and finds romance with Harvey Beaumont, who is like herself a misfit. Fortuitously for Heidi, Harvey grew up in a canine-dominated household.

Disciplined Writer

Wersba continued to produce nearly a novel a year well into the 1990s. Preferring to begin her workday before dawn, she is disciplined and for many years enjoyed the advantages of working with a top editor, Charlotte Zolotow. Yet despite Wersba's track record, "for every manuscript that succeeds there are five that fail," the author told *AAYA.* "But I can never bring myself to throw the failures away, and they are all kept in a trunk labeled *In Progress.*"

Wersba's later works include 1990's *The Best Place To Live Is the Ceiling* and *You'll Never Guess the End,* published in 1992. The latter features aspir-

ing Manhattan sleuth Joel Greenberg, who is intrigued by the much-publicized kidnaping case of an heiress who once dated his older brother. Soon he begins to suspect that his sibling, a much-feted new literary celebrity, is somehow involved. But perhaps Wersba's most acclaimed novel for young adults to emerge from this period is *Whistle Me Home.* This 1997 work features tomboyish Noli, who has problems with her mother and is already displaying a fondness for alcohol. Noli is at first perplexed and then entranced when the new, handsome rich kid in her class, T. J., finds her intriguing and zooms in on her for romance. The relationship is emotionally intimate, but physically platonic, and when Noli tries to seduce him on one occasion she discovers that T. J. is gay. Noli handles this badly, drinks even more, and loses

In this retelling of an original story by George Sand, a French boy who has a deep love for birds overcomes hardships as an apprentice to a nasty tailor.

If you enjoy the works of Barbara Wersba, you may also want to check out the following books:

Charles Ferry, *Binge*, 1992.
Lynn Hall, *The Solitary*, 1986.
Richard Peck, *Unfinished Portrait of Jessica*, 1991.
Jean Thesman, *Rachel Chance*, 1990.

the dog T. J. had given her. She finds help in Alcoholics Anonymous and eventually allows T. J. to give her the emotional support everyone needs from a trusted friend. "These characters are three-dimensional," noted Jacqueline Rose in a review for *Voice of Youth Advocates*. "It is easy to empathize with both characters' dilemmas, which is why this book is so worthwhile." *Whistle Me Home*, declared *Kirkus Reviews*, "isn't a perfect story, but its characters are perfectly human, and Wersba makes poetry of the arrival of unbidden love."

Long Island is the setting for many of Wersba's novels; she sold her Rockland County store and moved to the eastern tip of the island in 1983. Though she continues to write, she has slowed down the pace somewhat and has created her own small press, The Bookman Press. Wersba acknowledges that she has no family left at all. "My companion of fifteen years—a woman named Zue—died in the winter of 1994," Wersba told *SATA*. "I live alone in the large house we used to share, and the days are long. Zue was a small, gracious person, and her books and pictures and possessions—all still in place—speak of a world that has vanished."

Wersba also noted, "I find myself becoming acutely conscious of family groups, of people with grandchildren, of holidays," she told *SATA*. "As a young person I only wanted to escape the confines of family and lead my own life." Wersba remains firm in her conviction that for her, writing for young adults was the right choice. In a 1976 interview with Paul Janeczko for *English Journal*, she mused about the differences between young adult fiction from the previous generation and what was then being published. "When I was a child and read adult books there was a greater sense of hope, of humanity, of the goodness of

life. These things now seem to be the property of the young adult novel. . . . I am always the person who sees the sick cat on the side of the road, or who sees the lost child in the supermarket, or who is aware of people suffering," Wersba admitted. "I enter my workroom every morning to make sense of what I see."

■ Works Cited

Aswell, Joanne, review of *Just Be Gorgeous, School Library Journal*, November, 1988, pp. 133-34.

Druse, Judy, review of *Wonderful Me, Voice of Youth Advocates*, August, 1997, pp. 190-91.

Duncan, Marijo, review of *Crazy Vanilla, Voice of Youth Advocates*, December, 1986, p. 223.

Eaglen, Audrey, "Barbara Wersba," *Twentieth-Century Young Adult Writers*, first edition, St. James Press, 1994.

Edgerton, Cathi, review of *Beautiful Losers, Voice of Youth Advocates*, June, 1989, p. 108.

Feldman, Sari, review of *The Carnival in My Mind, Voice of Youth Advocates*, February, 1983, pp. 41-42.

Haas, Diane, review of *Tunes for a Small Harmonica, School Library Journal*, September, 1976, p. 127.

Janeczko, Paul, interview with Wersba in *English Journal*, November, 1976, pp. 20-21.

MacDonald, Eleanor K., review of *Beautiful Losers, School Library Journal*, March, 1988, p. 217.

McHargue, Georgess, review of *The Country of the Heart, New York Times Book Review*, January 4, 1976, p. 8.

Rose, Jacqueline, review of *Whistle Me Home, Voice of Youth Advocates*, August, 1997, p. 191.

Review of *Run Softly, Go Fast, Kirkus Reviews*, October 15, 1970.

Townsend, John Rowe, review of *Run Softly, Go Fast, New York Times Book Review*, November 22, 1970.

Review of *Tunes for a Small Harmonica, Publishers Weekly*, July 12, 1976, p. 72.

Vandergrift, Kay E., "Barbara Wersba," *Dictionary of Literary Biography*, Volume 52: *American Writers for Children since 1960: Fiction*, Gale, 1986, pp. 374-80.

Wersba, Barbara, *The Carnival in My Mind*, Harper & Row, 1982.

Wersba, Barbara, "Autobiography Feature," *Something about the Author*, Volume 103, Gale, 1999, pp. 186-96.

Weston, John, review of *The Dream Watcher, New York Times Book Review*, November 3, 1968.

Review of *Whistle Me Home, Kirkus Reviews*, March 1, 1997, p. 389.

■ For More Information See

BOOKS

Children's Literature Review, Volume 3, Gale, 1977.
Contemporary Literary Criticism, Volume 30, Gale, 1984.

PERIODICALS

Booklist, October 1, 1987, p. 255; November 15, 1992, p. 590.
Books for Keeps, July, 1991, p. 13.
Bulletin of the Center for Children's Books, February, 1977, p. 99; March, 1987, p. 137; June, 1987, p. 200; January, 1988, p. 105.
Children's Book News, September-October, 1969.
Five Owls, May-June, 1990, p. 90.
Horn Book, spring, 1993, p. 84; May-June, 1997.

Junior Bookshelf, April, 1987, p. 95.
Kirkus Reviews, May 15, 1989, p. 773.
Library Journal, September, 1968, p. 3328; February 15, 1973, pp. 620-23.
Los Angeles Times Book Review, August 24, 1980; November 20, 1988, p. 6.
New Statesman & Society, July 7, 1989, pp. 38-40.
New York Times Book Review, November 14, 1976, p. 29; October 24, 1982.
Publishers Weekly, July 12, 1976, p. 72; December 26, 1986, p. 57; June 12, 1987, p. 86; October 9, 1987, pp. 89-90; January 13, 1989; March 16, 1990, p. 72; October 12, 1992, p. 80; March 24, 1997, p. 84.
School Library Journal, June, 1997, pp. 128-29.
Voice of Youth Advocates, December, 1987, p. 239; April, 1988, p. 31; December, 1988, p. 244; April, 1993, p. 32.
Washington Post Book World, August 8, 1982, p. 6; September 12, 1982.
Wilson Library Bulletin, November, 1989, p. 16; January, 1991, p. 7.*

Kevin Williamson

■ Personal

Born March 14, 1965, in Oriental, NC; son of Wade (a fisherman) and Faye (a homemaker) Williamson. *Education:* Graduated from East Carolina University.

■ Addresses

Office—Outer Banks Entertainment, 8000 Sunset Blvd., Los Angeles, CA, 90046.

■ Career

Screenwriter, 1994—. Creator and executive producer of *Dawson's Creek*, WB Network, 1998—, and *WasteLand*, ABC, 1999—. Executive producer, *Scream 2*, 1997, and co-executive producer, *Halloween H20*, 1998. Also worked as an actor in New York City, 1987-91, including roles on *Another World*, and as a music video director's assistant in Los Angeles, CA.

■ Writings

FILM SCREENPLAYS

Scream, Dimension Films, 1996.
I Know What You Did Last Summer, Columbia, 1997.
Scream 2, Dimension Films, 1997.
The Faculty, Dimension Films, 1999.
(Uncredited story treatment, and executive co-producer) *Halloween H20: Twenty Years Later*, Dimension, 1998.
(And director) *Teaching Mrs. Tingle*, Miramax, 1999.

TELEVISION SCREENPLAYS

Dawson's Creek, WB, 1998—.

■ Work in Progress

Scream 3, for Miramax, expected 1999; *Her Leading Man*, a romantic comedy, for Universal.

■ Sidelights

The meteoric career of movie screenwriter Kevin Williamson, whose 1996 megahit horror film *Scream* won him instant wealth and celebrity, is the latest of the rags-to-riches tales which have always fueled the image of Hollywood as the epitome of the American dream. Williamson, the man *Time* has dubbed "the Bard of Gen-Y," was just another unemployed, unknown "wanna be" when in a rush of creative inspiration one momentous long weekend he hit upon an idea that forever changed his life. "[My] phone was about to be turned off. I didn't have enough money to buy a new ink cartridge for my printer," Williamson recalled in a 1997 interview with Pat Broeske of *Writer's Digest*. Then Williamson conjured up the outline for a trilogy of scary movies about a group of hip teenagers, most of whom end up as victims of a brutal psychopath. Two weeks later, he had completed a draft of the script for *Scream*, the movie which would jump-start his career, take in more than $103 million at the domestic box office alone, and single-handedly resuscitate and reinvent the moribund slasher film genre. It also earned Williamson a reported $20-million contract from Miramax and the creative

freedom to write and develop other movie and television projects, including *Dawson's Creek*, a hit weekly television series that is based on his own coming-of-age experiences in a small North Carolina town.

"On paper, the secret Williamson formula seems deceptively simple: Write Smart," observed Chris Nashawaty of *Entertainment Weekly*. "But the reason Williamson's been able to strike such a nerve with his young core audience is that instead of talking down to them, he compliments them." Doing so with wit and flair has enabled Williamson to achieve the kind of success that few people ever believed him capable of. Fifteen years after a high school English teacher told Williamson that he had no future as a writer, he had the last laugh when he suddenly found himself being hailed by the media as one of the movie

With *Scream* 2, the sequel to the blockbuster horror flick *Scream*, Williamson scored another hit.

industry's hottest and hippest young creative talents.

Williamson was born and raised in Oriental, North Carolina, a quiet fishing and tourist village on Pamlico Sound, an hour's drive southeast of Greenville. The younger of two brothers born to a blue-collar family, Williamson was a self-described "pop-culture junkie," as he explained in a 1998 interview with Ted Johnson of *TV Guide*. Williamson often fell asleep in front of the television set at night, and despite the fact the nearest theater was a half-hour drive away, he loved going to the movies.

Williamson was fourteen when he saw *Halloween*, the 1979 slasher film by director John Carpenter that's now regarded as a classic of the genre. "It was my revelation," he wrote in a foreword to the published version of his *Scream* screenplay. "I already knew my love of movies was bordering on obsessive, but I had no idea how fixated I was until the experience of *Halloween*. . . . I went to back to see the movie again and again. . . . It was a roller coaster ride from beginning to end, I knew from that first screening that I wanted to affect people like that. I wanted to make them scream and jump and then laugh at themselves for getting so worked up. *Halloween* was the film that opened my eyes."

Career Starts Slowly

Williamson attended Pamlico County High, where he wrote reviews for the student newspaper and plays for the drama club. He confided to Ted Johnson of *TV Guide* that he "always tried to talk bigger than I was and smarter that I was." Williamson hung out with various cliques at the school—sometimes with the smokers, other times with the "A students" or the "in-crowd." Doing so exposed him to a wide variety of characters and experiences, all of which eventually became grist for the creative mill in a writing career that almost never happened. According to Johnson, one of Williamson's high school English teachers doused his dreams by giving him an "F" grade and advising him that he would never make it as a writer. Fortunately for Williamson, he later received a much more positive assessment of his talents from one of his professors at East Carolina State University in nearby Greenville—even though he had been rejected by the journalism

department and was obliged to study theater and film as an alternative. Following his 1987 graduation, he moved to New York to seek his fame and fortune.

Williamson's life in the Big Apple followed a familiar script: enticing tastes of success, mostly in the bit parts he won on the NBC daytime soap *Another World*, followed by long periods of unemployment, struggling to pay the bills, and wondering where his next meal was coming from. Amidst his despair, Williamson engaged in the inevitable soul-searching that every aspiring young actor experiences. "I loved New York City," he told Johnson, "but I really had a hard time of it. Trying to find myself. Discover who I am." After four lean years of this, in 1991 Williamson started over. He packed his suitcases and headed west to Hollywood in hopes of becoming a movie star and of one day working with director Stephen Spielberg, whose phenomenally successful *Jaws* was another of the movies that had made an indelible impression on Williamson in his youth. "When I got [to Hollywood], I just soaked it up. I mean, the first day here I went to Universal Studios and met Bruce the shark [from *Jaws*]," Williamson told Ted Johnson. "I had to because that whole Spielberg thing [I have] is real."

Williamson supplemented his meager income from acting by working as an assistant to a music video director named Paris Barclay. At Barclay's urging, in 1994 he enrolled in a University of California at Los Angeles extension course in screenwriting. As part of the program Williamson wrote a portion of a screenplay for a teenage black comedy that he called "Killing Mrs. Tingle." The story, partly inspired by his own youthful experiences, was about a high school senior who will do anything to graduate as class valedictorian, even if it involves committing murder. When Williamson finished the screenplay it seemed for a time as though it might be his big break. According to Pat Broeske's *Writer's Digest* article, the industry newspaper *Daily Variety* reported that a Hollywood production company had bought the screen rights to "Killing Mrs. Tingle" for an amount "in the low six figures."

Assuming his luck had finally changed, Williamson went on a spending spree; he paid off his college loans, leased a new car, and found a better apartment. A year passed and he was still waiting for "Killing Mrs. Tingle" to be made. But the film was tied up in "development hell," and Williamson was again broke and feeling downcast. Dog walking and working as a word processing temp did not earn him enough to live on while he struggled to write another saleable screenplay.

Tragedy Sparks Idea for *Scream*

Around this same time, a serial killer was on the loose in Gainesville, Florida, and the brutal murders received national media attention; ironically, it was these grisly murders that provided Williamson with the creative spark he had been seeking. He was housesitting in the upscale Los Angeles neighborhood of Westwood one night when he chanced to see a Barbara Walters television special on the killings. "Then, suddenly I heard a noise. It was coming from another room," Williamson wrote in the foreword to his *Scream* screenplay. "I went to check it out and discovered an open window. I had been staying in the house for two days and hadn't noticed it." Williamson, badly shaken and in need of reassurance, grabbed a butcher knife and then called a friend on a cordless telephone while he checked the house for a possible intruder. But instead of offering words of reassurance, his wise-cracking friend began to joke about how Freddy, the infamous Elm Street slasher, or some other bloodthirsty movie fiend, was about to leap from the shadows to murder Williamson. "Before you know it, we were arguing over which killer was scarier and what horror movie worked best, mixing up all the movies together. The conversation turned into a movie debate where we started quizzing each other with our movie knowledge," he recalled.

Not long afterward, the same friend who owned the house that Williamson had been minding, offered him the use of a condominium in Palm Springs for a writing weekend. Williamson was quick to accept because he finally had an idea for a screenplay that he wanted to develop. The trauma of finding the unlocked window had inspired him to outline a plot and some key characters in his head; now he was ready to put his ideas down on paper. "I wrote around the clock and in three days I had a first draft. That . . . is pretty much the one that got made," he recalled. Williamson explained in a subsequent interview with Andy Mangelsfor for *Sci-Fi Entertainment*,

"My intention was just to make a scary movie. I wanted to be scared. I thought we hadn't had a scary movie in a really, really long time. Horror movies had just become so predictable and plot driven. The characters were always these stick figures that didn't really amount to anything. . . . So I kind of thought well, what if we had sort of a scary movie with a little touch of Agatha Christie in there?"

Williamson's agent loved the screenplay, and so did others. When he sent it out to potential producers, the result was a bidding frenzy involving four major studios. By the time the process ended, Williamson was left with two enticing offers to choose between. One promised a lot of money, but it contained no firm production time line; the other, from Miramax, was for less money, but it included a guarantee from studio boss Bob Weinstein that the film would be made "right away." Having experienced the frustrations—and hardships—of seeing his script for "Killing Mrs. Tingle" shelved indefinitely by production delays, Williamson opted for the Miramax deal, which according to Pat Broeske paid him about $500,000. That proved to be a wise decision because Weinstein, true to his word, immediately began work on the movie; what is more, he took a personal interest in the project.

It was Weinstein who shrewdly suggested changing the movie's title from "Scary Movie" to *Scream*, having decided that the former sounded too whimsical, too much like a comedy. It was also the Miramax owner who hired legendary horror film director Wes Craven—of *Nightmare on Elm Street* fame—to direct a talented young cast that included rising stars Drew Barrymore, Courtney Cox, Neve Campbell, David Arquette, and Skeet Ulrich. "Wes Craven in many ways was the perfect choice for [*Scream*]," Williamson concluded. "He loved the idea of exposing the conventions of the genre. Wes gave [the movie] its tone. He brought it to life with a perverse wickedness and I'm forever grateful."

Scream opens with a now-famous scene that had its creative origins in Williamson's own housesitting experience: an attractive young woman, played by Drew Barrymore, is home alone one night when the phone rings. She is standing in front of patio doors when she answers, and in the ensuing conversation it becomes clear that the unidentified male caller is a psy-

Williamson's quirky horror film *The Faculty* features aliens posing as teachers who are out to get their students.

chopath who is watching her; the question she and the audience then face is whether the man is inside the house or out. For the next ninety minutes, the costumed killer proceeds to dispatch one wise-cracking teenager after another with bloody efficiency. This sort of mayhem is familiar fare for slasher movie fans. The clever twist in Williamson's plot, and what sets *Scream* apart and above other films of the genre is that the characters are cool; they have all seen and been thrilled by—and joke about!—*Halloween, Nightmare on Elm Street, Friday the 13th,* and similar films. "[*Scream*] . . . for all of its ironic in-jokes, also functions as a horror film—a bloody and gruesome one, that uses as many cliches as it mocks," wrote *Chicago Sun-Times* critic Roger Ebert.

While *Scream* was in production, Williamson eagerly snapped up whatever work he was offered, fearing a repeat of his earlier career mistake. He worked on the rewrite of an ill-fated Fox Family Film called *Big Bugs,* and he developed a screen-

play for the Columbia studio, which was based on a 1973 teen novel by Lois Duncan called *I Know What You Did Last Summer.* All the while, Williamson prayed that *Scream* would be a hit with the high school- and college-age audience at whom it was aimed. It was, of course, but even he could not have even dared to predict that *Scream* would take off as it did following its December 1996 release. The movie, which cost just $15.3 million to make, earned more than $103 million at the box office. That qualified it as one of the year's biggest hits, a "sleeper" that became one of the top-grossing horror films of all time—right up there with the 1974 classic *The Exorcist.* Moviegoers and critics alike were thrilled by *Scream.* Richard Harrington of the *Washington Post* hailed *Scream* as "an instant classic, and not simply of the genre." Bruce Fretts of *Entertainment Weekly* noted, "Although [it] satirizes its cinematic antecedents, it never forgets its primary goal—to scare the crap out of you. That it does." Michael Krantz of *Time* agreed, observing that

Criticized for its portrayal of fourteen-year-olds who are too witty and sex-savvy to be real, Williamson's very personal television show *Dawson's Creek* has nevertheless gained a wide following among teen viewers.

Scream "reviv[ed] the moribund slasher genre and lift[ed] its author into Hollywood's screenwriting elite."

More Frights

In the wake of *Scream*'s success, Columbia forged ahead with the filming of Williamson's *I Know What You Did Last Summer* screenplay. The original book is about four teens who try to hide the truth when they kill a child with a car. Williamson recalled in his interview with Andy Mangelsfor of *Sci-Fi Entertainment* that he saw the story as "a morality tale." Studio executives were less lofty in their interpretation; they wanted a teenage slasher movie, and so that is what Williamson gave them. He changed the plot, and in the process also created a new character: a murderous fisherman who serves as a malevolent avenging angel. "And so I came up the Fisherman—my

dad was a fisherman, and I knew the boat; I knew the hooks; I knew the winch," Williamson told Mangelsfor.

While studio executives may have been delighted with this new plot wrinkle, author Lois Duncan was not. "I'd be upset if I was her, too. I can't blame her at all," Williamson added. No less irate were Miramax executives, who objected when Columbia began promoting *I Know What You Did Last Summer* as a movie "From the Creator of *Scream*"—namely Kevin Williamson. Miramax sued, arguing that Columbia's claim was misleading since it was director Wes Craven who had created *Scream*. As Andy Mangelsfor noted, "The situation is . . . a difficult one for Williamson, and he chooses not to talk about it."

When it opened in the fall of 1997, *I Know What You Did Last Summer* did brisk business at the box office despite the legal battles and some tepid reviews. A cynical Roger Ebert of the *Chicago Sun-Time* speculated that Kevin Williamson "hauled this one out of the bottom drawer after *Scream* passed the $100 million mark." He also noted, "After the screening was over and the lights went up, I observed a couple of my colleagues in deep and earnest conversation, trying to resolve twists in the plot. They were applying more thought to the movie than the makers did."

Hot on the heels of *I Know What You Did Last Summer*, Miramax released *Scream 2*. Many cynics naturally assumed that the film was created as a sequel intended solely to capitalize on *Scream*'s phenomenal success. Not so, Williamson told Andy Mangelsfor; he said that from the beginning he had envisioned *Scream* as Part One of a trilogy. Miramax owners Bob and Harvey Weinstein

The *Dawson's Creek* television show has also been adapted as original stories in book form.

had bought into Williamson's vision, agreeing to make the movie, and signing its author to a $20 million contract that will see him writing movies and television shows for Miramax into the next century. "Teens today have been exposed to so much," Michael Krantz of *Time* quoted Bob Weinstein as saying. "[Writers] that don't pander win the game. Kevin understands this brilliantly, and he's got the talent to go with it."

Scream 2 opened during the Christmas 1997 season to generally favorable reviews and a strong box office. Audiences were hungry for the same kind of thrills and chills the original film served up, and neither Williamson nor director Wes Craven, back for another go-around, wanted to disappoint them. *Scream 2* reunited the members of the original cast who had not been killed off in *Scream*: Neve Campbell, Courtney Cox, and David Arquette. "*Scream 2*, smarter still [than *Scream*] relocated chief damsel-in-distress Campbell to a college campus, where a copycat maniac begins carving up students the same weekend a cheapo Hollywood bloodfest, "Stab," arrives at theaters," reviewer Tom Gliatto of *People* wrote. Nonetheless, he found the on-screen mayhem much less shocking this time around. "What once was a fun house of twisting corridors is now as endlessly reflective as a hall of mirrors," Gliatto added. "*Scream 2* is a slasher film that mocks slasher films," wrote Walter Addiego of the *San Francisco Examiner*. "For people who like their amusement blood red, *Scream 2* will do the job. It's not as good as the original—which was fresher, funnier, and scarier—but if it were . . . it wouldn't be a genuine sequel."

Success on the Small Screen

With three successive hits to his credit, by early 1998 Williamson was on top of the entertainment world. Given the success of Williamson's slasher movies, some people were surprised by his next project: a weekly television series produced by Columbia TriStar for the fledgling WB Network. *Dawson's Creek*, a weekly "zits-and-all view of teen life," as Ken Tucker of *Entertainment Weekly* described it, harkened back to Williamson's own youth in North Carolina. He had devised the series in 1994 for Fox, only to have it rejected by the network because it seemed too much like the then-struggling *Party of Five*. Williamson has a special fondness for *Dawson's Creek*. He was con-

If you enjoy the works of Kevin Williamson, you may also want to check out the following books and films:

Lois Duncan, *Don't Look Behind You*, 1989.
Rob Thomas, *Rats Saw God*, 1996.
A Nightmare on Elm Street, a film directed by Wes Craven, 1984.

tractually obligated to work on the scripts for just the first twenty-two programs, but Williamson told Bruce Fretts of *Entertainment Weekly*, "I ain't ever leavin' *Dawson's Creek*. . . . It's too personal. I may have to put it more at arm's length, but I'll never be too far from it."

From the beginning, the show generated controversy. "The series was touted as shocking and too sexy, largely because its fourteen protagonists discussed sex in much the same manner you'd find in high school hallways all across the world . . . except they did so with smart—and tart—Williamson dialogue," Andy Mangelsfor wrote. Williamson himself was obviously aware of this aspect of the show, for he conceded to Bruce Fretts of *Entertainment Weekly*, "These kids talk like they've had ten years of therapy." However, if Williamson felt this posed a problem, he didn't let on. In fact, actress Katie Holmes, who plays Joey in the series, might well have been speaking for Williamson when she told Fretts, "[The dialogue is] a little heightened, but they'll understand it. Maybe they'll learn a few new words."

While *Dawson's Creek* was heavily promoted and found a receptive audience among its target age group, many television critics panned the show; in particular, they criticized the characters Williamson had created for being too cool. Reviewer Terry Kelleher of *People* observed, "Attractive as well as articulate, all these high schoolers qualify for some sort of advanced placement. They're easy to watch, just a little hard to believe." Rick Marin of *Newsweek* quipped, "*Dawson's Creek* is as much a marketing event as a small-town serial about overheated hormones." Among those in the media who liked *Dawson's Creek* was Andrew Billen of the *New Statesman*. Billen wrote that the show was "performed with aching conventionality by a quartet of clear-complexioned Hollywood actors who look nearer thirty than fif-

teen," but he hastened to add that "Williamson's script and premise, although bizarre, display the highest intelligence."

New Adventures in Horror

Despite his growing interest in expanding his creative horizons with projects such as *Dawson's Creek*, Williamson did not abandon his horror film roots, nor could he escape them. He was reminded of that while he was in Wilmington, North Carolina, for the filming of the series' pilot. Bob Weinstein had tried without success to convince Williamson to write the screenplay for a seventh—and final—installment of the *Halloween* saga; nicknamed "H20," the movie was intended to mark the twentieth anniversary of director John Carpenter's landmark 1979 film *Halloween*. While Williamson refused the job, he could not resist a chance to meet actress Jamie Lee Curtis, who had starred in that first film in the series. Curtis, one of Williamson's favorite film stars, also happened to be shooting a movie in Wilmington, and when *Scream's* creator went to meet her, Curtis too began trying to recruit him to join the H20 creative team. Williamson finally agreed to work on the story outline for H20, with input from Curtis. He also did some work on the final draft of the screenplay. His contribution went uncredited, although he did receive a credit as co-executive-producer.

Still working to broaden his career, Williamson moved in a new direction with his next movie. *The Faculty*, which opened on Christmas Day 1998, is a science fiction spoof about a group of small-town Ohio high school students who battle to save the world when they discover that aliens have taken over the bodies of the school's teachers; Elijah Wood stars. Williamson developed the story from a screenplay originally entitled "The Feelers." Originally, he was offered a chance to direct the film, however, he wisely decided against it. Williamson told Joshua Mooney of the *Milwaukee Journal Sentinel*, "I realized I didn't have a clue how to do this movie. It became apparent that this was probably not the best project with which to begin my directing career." Instead, on Williamson's recommendation, Miramax hired Robert Rodriguez, the director of the artfully violent *El Mariachi* to direct the movie. Even so, critics were generally unimpressed with the final results.

Reviewer Allan Ulrich of the *San Francisco Examiner* described *The Faculty* as "a grafting of *Invasion of the Body Snatchers* onto *Fast Times at Ridgemont High,* [which] yields gross-out scenes amid episodes of building self-esteem for the Clearasil set." The result, Ulrich concluded, is "a sporadically engaging science fiction fable of alien invasion among the high school set." Christopher Brandon, reviewing the film on-line for *Roughcuts,* was among the minority of critics who liked *The Faculty.* While he felt that much of the movie's "inside" humor about 1950s sci-fi movies was too obscure, he wrote that *The Faculty* still succeeded as "an entertaining scare fest that's packed with *Scream*-teen attitude and the type of pop-culture references we love."

As different as *The Faculty* was, Williamson's next movie promises to be even more of a career departure for him. In early 1999, he will make his long-awaited directorial debut with *Teaching Mrs. Tingle,* the film that was left unmade after he wrote it back in 1994 (as "Killing Mrs. Tingle"). In addition, Williamson has a variety of other projects underway. He is at work on a second season of *Dawson's Creek;* he has created a drama series for ABC called *WasteLand,* which is about a group of aimless twenty-somethings in Los Angeles; he is working on an action-adventure movie script; he is doing a romantic comedy for Universal Studios called her *Leading Man;* and the final installment of the *Scream* trilogy, *Scream 3,* will open in movie theaters for Christmas 1999. Asked by Andy Mangelsfor of *Sci-Fi Entertainment* why and how he is able—and willing—to write about such a wide range of story material—horror films, romantic comedies, teen dramas, and science fiction, Williamson explained, "I just love writing. I try to write sophisticated, smart, clever people."

■ Works Cited

Addiego, Walter, "I Scream, You Scream," *San Francisco Examiner,* Dec. 12, 1997, p. B1.

Billen, Andrew, "No sex please, we're American," *New Statesman,* May 8, 1998, p. 43.

Brandon, Christopher, review of *The Faculty, Roughcuts* on-line film reviews, http://www.roughcut/reviews/movies/vault.

Broeske, Pat, "Reinventing a Genre," *Writer's Digest,* November, 1997, p. 55.

Craven, Wes, and Williamson, Kevin, *Scream: A Screenplay,* Hyperion Books, 1997.

Ebert, Roger, review of *I Know What You Did Last Summer, Chicago Sun-Times* website, http://www.suntimes.com.

Ebert, Roger, review of *Scream, Chicago Sun-Times* website, http:www.suntimes.com.

Fretts, Bruce, review of *Scream, Entertainment Weekly,* June 27, 1997, pp. 127-128.

Fretts, Bruce, "High School Confidential," *Entertainment Weekly,* January 9, 1998, p. 34.

Gliatto, Tom, review of *Scream 2, People,* December 22, 1997, p. 22.

Harrington, Richard, "Go Ahead and *Scream,*" *Washington Post,* December 20, 1996.

Johnson, Ted, "His So-Called Life," *TV Guide,* March 7, 1998, pp. 25-26, 28-29.

Kelleher, Terry, review of *Dawson's Creek, People,* January 19, 1998, p. 14.

Krantz, Michael, "The Bard of Gen-Y," *Time,* December 15, 1997, pp. 105-106.

Mangelsfor, Andy, "His Voice Should be Heard: Talking With 'Scream King' Kevin Williamson," *Sci-Fi Entertainment,* on-line at http://www.h-y-p-e.com/kw/articles/1998/foreword.html.

Marin, Rick, "My So-Called Soap," *Newsweek,* January 19, 1998, p. 68.

Mooney, Joshua, "*Faculty* is to sci-fi what *Scream* was to horror," *Milwaukee Journal Sentinel,* January 1, 1999, p. 10E.

Nashawnty, Christ, *Entertainment Weekly,* December, 1997.

Tucker, Ken, review of *Dawson's Creek, Entertainment Weekly,* January 23, 1998.

Ulrich, Allan, "The Faculty Deserves an 'F' in Satire," *San Francisco Examiner,* December 25, 1998, p. B12.

■ For More Information See

PERIODICALS

Entertainment Weekly, August 1, 1997, p. 13; October 14, 1997, p. 44; November 14, 1997, p. 63; December 19, 1997, p. 57; December 22, 1997, pp. 22-23; January 9, 1998, p. 34; January 23, 1998, pp. 45-46.

Newsweek, December 23, 1996, p. 79; November 3, 1997, p. 84.

People, November 3, 1997, p. 22.

TV Guide, February 7, 1998, p. 16.

Variety, October 13, 1997, p. 78; December 8, 1997, p. 111*.

—Sketch by Ken Cuthbertson

Connie Willis

■ Personal

Born December 31, 1945, in Denver, CO; step-daughter of William and LaMarlys Crook Trimmer; married Courtney W. Willis (a physics teacher), August 23, 1967; children: Cordelia. *Education:* Colorado State College (now University of Northern Colorado), B.A., 1967.

■ Addresses

Home—1716 13th Ave., Greeley, CO 80631. *Agent*—Ralph Vicinanza, 111 Eighth Ave., Suite 1501, New York, NY 10011.

■ Career

Branford Public Schools, Branford, CT, teacher of fifth and seventh grades, 1967-69; freelance writer, 1969—; substitute teacher, Woodland Park, CO, 1974-81. *Member:* Science Fiction Writers of America.

■ Awards, Honors

National Endowment for the Humanities grant, 1980; Hugo Awards, World Science Fiction Convention, 1982, for novelette "Fire Watch," 1983, for short story "A Letter from the Clearys," 1988, for novella "The Last of the Winnebagos," 1993, for novel *Doomsday Book,* 1993, for short story "Even the Queen," and 1994, for "Death on the Nile"; Nebula Awards, Science Fiction Writers of America, 1982, for novelette "Fire Watch" and short story "A Letter from the Clearys," 1988, for novella "The Last of the Winnebagos," 1989, for novelette "At the Rialto," 1992, for novel *Doomsday Book* and short story "Even the Queen"; John W. Campbell Memorial Award, Science Fiction Research Association, 1988, for novel *Lincoln's Dreams; Locus* Awards, 1992, for novel *Doomsday Book* and short story "Even the Queen," and 1998, for short story "Newsletter."

■ Writings

SCIENCE FICTION AND FANTASY NOVELS

(With Cynthia Felice) *Water Witch,* Ace Books, 1982.
Lincoln's Dreams, Bantam, 1987.
(With Cynthia Felice) *Light Raid,* Ace Books, 1989.
Doomsday Book, Bantam, 1992.
Uncharted Territory, Bantam, 1994, expanded edition, New English Library, 1994.

Remake, M.V. Ziesing, 1994, Bantam, 1995.
Bellwether, Bantam, 1996.
(With Cynthia Felice) *Promised Land,* Ace, 1997.
To Say Nothing of the Dog, Bantam, 1997.

SCIENCE FICTION AND FANTASY STORIES

Fire Watch, Bluejay, 1984.
(With Poul Anderson, Ed Bryant, Stephen R.
 Donaldson, Larry Niven, Fred Saberhagen, and
 Roger Zelazny) *Berserker Base,* Tor Books, 1985.
Impossible Things, Bantam, 1994.
(Editor with Martin H. Greenberg) *The New Hugo
 Winners: Volume III,* Baen, 1994.
(Editor) *Nebula Awards 33,* Harcourt, 1999.

OTHER

Author of foreword, *Weird Women, Wired Women,*
by Kit Reed, University Press of New England,
1998. Contributor of short fiction to periodicals,
including *Isaac Asimov's Science Fiction Magazine,
Omni,* and *Magazine of Fantasy and Science Fiction.*

■ **Adaptations**

Several audio versions of Willis's works have been
recorded, including *Cibola* (short story), 1996; and
Even the Queen and Other Short Stories, Wyrmhole
Publishing, 1997.

■ **Sidelights**

"I think science fiction (SF) is the most free and
open of all the genres," award-winning author
Connie Willis said in a 1998 Cybling online interview. "Romances, you're tied to a single plot with
a couple of variations. Westerns, you're tied to a
locale and a lot of conventions of detail. Mystery,
the mystery has to be central, not the characterization. But in SF you can do anything! You can
rewrite fairy tales, you can do history, you can
do biology, you can do religion, you can do character driven stories . . . you can do adventures.
Or you can do deep philosophical stuff . . . you
can do anything!" Willis has taken advantage of
the wide possibilities of science fiction to earn a
dozen Hugo and Nebula Awards—more than any
other writer in the genre. She is "one of the least
predictable" writers in the field, Don D'Ammassa

noted in *Twentieth-Century Science-Fiction Writers,*
with works "ranging from science fiction to fantasy to horror." As a result, the critic explained,
"Willis has established a reputation as one of the
most reliably skillful writers in the genre, particularly at shorter length."

Willis was born in Colorado in 1945, and spent
her childhood there. When she was twelve years
old, her mother died, and "the world ended," the
author wrote in *Locus.* "Like Katherine Ann Por-
ter said in *Pale Horse, Pale Rider,* a knife came and
cut my life in half." However, Willis found some

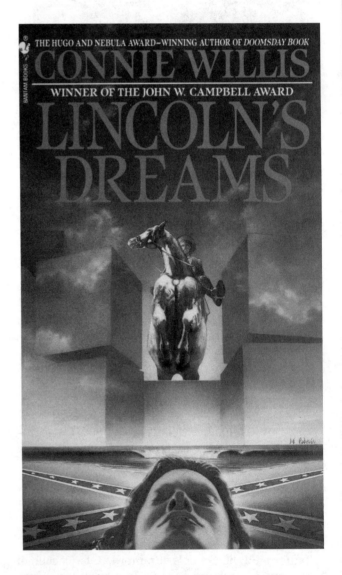

In her award-winning 1987 novel, Willis tells the romantic story of a modern-day woman haunted by realistic dreams of the Civil War and the research historian who goes on a quest to help her.

comfort in books, and at age thirteen she discovered Robert Heinlein's classic novel *Have Space Suit, Will Travel.* Willis became hooked on science fiction in general and Heinlein in particular. "I loved him from the minute I picked up *Have Space Suit, Will Travel,* because his characters were so smart and because his futures were so lived in and because there was so much humor in his books," she explained in answering a reader question posed to her during a *Science Fiction Weekly* online interview. Willis hoped to write similar works some day, and dreamed of having her own stories appear in one of the various "Year's Best Science Fiction" collections she enjoyed.

After graduating from high school, Willis attended Colorado State College (now the University of Northern Colorado), where she studied English and elementary education. She always planned to become a writer, but figured that she would need a regular job to support herself until she broke into the business. She earned her degree in 1967, the same year that she married Courtney Willis, and began teaching in Connecticut. She left teaching two years later when she had a baby, and planned to write at home while raising her daughter, Cordelia. For the next eight years she wrote science fiction, but only made a single sale in the genre. To combat the rejection slips, she also wrote "tawdry" confession stories for magazines such as *True Romance* and *True Confessions.* While the pieces were not what she really wanted to write, they gave her good experience as well as publication credits. As she explained in *Locus,* the "positive side" of writing confessions was that "I did nothing for ten years but plot, because there was nothing else to do. In the Confessions, there's no room for innovation or experimental literature or elaborate Jamesian characterizations or anything, so you just do plot. I do think it really helped me learn how to structure my stories."

Willis persisted, and by 1980 she was publishing short stories in science fiction magazines and anthologies; she also collaborated with Cynthia Felice on a novel, *Water Witch.* Although the science fiction field had been dominated by men prior to the 1970s, the author did not feel she was at any disadvantage because of her sex. "I suffered no discrimination ever that I know of," Willis noted in *Locus.* "I felt all I had to do was write better stories and I would break into the field. I wrote better stories, and I broke into the field. To me, there were no barricades. There had always been

women in the field, and I was going to be one of those women."

Travels in Time and Space

It was with her short stories that Willis finally made a breakthrough. Her 1982 novelette "Fire Watch" earned both the Hugo and Nebula Awards—given by science fiction fans and writers, respectively—while the same year her short story "A Letter to the Clearys" also swept science fiction's highest honors. "Fire Watch" is set in a future where history students conduct research by actually travelling back in time; one student is sent back to witness the London Blitz of World War II, where he battles alongside the volunteers who are trying to prevent the destruction of St. Paul's Cathedral. But the story is about more than war and time travel; as Gerald Jonas observed in the *New York Times Book Review,* Willis "is concerned with things that last and things that don't—and with admirable economy, she uses time travel to explore the distinction." Similarly, "A Letter from the Clearys" is about more than portraying the world after a nuclear war. In examining how a young woman struggles to deal with the aftermath of a nuclear holocaust, "Willis illustrates the strongest point of her fiction, her ability to create utterly convincing characters," D'Ammassa stated. Both these stories were published in the author's first story collection, titled *Fire Watch.* Writing of the collection's eleven stories, a *Publishers Weekly* critic noted that "Willis's range is impressive" and called *Fire Watch* "an exciting collection by one of the best new SF writers." Jonas similarly remarked that Willis's writing "is fresh, subtle and deeply moving," while *Booklist's* Roland Green concluded that the author's technique and "impressive command of the language make for accomplished readability."

In 1987, Willis brought out her first solo novel, *Lincoln's Dreams.* The story is about Jeff Johnston, a research assistant for a famous novelist who writes of the Civil War. Annie is a young woman whose increasingly detailed dreams of that conflict have brought her to Jeff's psychiatrist roommate. As Jeff hears Annie relate details about the war that only an expert would know, he takes her on a journey to discover the strange psychic connection behind her dreams. "The bones of the plot suggest little of the novel's clarity, its

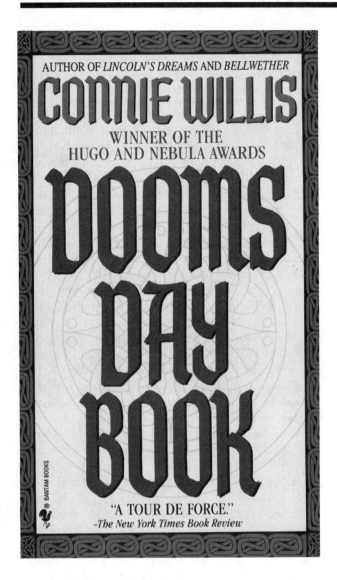

AUTHOR OF *LINCOLN'S DREAMS* AND *BELLWETHER*

CONNIE WILLIS

WINNER OF THE
HUGO AND NEBULA AWARDS

DOOMS DAY BOOK

"A TOUR DE FORCE."
–*The New York Times Book Review*

BANTAM BOOKS

Winner of the Hugo and Nebula awards, *Doomsday Book* is about a twenty-first-century history student who travels back to Europe at the time of the Black Death.

numinosity and depth of feeling," reviewer Gregory Feeley pointed out in the *Washington Post Book World*, adding that *Lincoln's Dreams* "is a novel of classical proportions and virtues, accessible, humane and moving." Gerald Jonas of the *New York Times Book Review* was equally impressed. "Willis's theme, as in her prize-winning story, 'Fire Watch,' is the persistent nature of time," he wrote. "The past is alive, not only in our memories, but in some super-real sense, and we ignore its claims on us at our peril." *Los Angeles Times Book Review* contributor David Brin wrote that *Lincoln's Dreams* "fulfills all the expec-

tations of those who have admired [the author's] award-winning short fiction." Brin went on to praise Willis's deftness in creating strong, believable characters, noting that "whether writing drama or witty humor or, in this case, a poignant examination of duty, [she] conveys through her characters a sense of transcendent pity that few modern authors ever attempt."

Although *Lincoln's Dreams* was a critical success— earning the John W. Campbell Memorial Award from the Science Fiction Research Association— Willis did not forsake the short story format. In 1988 she again won both the Hugo and Nebula Awards for her novella "The Last of the Winnebagos," while the following year she scored another Nebula for her novelette "At the Rialto." In "The Last of the Winnebagos," a photographer discovers clues about such obsolete items as dogs and recreational vehicles. D'Ammassa called this tale of extinction "one of the most poignant stories of the near future ever to appear in the field." On the other hand, the light-hearted "At the Rialto" showcases one of Willis's favorite techniques: that of "reflecting a scientific principle in the behavior and psychology of characters in a non-science-fictional situation," as Paul Kincaid described it in the *St. James Guide to Fantasy Writers*. "At the Rialto" illustrates chaos theory and the uncertainty principle of physics as it follows the troubles Dr. Ruth Baringer meets while attending a conference on quantum physics. The staff and equipment at the Rialto hotel never work properly, while the conference sessions are never in the assigned rooms and some speakers fail to show. Not only does "At the Rialto" speculate about theoretical physics, it "is a good example of effective humor, a device Willis uses consistently," Jane S. Bakerman observed in *Contemporary Novelists*. Both stories appeared in Willis's second collection, *Impossible Things*, which "displays a versatility of form and conception few in the genre can match," Carl Hays asserted in *Booklist*. Margaret Miles similarly hailed the collection in *Voice of Youth Advocates*, stating that "no story here is weak, no story fails to stand out in some way, and no story lacks Willis's inexorable, delicate, stylish touch."

An award-winning writer and an excellent speaker, Willis became a popular guest at science fiction conventions. It was at one of these conventions that she first conceived the idea for her highly regarded novel *Doomsday Book*. In a panel discussion on nuclear war, she found herself arguing against people who said that the results of a nuclear holocaust were unpredictable because nothing like it had ever happened before. "I said, 'Oh, yes, it has! The end of the world happened once before. You know, the Black Death,'" the author related in *Locus*. This viral plague, which killed over a third of Europe's population in the 1300s, "was kind of like radiation. It was everywhere. They didn't have any idea what had caused it. They couldn't stop it or see it or figure it out, and it was just killing people in droves." As Willis researched the era, she discovered her interpretation was fairly accurate, and she began to write a novel that recalled this long-ago "end of the world."

The First End of the World

Doomsday Book has the same initial setting as Willis's novelette "Fire Watch," with a twenty-first century Oxford history student being sent back in time as part of her degree requirement. However, instead of landing in the relatively safe year of 1320, Kivrin has arrived in 1348, at the height of the Black Death. Unfortunately for her, Kirvin's present-day supervisors have little time to spare to correct the mistake, for they are dealing with their own medical calamity: an outbreak of a virulent strain of flu. The brutal realities of the plague Kivrin faces in 1348 and the similar problems her colleagues confront in 2050 are intertwined throughout the novel. The author's research pays off in a realistic, believable portrayal of medieval life. As John Clute observed in the *Washington Post Book World*, "the world of 1348 burns in the mind's eye, and every character alive in that year is a fully realized being." Clute went on to state that the novel is "quite astonishingly gripping, cleverly constructed, cunningly hooked, narrated with such care that its momentum builds irresistibly." Reviewer Gary K. Wolfe of *Locus* echoed that praise, writing that the future tale of "academic politics and epidemiology" is both "convincing" and "a suspenseful counterpoint to the medieval narrative." Wolfe went on to write, "The essential form of *Doomsday Book* is not that of an historical novel or even of a time-travel story, but rather that of the end-of-the-world tale. That at least is the belief Willis' medieval characters come to adopt, and by the time we've lived with Kivrin through the harrowing series of tragedies that lead to the book's climax, we're convinced."

Other reviewers also lauded the compelling nature of *Doomsday Book*. "What makes this novel so outstanding . . . is that it lives and breathes," David V. Barrett remarked in *New Statesman & Society*, calling the work "one of the harshest yet most beautiful novels I have read for years." *Booklist*'s Roland Green likewise described *Doomsday Book* as "one of the best genre novels of the year," and he praised Willis's "deftness with language, superb characterization, and subtle wit." Calling *Doomsday Book* "a great accomplishment in storytelling," *Wilson Library Bulletin* writer Gene

This satire of corporate life brings together two scientists who decide to study sheep in order to understand chaos theory and end up revealing a lot about human stupidity.

LaFaille praised the characterization and observed that "the interweaving of past and future; the epidemiological information made understandable to the layperson; and the building, releasing, and rebuilding of tension are rarely so well written."

While *Doomsday Book* demonstrated Willis's ability to create a deeply moving story, her next works showcased her comic talents. The author's 1994 novel *Uncharted Territory* is a farcical romantic comedy set on an alien planet. Noted planetary explorers Finriddy and Carson are trying to survey the planet Boohte while still respecting the culture of the native species—who are all too willing to take financial advantage of their guests. Into the mix comes Evelyn Parker, a specialist in alien reproduction, and the discovery that hero-worshipping Evelyn is a male creates confusion throughout. "Willis handles all this with the high spirits and cheerful insensitivity of a Howard Hawks," Gary K. Wolfe noted in *Locus*, comparing the author to the noted film director of romantic comedies, "and gets off some genuinely funny lines along the way." However, Tim Sullivan wrote in the *Washington Post Book World* that "the comedy gracefully illuminates a number of contemporary issues quite painlessly," such as political correctness and gender roles. The critic observed that "the political and social satire is seamlessly integrated with the characters and setting," and concluded: "It's great to read a feminist work that appears to have no axe to grind."

Willis published another comic work in 1994, this time a send-up of Hollywood and the film industry. In *Remake*, it is the twenty-first century and films are no longer produced with live actors. Instead, classic works are endlessly remade using the digitally reproduced "performances" of proven talents. Tom is working in the industry carefully removing mentions or portrayals of alcohol consumption when he meets Alis, a dancer who wants to appear in films even though they no longer use real performers. As Tom tries to assist Alis with her dream, Willis creates a "discerning" portrayal of "the way movies inform our imaginations, giving us roles to play, and about desire, purpose and possibility," a *Publishers Weekly* critic commented. *Remake* "demonstrates a rare capacity for evoking both humor and regret," a *Library Journal* reviewer stated, while Charles de Lint of the *Magazine of Fantasy and Science Fiction* praised the author's attention to character and plot. "The heart of *Remake* is the timeless story of how we relate to one another and keep faith with our friends and ourselves," de Lint wrote. "And in that, as she has proved so often in the past, Willis excels."

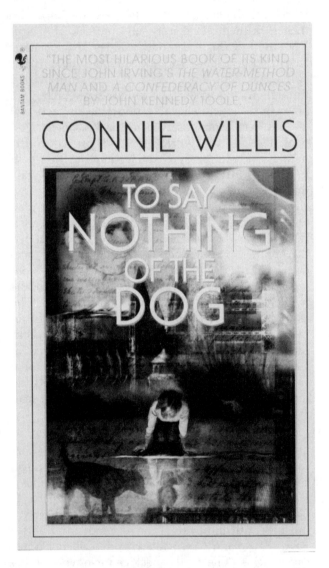

Taking a lighter look at time travel in this comical story, Willis tells how accidentally transporting a cat from the nineteenth to the twenty-first century threatens the fabric of the time-space continuum.

Chaos and Comedy

In her 1996 novel *Bellwether*, Willis satirizes corporate bureaucracy and modern-day fads while exploring the implications of chaos theory. In a giant, Dilbert-like corporation called HiTek, sociologist Sandra Foster is researching the formation

If you enjoy the works of Connie Willis, you may also want to check out the following books and films:

Orson Scott Card, *Maps in a Mirror,* 1990.
Nancy Kress, *The Aliens of Earth,* 1993.
Close Encounters of the Third Kind, a film directed by Steven Spielberg, 1977.

of fads so that HiTek can anticipate and thus profit from them. At the other end of the building is Bennett O'Reilly, an expert in chaos theory who is having difficulty maintaining funding for his research. The two are brought together by the terminally disorganized Flip, a mail clerk who causes trouble wherever she goes, and Sandra comes up with the idea of combining their research by studying the organizational behavior of sheep. This romantic comedy is "witty, thought-provoking, and a little too close to the bone to be considered a fantasy," Kathleen Beck observed in *Voice of Youth Advocates.* A *Publishers Weekly* reviewer noted that the plot's use of mix-ups, near-misses, and coincidence "neatly embodies [Willis's] theme of chaos," and adds that "the real pleasure [of the book] is the thick layers of detail . . . and the wryly disdainful commentary on human stupidity." "The analysis of humanity and the human condition are dead-on," a reviewer for the *Magazine of Fantasy and Science Fiction* likewise remarked, concluding that *Bellwether* "shows Willis in top form—again."

In her 1997 novel *To Say Nothing of the Dog,* Willis returned to the Oxford time-travel universe of "Fire Watch" and *Doomsday Book.* This novel is in a lighter vein than the previous time-travel stories, however, since the author tries "to make them as different from one another as I can," as she revealed in her *Science Fiction Weekly* online interview. Although the time-travel mechanism is supposed to prevent anything from the past from travelling into the present, in this instance a soft-hearted traveller has somehow brought a nineteenth-century cat into the twenty-first century. Ned Turner has been sent back to the year 1889 to return the cat and also recover from the effects of too many time jumps. As he travels in Victorian England, Ned meets Verity Brown, who herself has an unsettling knowledge of time travel. "No one mixes scientific mumbo jumbo and com-

edy of manners with more panache than Willis, who . . . is in one of her lighter moods in this novel," Jonas wrote in the *New York Times Book Review.* The novel makes reference to famous novels set in Victorian England, as Ned and Verity attempt to solve a mystery and prevent the collapse of the space-time continuum. "The elements of historical accuracy, mystery, and the convoluted nature of time travel are well balanced and convincing," Mary B. McCarthy commented in *Voice of Youth Advocates,* concluding that *To Say Nothing of the Dog* is "charming stuff-and-nonsense."

Although she has published six novels in the 1990s, Willis remains active in the short story genre, earning a *Locus* Award in 1998 for the story "Newsletter." She has said that she intends to continue working in the shorter genres, no matter how successful she becomes as a novelist. "I will never, even if it means the death of my career, abandon the short story and the novella," Willis wrote in *Locus.* "That's where my heart is. I think the future looks best when sort of glimpsed through a keyhole. You put a spotlight on one tiny little part of the future, the past, aliens, whatever, and then you have little hints of the vista that stretches out behind them. That's far more effective than working out the entire vista." "World-building" holds little interest for her, she explained, when the short story can actually convey a larger picture. "The short story tends to resonate beyond, it takes on an aura so it's bigger than it actually is." With the versatility of subject, mood, and length in her fiction, however, any new work from Willis is eagerly awaited by science fiction fans, and it is likely that she will maintain, as Paul Kincaid asserted in the *St. James Guide to Fantasy Writers,* her "formidable reputation as a fluent and often startling writer of science fiction."

■ Works Cited

Bakerman, Jane S., "Connie Willis," *Contemporary Novelists,* St. James Press, 1996, pp. 1054-56.

Barrett, David V., "Out of Time," *New Statesman & Society,* November 27, 1992, p. 38.

Beck, Kathleen, review of *Bellwether, Voice of Youth Advocates,* August, 1996, p. 173.

Review of *Bellwether, Magazine of Fantasy and Science Fiction,* April, 1996, p. 33.

Review of *Bellwether, Publishers Weekly,* January 29, 1996, p. 96.

Brin, David, review of *Lincoln's Dreams, Los Angeles Times Book Review,* February 7, 1988, p. 11.

Clute, John, review of *Doomsday Book, Washington Post Book World,* June 28, 1992, p. 8.

D'Ammassa, Don, "Connie Willis," *Twentieth-Century Science-Fiction Writers,* St. James Press, 1991, pp. 871-72.

de Lint, Charles, review of *Remake, Magazine of Fantasy and Science Fiction,* May, 1995, pp. 35-36.

Feeley, Gregory, "Cyberpunks and Humanists," *Washington Post Book World,* May 24, 1987, p. 6.

Review of *Fire Watch, Publishers Weekly,* January 18, 1985, p. 64.

Green, Roland, review of *Fire Watch, Booklist,* February 15, 1985, p. 824.

Green, Roland, review of *Doomsday Book, Booklist,* June 15, 1992, p. 1811.

Hays, Carl, review of *Impossible Things, Booklist,* December 15, 1993, p. 741.

Jonas, Gerald, review of *Fire Watch, New York Times Book Review,* March 10, 1985, p. 31.

Jonas, Gerald, review of *Lincoln's Dreams, New York Times Book Review,* June 7, 1987, p. 18.

Jonas, Gerald, review of *To Say Nothing of the Dog, New York Times Book Review,* December 21, 1997, p. 21.

Kincaid, Paul, "Connie Willis," *St. James Guide to Fantasy Writers,* St. James Press, 1996, pp. 621-22.

LaFaille, Gene, "Science Fiction Universe," *Wilson Library Bulletin,* September, 1992, pp. 98-99.

McCarthy, Mary B., review of *To Say Nothing of the Dog, Voice of Youth Advocates,* April, 1998, p. 62.

Miles, Margaret, review of *Impossible Things, Voice of Youth Advocates,* June, 1994, p. 102.

Review of *Remake, Library Journal,* December, 1994, p. 139.

Review of *Remake, Publishers Weekly,* December 19, 1994, p. 51.

Sullivan, Tim, review of *Uncharted Territory, Washington Post Book World,* June 26, 1994, p. 11.

Willis, Connie, "Connie Willis: Talking Back to Shakespeare," *Locus,* July, 1992, pp. 4, 72-73.

Willis, Connie, online interview with *Science Fiction Weekly,* http://www.scifi.com/sfw/issue17/interview.html, 1996.

Willis, Connie, online interview with Cybling, http://www.cybling.com, August, 1998.

Wolfe, Gary K., review of *Doomsday Book, Locus,* March, 1992, p. 27.

Wolfe, Gary K., review of *Uncharted Territory, Locus,* June, 1994, p. 62.

■ For More Information See

ON-LINE

Connie Willis Homepage, http://www.geocities.com.

PERIODICALS

Locus, July, 1992, p. 36; January, 1995, p. 21.

New York Times Book Review, August 14, 1994, p. 30.

Publishers Weekly, April 14, 1989; November 29, 1993, p. 59; June 6, 1994, p. 62.

Voice of Youth Advocates, October, 1987, p. 182.

Washington Post Book World, July 31, 1988; May 28, 1989.

—Sketch by Diane Telgen

Acknowledgments

Acknowledgments

Grateful acknowledgment is made to the following publishers, authors, and artists for their kind permission to reproduce copyrighted material.

SHERWOOD ANDERSON. Benton, Thomas Hart, illustrator. From a cover of *Poor White,* by Sherwood Anderson. New Directions, 1993. Copyright © 1999 by New Directions Publishing Corp. Art © T. H. Benton and R. P. Benton Testamentary Trusts/Licensed by VAGA, New York, NY. Reproduced by permission of Visual Artists and Galleries Association, Inc. in North America by New Directions Publishing Corp. / Cover of *Winesburg, Ohio,* by Sherwood Anderson. Signet Classics, 1993. Reproduced by permission of Viking Penguin, a division of Penguin Putnam Inc. / "Adolescence," 1933-1940, painting by Grant Wood. From a cover of *The Egg and Other Stories,* by Sherwood Anderson. Penguin Books, 1998. Art © Estate of Grant Wood/Licensed by VAGA, New York, NY. Reproduced by permission. / Anderson, Sherwood, 1984, photograph by Alfred Stieglitz. The Library of Congress.

T. A. BARRON. Barron, T. A., photograph by Currie C. Barron. Reproduced by permission of the author.

JAMES BERRY. Fuchs, Bernie. From a jacket of *Ajeemah and His Son,* by James Berry. HarperTrophy, 1994. Jacket copyright © 1991 by Bernie Fuchs. Jacket copyright © 1991 by HarperCollins Publishers. Reproduced by permission of HarperCollins Publishers. / Gilbert, Yvonne, illustrator. From a cover of *Classic Poems to Read Aloud,* by James Berry. Larousse Kingfisher Chambers Inc., 1997. Cover illustration © 1997 Yvonne Gilbert. Reproduced by permission of Larousse Kingfisher Chambers, New York. / Cover of *Everywhere Faces Everywhere: Poems,* by James Berry. Simon & Schuster Books for Young Readers, 1997. Reproduced by permission of Simon & Schuster Books for Young Readers, an imprint of Simon & Schuster's Children's Publishing Division. / Berry, James, photograph. Peters, Fraser & Dunlop Group, Ltd. Reproduced by permission.

DEE BROWN. Cover of *Bury My Heart at Wounded Knee: An Indian History of the American West,* by Dee Brown. Henry Holt and Company, 1991. Reproduced by permission of Henry Holt and Company, LLC. / Cover of *Hear That Lonesome Whistle Blow: Railroads in the West,* by Dee Brown. Photograph from Corbis-Bettmann. Touchstone Books, 1994. Reproduced by permission of Corbis-Bettmann. / Cover of *Conspiracy of Knaves,* by Dee Brown. Wings Books, 1996. Reproduced by permission of Wings Books, a division of Crown Publishers, Inc. / "Tennessee (Mohawk Valley)," oil painting by Alexander Helwig Wyant. From a jacket of *The Way to Bright Star,* by Dee Brown. Tom Doherty Associates Book, 1998. Painting gift of Mrs. George E. Schank in memory of Arthur Hoppock Hearn. Photo © 1984 by The Metropolitan Museum of Art. Reproduced by permission. / Brown, Dee, photograph. Reproduced by permission of the author.

JUDITH ORTIZ COFER. Cover of *Silent Dancing: A Partial Remembrance of a Puerto Rican Childhood,* by Judith Ortiz Cofer. Arte Publico Press—University of Houston, 1990. Reproduced by permission. / Sanchez, Juan, illustrator. From a cover of *The Latin Deli: Prose and Poetry,* by Judith Ortiz Cofer. W. W. Norton & Company, Inc., 1995. Reproduced by permission of the illustrator. / Brisson, James F., illustrator. From a cover of *The Year of Our Revolution,* by Judith Ortiz Cofer. Arte Publico Press—University of Houston, 1998. Reproduced by permission. / Cofer, Judith Ortiz, photograph. Arte Publico Press Archives, University of Houston. Reproduced by permission.

DIANE DUANE. Jensen, Bruce, illustrator. From a cover of *Spiderman: The Venom Factor,* by Diane Duane. Byron Preiss Multimedia Company, Inc., 1995. TM & © 1999 Marvel Characters, Inc. All rights reserved. Reproduced by permission of Marvel Entertainment Group, Inc. / Goldstrom, Robert, illustrator. From a cover of *The Book of Night with Moon,* by Diane Duane. Warner Books, 1997. Reproduced by permission. / Bowers, David, illustrator. From a cover of *High Wizardry,* by Diane Duane. Magic Carpet Books, 1997. Cover illustration © 1997 by David Bowers. Reproduced by permission of Scott Hull Associates for David Bowers. / Post, R. K., illustrator. From a cover of *Starrise at Corrivale,* by Diane Duane. TSR, Inc., 1998. Reproduced by permission. / Duane, Diane, photograph. Reproduced by permission of the author.

JACK FINNEY. Cover of *Three by Finney,* by Jack Finney. Fireside Books, 1987. Reproduced by permission of Simon & Schuster, Inc. / Ratzkin, Lawrence, photographer. From a cover of *Time and Again,* by Jack Finney. Scribner Paperback Fiction, 1995. Reproduced by permission of the photographer. / Cover of *About Time: 12 Short Stories,* by Jack Finney. Scribner Paperback Fiction, 1998. Cover photograph © Archive Photos. Reproduced by permission of Archive Photos, Inc. / McCarthy, Kevin and Dana Wynter, in the film "Invasion of the Body Snatchers," 1956, photograph. The Kobal Collection. Reproduced by permission. / Finney, Jack, photograph by Darcy Padilla/NYT Pictures. Reproduced by permission.

STANLEY KUBRICK. Scene from the film "2001: A Space Odyssey," 1968, photograph. The Kobal Collection. Reproduced by permission. / Nicholson, Jack, in the film "The Shining," 1980, photograph. The Kobal Collection.

Reproduced by permission. / Modine, Matthew, and Adam Baldwin, in the film "Full Metal Jacket," 1987, photograph. The Kobal Collection. Reproduced by permission. / Kubrick, Stanley, photograph. Archive Photos, Inc. Reproduced by permission.

CHRISTA LAIRD. Duffy, Daniel Mark, illustrator. From a cover of *Shadow of the Wall,* by Christa Laird. Beech Tree Books, 1997. Cover illustration © 1997 by Daniel Mark Duffy. Reproduced by permission of Beech Tree Books, a division of William Morrow and Company, Inc. / Duffy, Daniel Mark, illustrator. From a cover of *But Can the Phoenix Sing?,* by Christa Laird. Beech Tree Books, 1998. Cover illustration © 1998 by Daniel Mark Duffy. Reproduced by permission of Beech Tree Books, a division of William Morrow and Company, Inc. / Laird, Christa, photograph. Reproduced by permission of the author.

JACOB LAWRENCE. "Christmas Pageant," painting by Jacob Lawrence. Corbis-Bettmann. Reproduced by permission of Corbis-Bettmann and Jacob Lawrence. / "Depression," painting by Jacob Lawrence, photograph by Geoffrey Clements. Whitney Museum of American Art. Reproduced by permission of Whitney Museum of American Art and Jacob Lawrence. / "Tombstones," painting by Jacob Lawrence, photograph by Geoffrey Clements. Whitney Museum of American Art. Reproduced by permission of Whitney Museum of American Art and Jacob Lawrence. / Lawrence, Jacob, photograph by Frank Stewart. AP/Wide World Photos. Reproduced by permission.

JOAN MIRÓ. "The Gold of the Azure," 1967, oil painting by Joan Miró. From a jacket of *Miró,* by Walter Erben. Taschen, 1998. © 1999 by Artists Rights Society (ARS), New York/ADAGP, Paris. Reproduced by permission of the Artists Rights Society, Inc. / "The Hunter (Catalan Landscape)," 1923-24, oil on canvas, 25 ½ x 39 ½" (64.8 x 100.3 cm), painting by Joan Miró. The Museum of Modern Art, New York. © 1999 The Museum of Modern Art, New York. © Artists Rights Society (ARS), New York/ADAGP, Paris. Reproduced by permission of The Museum of Modern Art, New York, and Artists Rights Society, Inc. / "The Port," painting by Joan Miró, photograph. Art Resource, NY. © 1999 Artists Rights Society (ARS), New York/ADAGP, Paris. Photograph © ARS, NY. Reproduced by permission of Art Resource and Artists Rights Society, Inc. / Miró, Joan, photograph. AP/Wide World Photos. © 1999 by Artists Rights Society (ARS), New York/ADAGP, Paris. Reproduced by permission of AP/Wide World Photos and the Artists Rights Society, Inc. / Miró, Joan, photograph by Carl Van Vechten. Reproduced by permission of the Estate of Carl Van Vechten.

PERRY NODELMAN. Cieslawski, Steve, illustrator. From a jacket of *A Completely Different Place,* by Perry Nodelman. Simon & Schuster Books for Young Readers, 1997. Jacket illustration © 1997 by Steve Cieslawski. / Cover of *Of Two Minds,* by Carol Matas and Perry Nodelman. Scholastic, 1998. Cover illustration © 1998 by Scholastic Inc. Reproduced by permission. / Nodelman, Perry, photograph by Peter Tittenberger. Reproduced by permission of the author.

JANETTE OKE. Thornberg, Dan, illustrator. From a cover of *Once Upon a Summer,* by Janette Oke. Bethany House Publishers, 1981. Reproduced by permission. / Cover of *Love's Long Journey,* by Janette Oke. Bethany House Publishers, 1982. Reproduced by permission. / Jacket of *Janette Oke: A Heart for the Prairie,* by Laurel Oke Logan. Bethany House Publishers, 1993. Reproduced by permission. / Thornberg, Dan, illustrator. From a cover of *Drums of Change: The Story of Running Fawn,* by Janette Oke. Bethany House Publishers, 1996. Reproduced by permission. / Cover of *The Tender Years,* by Janette Oke. Bethany House, 1997. © Bethany House Publishers, 1997. Reproduced by permission. / Oke, Janette, photograph. Bethany House Publishers. Reproduced by permission.

SARA PARETSKY. Cover of *Burn Marks,* by Sara Paretsky. Dell, 1991. Reproduced by permission of Dell Publishing, a division of Random House, Inc. / Cover of *Guardian Angel,* by Sara Paretsky. Dell, 1993. Reproduced by permission of Dell Publishing, a division of Random House, Inc. / Cover of *Tunnel Vision,* by Sara Paretsky. Dell, 1995. Reproduced by permission of Dell Publishing, a division of Random House, Inc. / Cover of *Women on the Case,* edited by Sara Paretsky. Dell, 1997. Reproduced by permission of Dell Publishing, a division of Random House, Inc. / Paretsky, Sara, photograph. Reproduced by permission of the author.

LISA SCOTTOLINE. Griffin, Jim, illustrator. From a cover of *Everywhere That Mary Went,* by Lisa Scottoline. HarperPaperbacks, 1993. Reproduced by permission of HarperCollins Publishers. / Gerber, Mark, illustrator. From a cover of *Legal Tender,* by Lisa Scottoline. HarperPaperbacks, 1997. Reproduced by permission of HarperCollins Publishers. / Cover of *Rough Justice,* by Lisa Scottoline. HarperPaperbacks, 1998. Reproduced by permission of HarperCollins Publishers. / Ducak, Danilo, illustrator. From a cover of *Running from the Law,* by Lisa Scottoline. HarperPaperbacks, 1996. Reproduced by permission of HarperCollins Publishers. / Scottoline, Lisa, photograph. Reproduced by permission of the author.

J. MICHAEL STRACZYNSKI. Cover of *The Complete Book of Scriptwriting,* by J. Michael Straczynski. Writer's Digest Books, 1996. Reproduced by permission. / Boxleitner, Bruce, and others, in the television series "Babylon 5," 1996, photograph. The Kobal Collection. Reproduced by permission. / Straczynski, J. Michael, photograph by Byron J. Cohen. AP Photo/Pten Consortium. Reproduced by permission.

ERIKA TAMAR. Brennan, Steve, illustrator. From a cover of *The Things I Did Last Summer,* by Erika Tamar. Harcourt, 1994. Cover illustration © 1994 by Steve Brennan. Reproduced by permission of the illustrator. / Kahl, David, illustrator. From a cover of *Fair Game,* by Erika Tamar. Cover illustration © 1993 by David Kahl. Reproduced by permission of the illustrator. / Tamar, Erika, photograph. Reproduced by permission of the author.

CYNTHIA VOIGT. Cover of *Dicey's Song,* by Cynthia Voigt. Fawcett Juniper, 1984. Reproduced by permission of Random House, Inc. / Cover of *The Runner,* by Cynthia Voigt. Scholastic, 1994. Cover illustration © 1994 by Scholastic Inc. Reproduced by permission. / Voigt, Cynthia, photograph by Walter Voigt. Reproduced by permission of the author.

WILL WEAVER. Carroll, Jim, illustrator. From a jacket of *Farm Team,* by Will Weaver. HarperCollins, 1995. Jacket art copyright © 1995 by Jim Carroll. Jacket copyright © 1995 by HarperCollins Publishers. Reproduced by permission of HarperCollins Publishers. / From a cover of *Striking Out,* by Will Weaver. HarperTrophy, 1995. Cover © 1999 by HarperCollins Publishers. Reproduced by permission of HarperCollins Publishers. / Koelsch, Michael, illustrator. From a jacket of *Hard Ball,* by Will Weaver. HarperCollins, 1998. Jacket art © 1998 by Michael Koelsch. Jacket © 1998 by HarperCollins Publishers. Reproduced by permission of HarperCollins Publishers. / Weaver, Will, photograph by Image Photography. Reproduced by permission of the author.

BARBARA WERSBA. Robbins, Ken, illustrator. From a jacket of *Whistle Me Home,* by Barbara Wersba. Henry Holt and Company, 1997. Jacket art © 1997 by Ken Robbins. Reproduced by permission of Henry Holt and Company, LLC. / Frasconi, Antonio, illustrator. From a jacket of *The Wings of Courage,* by George Sand, retold by Barbara Wersba. George Braziller, Inc., 1998. Cover illustration © 1998 by Antonio Frasconi. Reproduced by permission of the illustrator. / Wersba, Barbara, photograph. Reproduced by permission of the author.

KEVIN WILLIAMSON. Cover of *Major Meltdown,* by K. S. Rodriguez. Pocket Books, 1999. Cover photograph © 1999 by Columbia TriStar Television, Inc. Reproduced by permission. / Arquette, David and Courteney Cox, in the film "Scream 2," 1997, photograph by Kimberly Wright. The Kobal Collection. Reproduced by permission. / Van Der Beek, James and Michelle William, in the television series "Dawson's Creek," 1998, photograph. Fotos International/Archive Photos, Inc. Reproduced by permission. / Laurie, Piper, Salma Hayek and Robert Patrick, in the film "The Faculty," 1998, photograph by Rico Torres. The Kobal Collection. Reproduced by permission. / Williamson, Kevin, photograph. Corbis-Bettmann. Reproduced by permission.

CONNIE WILLIS. Poderin, Jean-Francois, illustrator. From a cover of *Lincoln's Dreams,* by Connie Willis. Bantam, 1992. Cover art © 1992 by Jean-Francois Poderin. Reproduced by permission of Bantam Books, a division of Random House, Inc. / Cover of *Doomsday Book,* by Connie Willis. Bantam, 1993. Reproduced by permission of Bantam Books, a division of Random House, Inc. / Jensen, Bruce, illustrator. From a cover of *Bellwether,* by Connie Willis. Bantam, 1996. Cover art © 1996 by Bruce Jensen. Reproduced by permission of Bantam Books, a division of Random House, Inc. / Dinyer, Eric, illustrator. From a cover of *To Say Nothing of the Dog,* by Connie Willis. Bantam, 1998. Cover art © 1998 by Eric Dinyer. Reproduced by permission of Bantam Books, a division of Random House, Inc. / Willis, Connie, photograph. Reproduced by permission of the author.

Cumulative Index

Author/Artist Index

The following index gives the number of the volume in which an author/artist's biographical sketch appears.